NARRATIVE OF THE LIFE OF

FREDERICK DOUGLASS,

AN AM

D0283050

Frederick Douglass

Frontispiece of 1845 edition of *Narrative of the Life of Frederick Douglass, an American Slave* (Boston: Published at the Anti-Slavery Office, 1845).

Narrative of the Life

of Frederick Douglass,

An American Slave

Written by Himself

John W. Blassingame,
John R. McKivigan,
and Peter P. Hinks,

EDITORS

Gerald Fulkerson,

TEXTUAL EDITOR

James H. Cook, Victoria C. Gruber,
and C. Jane Holtan,
EDITORIAL ASSISTANTS

Yale Nota Bene

Yale University Press

New Haven & London

First published as a Yale Nota Bene book in 2001.

This edition is based on *The Frederick Douglass Papers,* Series Two: *Autobiographical Writings,* Volume 1: *Narrative,* ed. John W. Blassingame, John R. McKivigan, and Peter P. Hinks (New Haven: Yale University Press, 1999), published with assistance from the National Historical Publications and Records Commission.

For information about this and other Yale University Press publications, please contact:

    U.S. office   sales.press@yale.edu
    Europe office sales@yaleup.co.uk

Printed in the United States of America.

Library of Congress card number: 00-103556
ISBN 0-300-08831-0 (cloth : alk. paper)
ISBN 0-300-08701-2 (pbk.)

A catalogue record for this book is available from the British Library.

10 9 8 7 6 5 4 3 2 1

COMMITTEE ON
SCHOLARLY EDITIONS

AN APPROVED TEXT

MODERN LANGUAGE
ASSOCIATION OF AMERICA

Contents

Abbreviations   vi
Chronology   vii
Introduction   ix
Narrative   3
Historical Annotation   87
Reader Responses, 1845–49   123
Index   138

Abbreviations

ACAB	*Appleton's Cyclopaedia of American Biography*
ASB	*Anti-Slavery Bugle*
BDAC	*Biographical Directory of the American Congress*
DAB	*Dictionary of American Biography*
DANB	*Dictionary of American Negro Biography*
DHU	Moorland-Spingarn Library, Howard University
DLC	Library of Congress
DNB	*Dictionary of National Biography*
FDP	*Frederick Douglass' Paper*
JNH	*Journal of Negro History*
Lib.	*Liberator*
MdAA	Hall of Records Commission, Annapolis, Md.
MdHi	Maryland Historical Society
MdHM	*Maryland Historical Magazine*
MdTCH	Talbot County, Maryland, Courthouse
NASS	*National Anti-Slavery Standard*
NCAB	*National Cyclopaedia of American Biography*
NHi	New-York Historical Society
NS	*North Star*
PaF	*Pennsylvania Freeman*

Brief Chronology of the Life of Frederick Douglass

February 1818	Born at Holme Hill Farm, Talbot County, Maryland.
August (?) 1824	Sent to live on Wye House, the Lloyd family's home plantation.
March 1826	Sent to live with Hugh Auld's family in the Fells Point neighborhood of Baltimore.
14 November 1826	Master Aaron Anthony dies.
March 1833	Sent to live with Thomas Auld at St. Michaels, Maryland.
1 January 1834	Begins year as field hand hired out to Talbot County "slave breaker," Edward Covey.
2 April 1836	Escape plot exposed and Douglass jailed in Easton, Maryland.
Mid-April 1836	Returned to Thomas Auld in Baltimore.
3 September 1838	Departs Baltimore on successful escape attempt to the North.
15 September 1838	Marries Anna Murray in New York City.
18 September 1838	Settles in New Bedford, Massachusetts.
August 1841	Addresses antislavery meeting in Nantucket, Massachusetts, and is hired as lecturer by Garrisonian abolitionists.
May 1845	Publishes his first autobiography, *Narrative of the Life of Frederick Douglass, an American Slave.*
August 1845–April 1847	Travels in Great Britain as abolitionist lecturer.

3 December 1847	From new home in Rochester, New York, publishes first issue of weekly newspaper, *North Star.*
May–June 1851	Breaks with Garrisonian abolitionists and revamps newspaper into *Frederick Douglass' Paper,* a Liberty party vehicle.
August 1855	Publishes second autobiography, *My Bondage and My Freedom.*
October 1859–April 1860	Following Harpers Ferry Raid, flees first to Canada and then Great Britain for safety.
February–July 1863	Recruits black troops for the Union Army.
June 1872	Moves family to Washington, D.C.
March–July 1874	President of the Freedman's Savings Bank.
17 March 1877	Becomes U.S. marshal of the District of Columbia.
March 1881	Appointed recorder of deeds for the District of Columbia.
4 August 1882	Wife Anna dies.
24 January 1884	Marries Helen Pitts.
September 1886–August 1887	Tours Europe and Near East with new wife.
July 1889–August 1891	Serves as U.S. resident minister and consul general to Haiti.
October 1892–December 1893	Commissioner of Haitian pavilion at the World's Columbian Exposition in Chicago.
20 February 1895	Dies at Cedar Hill home in Washington, D.C.

Introduction

John W. Blassingame

Frederick Douglass's antebellum reputation as a writer rests firmly on the autobiography he published when he was twenty-seven years old. At first glance, Douglass's incomparable literary success is inexplicable. During the two decades he spent as a Maryland slave, for example, Douglass displayed few of the talents that would mark his later literary career. Indeed, one observer who knew Douglass during the years he spent in bondage recalled that he was "an unlearned, and rather ordinary negro." However ordinary Douglass appeared as a slave, he had become an extraordinary man by 1845, seven years after his escape from bondage. If not yet learned, Douglass was at least highly literate by 1845.[1]

In typical nineteenth-century fashion, Douglass was fond of referring to his autobiography in self-effacing terms. Speaking of his *Narrative* in 1845, for instance, he asserted that "a person undertaking to write a book without learning will appear rather novel, but such as it was I gave it to the public."[2] Like many authors, Douglass did not often reflect on or clearly elucidate the nature of his "learning" or the various literary influences bearing upon his writing. Nevertheless, it is obvious that when Douglass began writing his autobiography in the winter of 1844–45, he understood the conventions and literary canons that applied to the genre.[3]

The manifold influences bearing upon Douglass's autobiography included antebellum literary criticism, previously published black and white slave narratives, his knowledge of other autobiographical writings, and several events that took place between 1838 and 1845. Many of the conventions followed by Douglass were similar to those of other nineteenth-

---

1. John W. Blassingame et al., eds., *The Frederick Douglass Papers,* Series 1: *Speeches, Debates, and Interviews,* 5 vols. (New Haven, 1979–92), 1 : 201.

2. Ibid.

3. The paucity of studies of nineteenth-century American criticism of autobiographies forces the interested student systematically to examine the magazines of the period and the collected essays on the literary critics active between 1800 and 1860. A brief overview of nineteenth-century English criticism of autobiographies can be found in Keith Rinehart, "The Victorian Approach to Autobiography," *Modern Philology,* 51 : 177–86 (February 1954); and George P. Landow, ed., *Approaches to Victorian Autobiography* (Athens, Ohio, 1979), 3–26, 39–63, 333–54. The most useful bibliography of works revealing the nature of autobiographies appears in James Olney, ed., *Autobiography: Essays Theoretical and Critical* (Princeton, N.J., 1980).

century American and English autobiographers, black and white. The similarities between black and white autobiographers were most evident in the narratives of those who had been enslaved or captured by Indians in the Americas or of white Europeans and Americans who were shipwrecked and enslaved in Africa.[4]

Because antebellum Americans frowned upon the reading of novels, they avidly read personal accounts of shipwrecks, slavery, and Indian captivities that had all of the characteristics of romanticized adventures. Between 1682 and 1860, for instance, some Indian captivity narratives went through as many as forty-one editions. Among the earliest forms of American literature, these narratives expressed the religious sentiment of the age, employed biblical allusions extensively, exemplified the redemptive power of suffering, and illustrated divine providence. Authors stressed the didactic purposes served by their accounts. Frequently serialized in nineteenth-century newspapers and magazines, the narratives had become stylized, sentimental, melodramatic, and sensational tales containing exaggerated accounts of the barbarities, tortures, and manifold horrors suffered by the captives. Journalists fabricated many nineteenth-century accounts, and true stories had to compete with fiction parading as truth.[5]

Perhaps the clearest indication of the merging of black and white autobiographical traditions at an early point in American literary history is that some of the first black autobiographies were also, in part, Indian captivity narratives. Among the African-American autobiographers to detail their captivity by and deliverance from Indians were Briton Hammon and Joseph Marrant in *A Narrative of the Uncommon Sufferings and Surprising Deliverance of Briton Hammon, a Negro Man* (1760) and *A Narrative of the Lord's Wonderful Dealings with John Marrant, a Black, Taken Down from His Own Relation* (1785).

4. C. Marius Barbeau, "Indian Captivities," *Proceedings of the American Philosophical Society,* 94 : 522–48 (December 1950); Richard Van Der Beets, "A Surfeit of Style: The Indian Captivity Narrative as Penny Dreadful," *Research Studies,* 39 : 297–306 (December 1971); Roy Harvey Pearce, "The Significance of the Captivity Narrative," *American Literature,* 19 : 1–20 (March 1947); Joseph Bruchac, "Black Autobiography in Africa and America," *Black Academy Review,* 2 : 61–70 (Spring–Summer, 1971); Mutulu K. Blasing, *The Art of Life: Studies in American Autobiographical Literature* (Austin, Tex., 1977); James Riley, *An Authentic Narrative of the Loss of the American Brig Commerce* (Hartford, Conn., 1836), iii–xiv; Eliza Bradley, *An Authentic Narrative of the Shipwreck and Sufferings of Mrs. Eliza Bradley* (Boston, 1821); John W. Blassingame, *The Slave Community: Plantation Life in the Antebellum South,* rev. ed. (New York, 1979), 376–77.

5. Richard Van Der Beets, ed., *Held Captive by Indians: Selected Narratives, 1642–1836* (Knoxville, Tenn., 1973), xi–xxxi.

A group of powerful literary critics in the United States and the United Kingdom shaped the nineteenth-century autobiographical convention followed by Douglass and other authors. One of the most influential of these critics was an Englishman, the Reverend John Foster, a prolific and popular essayist. An ardent republican, Foster wrote widely on theological and biographical subjects and contributed 184 articles to the *Eclectic Review* between 1806 and 1839. Among the most frequently reprinted of Foster's works was the 1805 collection of his early essays. The book, appearing in several American editions between 1807 and 1845, contained Foster's twenty-one-page essay "On a Man's Writing Memoirs of Himself," which played a primary role in establishing the conventions of English and American autobiography.[6]

Concerned in most of his numerous essays with the formation and evidence of character, Foster drew a distinction between the exterior and the interior of a person's life. He admired "simple conviction" and despised "the sly deceit of self-love" and the "self-describers who . . . think the publication of their vices necessary to crown their fame." As much as he disliked the "confessions" of courtesans, debauchees, drunkards, and criminals, Foster delighted in accounts tracing the various stages that marked an individual's moral, spiritual, and intellectual progress. Above all, he viewed the end of autobiography to be self-understanding, a way for a person "to acquire a complete knowledge of himself" and the course of his growth. It was, of course, axiomatic that a person's self-history differed significantly according to the stage at which it was written, since "in the course of a long life a man may be several moral persons." Recognition of moral, religious, and intellectual advancement and retrogression was essential, according to Foster, because of the lessons they provided and because they constituted a record to compare "with the standard of perfection." Conscience required that there be explicit admission of delinquencies to cultivate humility and diminish vanity and "self-love."[7]

Realizing how difficult it was for people to parade their errors, Foster returned again and again in his essay to the distinction between inner and

---

6. Walter Graham, *Tory Criticism in the Quarterly Review, 1809–1853* (New York, 1921); William Charvat, *The Origins of American Critical Thought, 1810–1835* (1936; New York, 1961), 1–26, 164–205. *Dictionary of National Biography*, 21 vols. (London, 1921–22), 7 : 497–99. John Foster, *Essays in a Series of Letters* (New York, 1853), 66–81. The first edition of Foster's book was published in London in 1805. The American editions available to Douglass appeared in Hartford, 1807, 1844, 1845; Boston, 1811, 1833, 1839; Utica, 1815; Andover, 1826; and New York, 1835.

7. Foster, *Essays in a Series of Letters*, 69, 71–72, 73, 78.

outer character. Inner character he considered more important because an attempt to represent it exposed one to the powerful temptation to be dishonest. Without a truthful recounting of this hidden compartment, autobiography would lose much of its power for self-instruction. Foster also felt that dishonesty in this area would make an autobiography less interesting or capable of eliciting sympathy from readers. Truth, history, and divinity met as the autobiographer struggled to reveal his or her inner character:

> Each mind has an interior apartment of its own, into which none but itself and the Divinity can enter. In this secluded place, the passions mingle and fluctuate in unknown agitations. Here all the fantastic and all the tragic shapes of imagination have a haunt, where they can neither be invaded nor descried. . . . Here projects, convictions, vows, are confusedly scattered, and the records of past life are laid. Here in solitary state sits Conscience, surrounded by her own thunders, which sometimes sleep, and sometimes roar, while the world does not know. . . . If, in a man's own account of himself, written on the supposition of being seen by any other person, the substance of the secrets of this apartment be brought forth, he throws open the last asylum of his character. . . . And if it be not brought forth, where is the integrity or value of the history . . . ?[8]

Although actually offering little advice about how to structure autobiography, his few remarks nevertheless resonated through hundreds of prefaces, reviews, and critical essays for the next century. Again and again the critics upheld his singular directive that "the *style* should be as simple as possible."[9]

The critics who followed Foster exhibited far more interest in the readers than the writers of autobiographies. In contrast to Foster, they stressed the autobiography's power to acquaint the reader with human virtues as well as to furnish relaxation and entertainment. Many critics contended that the chief value of the autobiography was that it was a historical document. Through autobiographies—especially those of public figures—readers could see behind the public facades of great figures and learn in detail from the events and influences that shaped their characters.[10]

Writing for an increasingly literate society, American critics valued autobiographies as instructive books for the education of youth. It was

8. Ibid., 76.
9. Ibid., 74.
10. *New York Review,* 1 : 475–76 (October 1837), 9 : 531–33 (October 1841).

infinitely better, they contended, for youths to read autobiographies than novels. Because autobiographers sketched their lives from childhood to their attainment of eminence and stressed "the cultivation of intellectual and moral power," they could provide lessons, examples, and inspirations to the young.[11]

But what was of special concern to antebellum critics was the credibility of any autobiography. Detailing the factors that limited credibility (senility, egotism, and vanity), the critics tried to develop a series of tests to determine where it existed. As critics became more familiar with the genre, they became more confident of their ability to determine the veracity of autobiographies. By concentrating on the patterns of revelation and concealment in a work, the critics believed that they could uncover an author's true self-portrait. A *New York Review* critic, for instance, writing in October 1838, insisted that by a close reading of an autobiography, one could determine whether it was true because "in autobiography we study character in two modes at once. We have, first, what the individual *says* of himself, and secondly, the *unconscious* revelation which he makes of himself as narrator; the picture in the glass, and the real man seen behind it."[12]

A number of critics drew upon their own experience or sought the proof of the credibility of an autobiography in its narrative technique. Frequently they combined the two tests. A *North American Review* critic, for example, argued in 1844 that the most believable autobiographies were those in which minuteness of detail was a salient feature: "Minuteness of narration, whether in fiction or in real life, has a singular charm for all readers. . . . Now, the *only* truth is the *whole* truth. The complete portrait is the only faithful portrait. The only true history or biography is that which tells all." For most readers the credibility of such accounts would be "attested by our experience, which necessarily comprehends the whole of our own thoughts, motives and actions." The "vast edifice" of a life had to be portrayed because the "piecemeal exhibition of another's life finds no counterpart in our own memories, which embrace every incident in our own career."[13]

11. *New England Magazine,* 5 : 32–33 (July 1833), 9 : 140–41 (August 1835); *New York Review,* 7 : 535–37 (July 1840); *North American Review,* 10 : 1–14 (January 1820).

12. *New York Review,* 3 : 403 (October 1838). See also: *North American Review,* 9 : 58–59 (June 1819); *New York Review,* 8 : 1–50 (January 1841); Howard Helsinger, "Credence and Credibility: The Concern for Honesty in Victorian Autobiography," in Landow, ed., *Approaches to Victorian Autobiography,* 39–63.

13. *North American Review,* 54 : 452–53 (October 1844).

Much of what critics thought was likely to be incredible about auto-biographies was, they contended, inherent in the genre. Since an auto-biography involved revelations about the frequently inaccessible interior of life, it often raised unanswerable questions about credibility. The personal secrets of the autobiographer represented what most critics believed consti-tuted the most instructive aspect of his or her self-portrait—thoughts, feel-ings, imaginations, motives. Critics longed to see what they described as the autobiographer's "thoughts and feelings in their nakedness . . . his envy, jealousy, malice, and uncharitableness." They wanted to read the works of autobiographers willing to risk notoriety and "lay open to the world the deepest and darkest nooks of their own hearts, however ugly and loathsome may be the things which dwell therein." True histories of the inner person would always be rare, however, the critics argued, because most autobiographers lacked the necessary discrimination, analytical skills, sincerity, and self-knowledge to write them. A *New England Maga-zine* writer sadly concluded in 1834, we "know our enemies better than ourselves, because we judge them with more severity; we can write better lives of them than memoirs of ourselves."[14]

Yet they also imposed limits on such exposure. Self-revelation must not be a promiscuous exercise intended merely to shock and arouse the audi-ence but must promote a moral life and show an eventual turning away from things bad even as they are described in detail.

Nevertheless, the author must have a proper and unavoidable dose of egotism. Many of the critics argued that egotism naturally determined both the focus and the design of life histories. Reviewing Johann Wolfgang von Goethe's autobiography in October 1838, a *New York Review* critic pro-fessed that in autobiography "if the author is himself the central point around which all seems to revolve, this is in conformity with the idea of an autobiography, and is necessary to unity of design . . . egotism is the very thing to be desired in such a work."[15]

Following Foster's injunctions, critics also expressed a desire for a "simple" style in autobiographies. Increasingly, critics translated "simple" into "appropriate," a variable standard dependent on the times, incidents, and the lives being described. What was, under this standard, misplaced ornamentation in one author would be appropriate in another. Critics ex-

14. *New England Magazine,* 6 : 497 (June 1834); *New York Review,* 8 : 1–50 (January 1841); *North American Review,* 9 : 58–59 (June 1819), 9 : 341–43 (October 1820).
15. *New York Review,* 3 : 404 (October 1838).

pected an autobiographer to demonstrate lucidity, modesty, honesty, and economy. Repeatedly, critics praised those self-portraits that were "plain, unaffected" narratives marked by unity of design and artful symmetry. Especially ornate language suggested that the author was insincere.[16]

Many American critics identified Benjamin Franklin as the model autobiographer because of the clarity and economy of his writing. A *North American Review* evaluation of Benjamin Franklin's autobiographical writings in 1818 varied little from the positive assessments of numerous other critics. In spite of "some trifling blemishes," Franklin's work was "always admirable for its precision and perspicuity. It is as transparent as the atmosphere; and his thoughts lie before us like objects seen in one of our finest and clearest days, when their very brightness and distinctness alone give us pleasure."[17]

In the 1830s Douglass first encountered Franklin indirectly in Caleb Bingham's *Columbian Orator*. In his primer, Bingham reprinted Abbé Fauchet's 1790 eulogy of Benjamin Franklin. Fauchet praised Franklin for having "presented new and sublime ideas, in a style simple as truth, and as pure as light." Further he contended that Franklin "laid the sacred foundations of social morality. . . . This amiable moralist descended, in his writings, to the most artless details; to the most ingenuous familiarities; to the first ideas of a rural, a commercial, and a civil life; to the dialogues of old men and children; full at once of all the verdure and all the maturity of wisdom." Fauchet stamped the essentials of antebellum American autobiography in his paean to Franklin and assuredly made his impress upon the young Douglass as well.[18]

Although the *Columbian Orator* was Douglass's key textbook during the time of his enslavement in Maryland, his central texts once he escaped from slavery were abolitionist newspapers, magazines, books, and pamphlets and slave narratives. Such works greatly expanded his knowledge of autobiographies. In abolition sources alone, Douglass read dozens of narratives of fugitive slaves before he sat down to write his autobiography in 1844.

Between 1838 and 1844 Douglass avidly read such antislavery publications as the *Liberator, National Anti-Slavery Standard, Liberty Bell, Emancipator, Anti-Slavery Almanac,* and *American and Foreign Anti-Slavery*

---

16. *New England Magazine,* 5 : 31–33 (July 1833); *New York Review,* 7 : 535–37 (July 1840).

17. *North American Review,* 7 : 321 (September 1818).

18. Caleb Bingham, ed., *The Columbian Orator* (1797; Boston, 1831), 65–68.

Reporter that contained speeches, interviews, and autobiographies of dozens of fugitive slaves including Lunsford Lane, James Curry, Lewis Clarke, and the *Amistad* rebels. Equally significant, the abolition newspapers and magazines published reviews of the autobiographies of blacks and whites and furnished Douglass with further advice on the elements of the proper autobiography. At a very early period, Douglass also came to know the "slave's biographer," Isaac T. Hopper, who published a long-running popular column of slave narratives in the *National Anti-Slavery Standard* under the heading "Tales of Oppression."[19]

Another source of information about the autobiographical canon that Douglass read repeatedly was Theodore Dwight Weld's *American Slavery As It Is*. Douglass quoted frequently from Weld's work in the speeches he gave between 1841 and 1845. Indeed, *American Slavery As It Is* long represented for Douglass the standard by which to measure all statements about the character of America's peculiar institution. The book was, Douglass wrote in 1853, the "repository of human horrors."[20]

Douglass relied so extensively on personal narratives in *American Slavery As It Is* that they undoubtedly formed the structure, focus, and style of his *Narrative*. He learned, for instance, that most of the accounts that Weld published followed letters vouching for the author's integrity and veracity. Weld himself repeatedly stressed the importance of a truthful portrayal of slavery, urged witnesses to "'speak what they know, and testify what they have seen,'" and commanded them to demonstrate a "fidelity to truth." Conscious of the incredulity of his northern readers, Weld insisted on making a clear distinction between opinion and fact: "Testimony respects matters of *fact*, not matters of opinion: it is the declaration of a witness as to *facts*, not the giving of an opinion as to the nature or qualities of actions, or the *character* of a course of conduct."[21]

American Slavery As It Is may also have played a crucial role in Douglass's original decision to write and publish his *Narrative*. Signi-

19. For examples of these autobiographical accounts, see: John W. Blassingame, ed., *Slave Testimony: Two Centuries of Letters, Speeches, Interviews, and Autobiographies* (Baton Rouge, 1977), 128–64, 198–245, 690–95; Lydia Maria Child, "Charity Bowery," *Liberty Bell* (Boston, 1839), 26–43; Isaac T. Hopper, "Story of a Fugitive," *Liberty Bell* (Boston, 1843), 163–69; "Story of Anthony Gayle," in *The American Anti-Slavery Almanac, for 1838* (Boston, 1838); 44; "The Conscientious Slave," in *The American Anti-Slavery Almanac, for 1843* (New York, 1843), 42–44; Lydia Maria Child, *Isaac T. Hopper: A True Life* (Boston, 1853).

20. *FDP,* 29 April 1853; Blassingame, *Douglass Papers,* 1 : 42, 52, 75.

21. [Theodore Dwight Weld], *American Slavery As It Is: Testimony of a Thousand Witnesses* (New York, 1839), 9–10, 122; Blassingame, *Douglass Papers,* 1 : 41, 51–52, 254, 279–81, 322, 485.

ficantly, in a prefatory "Note" to his book, Weld announced that the American Anti-Slavery Society intended to publish other "TRACTS, containing well authenticated facts, testimony, personal narratives, etc. fully setting forth the *condition* of American slaves." Each prospective author unknown to the Executive Committee of the Society had to furnish references. Weld specified exactly the kinds of narratives in which the society had an interest:

> Facts and testimony respecting the condition of slaves, in *all respects,* are desired; their food, (kinds, quality, quantity), clothing, lodging, dwellings, hours of labor and rest, kinds of labor, with the mode of exaction, supervision, &c.—the number and times of meals each day, treatment when sick, regulations respecting their social intercourse, marriage and domestic ties, the system of torture to which they are subjected, with its various modes; and *in detail,* their *intellectual* and *moral* condition. Great care should be observed in the statement of facts. Well-weighed testimony and well-authenticated facts, with a responsible name, the Committee earnestly desire and call for.[22]

Given this note, it is probably no accident that the publisher Douglass chose for his first autobiography was the American Anti-Slavery Society and that he found two people, William Lloyd Garrison and Wendell Phillips, "personally known" to its executive committee to write prefatory notes to his *Narrative*.

Although the other autobiographical works Douglass read were probably somewhat less influential than *American Slavery As It Is,* they were no less significant. The most salient features of the slave narratives he read in the abolition press were their brevity, directness, simplicity, and lack of specificity. Often editors prefaced the accounts with declarations that publication had been delayed until the fugitive had reached Canada. Editors of the accounts of fugitives who remained in the United States frequently tried to guarantee their anonymity by giving them fictional names, deleting specific references to their masters and places of enslavement, or citing initials for all personal and place names that might possibly serve as keys to the real identity of the narrator. While helping to ensure the safety of the fugitive, such practices, the amanuenses realized, seriously undermined the

22. Weld, *American Slavery,* iv.

credibility of the accounts. In many cases, however, the guarantee of anonymity was the sine qua non for obtaining accounts from frightened fugitives.[23]

Significantly, Douglass had some of his first exposures to the narratives of fugitive slaves in oral rather than written form at the home of the
most prolific of the slaves' amanuenses, Isaac T. Hopper. Reflecting in
1853 on his introduction to Hopper, Douglass asserted that he first saw him
in September 1838 when Hopper was a witness in a fugitive slave case. In a
review of Lydia Maria Child's biography of Hopper, Douglass discussed
his "intimate acquaintance with the venerable, Quakerly gentleman" and
his visits to Hopper's home in the early 1840s, where he "listened to some
of the admirable stories and adventures in the matter of rescuing fugitives."[24]

Possessing a nearly photographic memory and being totally fearless,
Hopper aided hundreds of fugitive slaves, first in Philadelphia and later in
New York. Recording the minutest details from the tales of fugitives,
Hopper published about sixty of the stories in his "Tales of Oppression"
column in the *Standard*. Occasionally, when introducing these narratives,
Hopper explained the techniques he employed and taught Douglass much
about the art of autobiography.[25]

What impressed critics were "unvarnished" stories of the slaves' lives
filled with "unstudied pathos" and "touching" incidents that only an actual
observer could describe. Credibility and plainness were everything.[26]

Thus when the scandal over the narratives of Archy Moore and James
Williams broke in the late 1830s, the continuing viability of the slave
autobiographies was threatened. Published anonymously in 1836, the
Memoirs of Archy Moore produced disarray among the abolitionists when
southerners protested that it was fictional. Reviewers—uncertain about the
work's reliability—wavered between describing it as the factual account of
a slave and a fictional work. In 1837, however, a historian and abolitionist,
Richard Hildreth, admitted that he had created the narrative and disguised it
as genuine autobiography. Deeply embarrassed by this affair, the antislav-

23. Blassingame, *Slave Testimony,* 145–50, 151–64, 213–16; Hopper, "Story of a Fugitive,"
163–69.

24. Blassingame, *Slave Testimony,* 151, 158–59; *FDP,* 25 November 1853.

25. *NASS,* 22, 29 October, 5, 12, 26 November, 3, 10, 24, 31 December 1840, 7 January, 4
February 1841.

26. *Lib.,* 9, 30 March 1838.

ery societies had to rescue this critical tool in their crusade from the refuse pile to which the slaveholders wanted permanently to consign it.[27]

There could not have been a worse time, then, for another crisis of credibility to arise as it did in 1838 with the *Narrative of James Williams,* published by the Massachusetts Anti-Slavery Society and edited by John Greenleaf Whittier. Abolitionists spent much of 1838 countering the attacks on Williams's story. The most systematic defense came from the pen of "Memento." Reminding *Liberator* readers of the general skepticism of Whittier, "Memento" noted that former slaveholder James Birney of Alabama confirmed Williams's characterization of slave life in that state, praised the account of valuable "documentary evidence," and concluded that it was "incontrovertibly true; and is additionally valuable, because it so powerfully corroborates other evidence and facts which have been published."

Because it was "incontrovertibly true," the publication of Williams's story should be followed, "Memento" contended, by a flood of similar ones: "a few more such personal narratives as the life and experience of James Williams will render the boasted 'Southern domestic institutions' as loathsome, as they are cruelly malignant and criminal." What was most significant in the defense was a clear elaboration of the general credibility problem facing all abolitionist writers:

> Amid the strange characteristics of mankind, no one of their moral features is more unaccountable than their complex credulity in some cases, and in others, their marvelous unbelief. This general position is illustrated in an astonishing manner, upon the subject of slavery. It seems as if our northern citizens had determined to resist all evidence respecting the practical concerns of slaveholding, until they are ocularly convinced; while they have resolved never to witness *Life in the Negro Quarters*. It is yet more perplexing, that many of our anti-slavery friends are incredulous respecting the facts which are stated by professed eye-witnesses, and the few competent narrators of slavery as it exists in our country. Thus the only citizens, who personally know what slavery is from their own observation, and who are sufficiently independent to disclose the truth, are not only disbelieved, but are also

---

27. Richard Hildrith, ed., *Archy Moore, the White Slave; Or Memoirs of a Fugitive* (1856; New York, 1969); Marion Wilson Starling, *The Slave Narrative: Its Place in American History* (Boston, 1981), 227–33.

suspected of untruth, or reproached with falsehood, by the silly retort—
"I will not believe it; it cannot be true."[28]

In spite of the complaints and defense of people like "Memento," the
Executive Committee of the Massachusetts Anti-Slavery Society eventually had to consider the possibility that Williams had fabricated his story.
The committee checked many of the personal and place names mentioned
in Williams's account with knowledgeable southerners who almost universally disputed his claims. After its investigation, the committee published a
full retraction in November 1838 in which it came "fully to the conclusion,—that the statements of the narrative . . . are wholly false" and withdrew the book from sale. The Williams debacle forced all abolitionist
amanuenses to be more cautious, to state whether they were using real or
fictitious personal and place names, and to search systematically for cor-
roborating evidence and authenticating testimony for the oral accounts of
fugitive slaves. Williams haunted Theodore Weld; he sought to exorcise
fraudulent statements from the eyewitness accounts he published in *American Slavery As It Is*. The import of this crisis could not have been lost on
Douglass.[29]

Many of Douglass's views of the purpose and structure of autobiographies were those traditionally expressed by black authors since the eighteenth century. Antebellum black authors were well aware of contemporary
autobiographical canons and especially the didactic purposes served by
such works. Like their white contemporaries, black autobiographers often
reflected on the genre and frequently explained their motives for writing in
their preface and introductions. For example, Olaudah Equiano began his
narrative of 1789 by acknowledging that it was "a little hazardous in a
private and obscure individual" to publish his memoirs, establish the credibility of his account, and "to escape the imputation of vanity." Significantly, the "preface" to Equiano's narrative consisted of his open letter to
the British Parliament petitioning for the abolition of the African slave
trade and presenting his narrative as the evidence he hoped would convince
the members to answer his prayer.[30]

28. *Lib.,* 9 March 1838. See also: Starling, *Slave Narrative,* 115–17, 228–33; *Lib.,* 23 September
1838. See also *Narrative of James Williams, An America Slave, Who Was for Several Years A Driver on
a Cotton Plantation in Alabama* (New York, 1838).

29. *Lib.,* 2 November 1838; *African Repository,* 15 : 161–63 (June 1839). See also: Moses
Grandy, *Narrative of the Life of Moses Grandy; Late a Slave in the United States of America,* ed. George
Thompson (London, 1843), ii.

30. For a list of black autobiographies published between 1837 and 1845, see: George P. Rawick,

The sentiments expressed in Equiano's open letter would resonate in all of the autobiographies written by antebellum African Americans. Antebellum black autobiographers consistently asserted that the chief reason for portraying their lives was the need to bear witness against slavery, to wake their fellow Americans to its evil, and to cheer on those who labored in the cause of human freedom. Truth, the antebellum black autobiographers contended, would expose the evil of slavery and contribute to its destruction. Interestingly, American whites formerly enslaved in Africa wrote autobiographies with the same didactic purposes and expectations in mind. Although the experiences of white authors formerly enslaved or held captive were recorded in published reminiscences, the autobiographical writings of black slaves grew out of their own lectures. Once published, the autobiography led to more frequent trips to the lectern as the black's *written* and *spoken* voice moved in easy tandem.[31]

Moses Roper, the former North Carolina slave, illustrated many of the conventions of black autobiographies in his "Introduction" to the successive editions of his *Narrative of the Adventures and Escape of Moses Roper, from American Slavery*. In the first edition published in the United States in 1838, Roper declared that he wrote his autobiography "with the view of exposing the cruel system of slavery" and with the hope that it would become "the instruments of opening the eyes of the ignorant to this system; of convincing the wicked, cruel, and hardened slave-holder; and of befriending generally the cause of oppressed humanity." His decision to publish his life story, Roper assured his readers, "did not arise from any desire to make myself conspicuous." Roper was conscious not only of the possible imputation of vanity to an autobiographer but also of the conventional rules for determining the credibility of such stories. After Thomas Price, the editor of the volume, had quoted from the letters of

---

From Sundown to Sunup: The Making of the Black Community (Westport, Conn., 1972), 179–89; Starling, *Slave Narrative*, 39–50. See also [Olaudah Equiano], *The Interesting Narrative of the Life of Olaudah Equiano, or Gustavus Vassa, the African* (1789; Dublin, 1791), 1–2; Smith, *Where I'm Bound*, 3–27; Charles H. Nichols, *Many Thousand Gone: The Ex-Slaves' Account of Their Bondage and Freedom* (Leiden, Netherlands, 1963); Gilbert Osofsky, ed., *Puttin' On Ole Massa: The Slave Narratives of Henry Bibb, William Wells Brown, and Solomon Northrup* (New York, 1969), 9–44; Frances Smith Foster, *Witnessing Slavery: The Development of Ante-bellum Slave Narratives* (Westport, Conn., 1979); Arna Bontemps, ed., *Great Slave Narratives* (Boston, 1969), vii–xix; John F. Bayliss, ed., *Black Slave Narratives* (London, 1970), 7–21; Butterfield, *Black Autobiography in America*, 11–89; Charles H. Nichols, ed., *Black Men in Chains: Narratives by Escaped Slaves* (New York, 1972), 9–24.

31. Stephen Clissold, *The Barbary Slaves* (London, 1977); Blassingame, *Slave Community*, 367–82; Riley, *Authentic Narrative*, x–xxii; Blassingame, *Slave Testimony*, xxxiv–xxxvii, 145–64.

introduction written by American abolitionists that Roper brought to England and noted the narrative's "internal evidence of truth," the former slave confronted directly the possibility that many readers might feel that his account was "somewhat at variance with the dictates of humanity." Roper assured his readers that he did not present facts "unsubstantiated by collateral evidence, nor highly colored to the disadvantage of cruel task-masters." Finally, Roper observed that his master and other slaveholders would have an opportunity to read and contradict any aspect of his autobiography.[32]

Usually, autobiographers present their views of the genre in the prefaces of their life stories. Unfortunately, during the antebellum period autobiographers often had friends and acquaintances write prefaces, and Douglass followed this route in 1845. Only later in his speeches did Douglass publicly explain why he had written his autobiography. Essentially, Douglass contended, he wrote the autobiography to authenticate his antislavery speeches—and thus his voice. Douglass delivered a typical exposition of this theme in his speech of 18 May 1846 in London in which he pointed out that after delivering antislavery lectures for four years

> my manner was such as to create a suspicion that I was not a runaway slave, but some educated free negro, whom the abolitionists had sent forth to attract attention to what was called there a faltering cause. They said, he appears to have no fear of white people. How can he ever have been in bondage? But one strong reason for this doubt was, the fact that I never made known to the people to whom I spoke where I came from . . . But it became necessary to set myself right before the public in the United States, and to reveal the whole facts of my case. I did not feel it safe to do so till last spring, when I was solicited to it by a number of anti-slavery friends, who assured me that it would be safe to do so. I then published a narrative of my experience in slavery, in which I detailed the cruelties of it as I had myself felt them.[33]

Douglass knew well that perhaps the central problem he faced was to establish his credibility. To do so, he adopted several strategies. First, he placed a daguerreotype of himself on the book's frontispiece and signed his name below it. Before the reader had even begun the *Narrative,* they had seen a reproduction of the author and of his handwriting, evidence of his

32. Moses Roper, *A Narrative of the Adventures and Escape of Moses Roper, From American Slavery* (Philadelphia, 1838), 5, 7–8.

33. Blassingame, *Douglass Papers,* 1 : 37–38, 82, 88–89, 132–33.

literacy. Next he preceded his text with letters from William Lloyd Garrison and Wendell Phillips, who served as witnesses to his veracity. Finally, in the text of the *Narrative* Douglass used real names when referring to people and places and described how he came to know Garrison and Phillips.[34]

The letters of Garrison and Phillips afforded powerful confirmation of Douglass's "many sufferings" and his several attainments. Acknowledging the popular misconception of slavery in Maryland as being less severe than in the Deep South, Garrison proclaimed that Douglass's lived experience belied that stereotype and proved that slavery in whatever form still degraded blacks, leaving nothing "undone to cripple their intellects, darken their minds, debase their moral nature, obliterate all traces of their relationship to mankind." Garrison further asserted that he was deeply moved by the way Douglass had emerged from this prison house to "consecrate" his life as an antislavery lecturer with an "intellect richly endowed" and a character filled with "gentleness," "meekness," "manliness." Douglass had passed through all that he claimed. Reiterating some of the points Garrison made, Phillips wrote of his personal acquaintance with Douglass and emphasized his "truth, candor, and sincerity." The *Narrative,* Phillips argued, gave "a fair specimen of the whole truth. No one-sided portrait,—no wholesale complaints,—but strict justice done."[35]

But Douglass did not rest even here in promoting his authenticity. Soon after the publication of the *Narrative,* he took a bold and unprecedented step: he mailed a copy of the *Narrative* to his master Thomas Auld, and thereby challenged him publicly to refute it. Auld obviously had the greatest motive and was in the best position to disprove Douglass's *Narrative* if it were untrue. Although Douglass relished this gesture, he also compounded his risk of realizing the fugitive's greatest fear—recapture. At a time when many of his fellow fugitives recounted the story of their lives only on condition that their anonymity be maintained by suppressing their true names, those of their masters, and the places of their enslavement, Douglass's revelations of such details in the face of the obvious threat their publication posed represented the greatest authentication of his text.[36]

---

34. Stepto, *From Behind the Veil,* 4–5, 17–26.

35. *Narrative* (Boston, 1845), iii, iv, v, vi, vii, xiv.

36. On kidnappings and renditions of fugitive slaves, see: *NASS,* 29 October 1840, 25 November 1841, 3 February, 15 August, 29 September, 13 October, 17, 24 November, 8, 15 December 1842, 2 February 1843, 9 May, 25 July, 26 September, 7 November 1844, 22 May 1845.

The swift acclaim Douglass's work achieved attested to the success of these verifying methods. Of all of the other twenty-seven black autobiographies published before 1846, only six went through four or more editions during the nineteenth century and only three of these were translated into foreign languages. The most successful of them were the narratives of Charles Ball (six English-language editions), James A. Gronnisaw (six English-language and one Swedish edition), Moses Roper (seven English-language and one Celtic edition), and Olaudah Equiano (twelve English-language, one Dutch, and one German edition).

The *Narrative* far outstripped any of its predecessors. Between its appearance in May and September 1845, more than 4,500 copies of the *Narrative* had been sold. Three years later it had been translated into French, German, and Dutch. Between 1845 and 1847, two Irish and four English editions were published. According to Douglass, the *Narrative* had "passed through nine editions in England" by January 1848. Nine American editions had been published by 1850. In six years a total of twenty-one editions of the book had been published in the United States, the United Kingdom, and Europe. By 1853, at least 30,000 copies of the book had been sold. The price of the American editions varied between 25 and 35 cents.[37]

The *Narrative* served several extraliterary purposes. Published just as Douglass was leaving the United States for an extended tour of England, Scotland, and Ireland, the *Narrative* promoted his lectures. Sales of the book before and after his appearance in a town helped him meet his expenses. To the extent that readers in the United Kingdom believed the *Narrative,* they were that much more prepared to accept Douglass's lectures castigating America and American slavery. Douglass added further drama to his highly publicized "flight" to Great Britain to avoid the certain recapture assured by the publication of his *Narrative* by constantly alluding to this threat in his speeches.[38]

At the beginning of his tour of the United Kingdom, references to the *Narrative* became stock rhetorical devices in Douglass's speeches. Doug-

---

37. *NS,* 7 January, 21 April, 29 September 1848; *NASS,* 29 April 1847; *Lib.,* 20 June 6, 12, 19 September, 24, 31 October 1845, 2 January 1846, 12 November 1847, 24 May 1850. The foreign-language editions were: *Levensverhaal van Frederik Douglass, een' gewezen' slaaf (door hem zelven geschreven); Uit het Engelsch* (Rotterdam: H. A. Kramers, 1846); *Vie de Frédéric Douglass, esclave americain, écrite par lui-même, traduite de l'anglais par S.-K. Parkes* (Paris: Pagnerre, 1848).

38. *Lib.,* 25 July 1845, 10 July 1846; Cork *Examiner,* 22 October 1845; *NASS,* 4 December 1845; *British Friend,* 3 : 191 (December 1845); Bristol *Mercury,* 6 January 1846; *ASB,* 9 January 1846; *Littell's Living Age,* 9 : 50 (4 April 1846); Newcastle *Guardian,* 11 July 1846.

lass frequently emphasized the threat of recapture when he began a speech. Typical was his assertion in a speech in Cork, Ireland, in October 1845 that although publication of the *Narrative* removed doubts that he had been a slave, it produced some excitement in the South, endangering his safety: "The excitement at last increased so much that it was thought better for me to get out of the way lest my master might use some stratagems to get me back into his clutches. I am here then in order to avoid the scent of the blood hounds of America, and of spreading light on the subject of her slave system."[39]

The *Narrative* was the most widely reviewed of all antebellum black autobiographies. Dozens of newspapers and magazines published in the United States, the United Kingdom, and Europe praised the book, and reviews exceeding three thousand words were not unusual. Varying from long summaries containing numerous extracts to thoughtful essays on the nature of black autobiographies, the reviews generally accepted Douglass's self-portrait as true, interesting, and instructive.[40]

Reviewers in the antislavery press flocked to celebrate the *Narrative*. The *Liberator* inaugurated the campaign while the *Narrative* was still being printed. Announcing the forthcoming book in a lead editorial on 9 May 1845, the *Liberator* stressed that Douglass alone wrote the account. The acting editor of the newspaper then reprinted in full Garrison's preface. The reviewer for the *National Anti-Slavery Standard* attested that the book was "illustrated by a remarkably good engraving of the author" and buttressed this authenticating device with an indication of his personal acquaintance with the author. The *Liberator* added that the *Narrative* "was written entirely by Mr. Douglass, and reveals all the facts in regard to his birthplace,—the names of his mother, master, overseer, &c &c."[41]

The May 1845 annual meeting of the New England Anti-Slavery Society was also used to advance the *Narrative*. Attended by Garrison, Phillips, and Douglass, the convention was extensively covered in the press. Quickly taking advantage of free advertising, the first motion of the business committee offered by Wendell Phillips on 27 May welcomed the *Narrative* as "The new Anti-Slavery lecturer" and commended it to "all

---

39. Blassingame, *Douglass Papers,* 1: 37–45, 76, 81–90, 109, 128, 132–33, 291, 399.

40. For an overview of critical reception of books by nineteenth-century black authors, see: Julian D. Mason, "The Critical Reception of American Negro Authors in American Magazines, 1800–1885" (Ph.D. diss., University of North Carolina, 1962).

41. *Lib.,* 23 May 1845; *NASS,* 12 June 1845. See also: Concord (N.H.) *Herald of Freedom,* 9 May 1845; Chicago *Western Citizen,* 19 June 1845.

those who believe the slaves of the South to be either well treated, or happy, or ignorant of their right to freedom, or in need of preparation to make them fit for freedom; and that we urge upon the friends of the cause the duty of circulating it among all classes."[42]

Abolitionist critics contended the *Narrative* exposed slavery where it was allegedly "mildest" and that it would be an important "auxiliary" in the abolition crusade. The *Liberator* review of 23 May 1845, asserted that the *Narrative* "cannot fail to produce a great sensation wherever it may happen to circulate, especially among the slavocracy. . . . What a lifting of the veil is this, to convince the skeptical that it is impossible to exaggerate the horrors and enormities of that impious system!"[43]

The *Narrative* substantiated the intellectual capacity of African Americans for many critics. The growth of moral sensibilities, acquisition of a rudimentary education, and evidence of courage in the midst of slavery's degradation recounted by Douglass indicated that he was an exceptional man and that all blacks freed of the slave's fetters could improve themselves. The abolitionist editor of the Oberlin *Evangelist* found in Douglass's autobiography an expression of "some of the noblest sentiments of the human heart," a harbinger that "the days of Oppression are numbered," and an example of the potentiality of blacks once emancipated. Abolitionist Mary Howitt in her review of 1847 in London's *People's Journal* described Douglass as "a noble human being" and viewed his *Narrative* as an incomparable catalog of slavery's horrors: "If we were to write ten volumes on the atrocities and miseries of slavery in the abstract, we could say nothing half so impressive and conclusive as is the simple, honest narrative of a real slave, written by himself."[44]

Several critics declared how instructive the book would be to all classes or readers. "This little book taught by examples the cruel workings of the systems of Slavery, in a region where its burden is comparatively light, and the plainness of the narration and the simplicity of the style made it attractive to all classes of readers." One of the most enthusiastic critiques was in the *National Anti-Slavery Standard* of 12 June 1845. Contending that the book would enlighten even slavery's defenders, the reviewer observed: "This book ought to be read by all before whose mental blindness visions of happy slaves continually dance. It is the story of the life of a man of great

---

42. *Lib.,* 6 June 1845; *NASS,* 26 June 1845.
43. *Lib.,* 9, 23, 30 May 1845; *NASS,* 5 June 1845.
44. Oberlin *Evangelist,* 29 April 1846; (London) *People's Journal,* 2 : 302 (1847).

intellectual power, in the very circumstances of Slavery,—in the Northernmost of the slave states, and under kind masters."[45]

Nonabolitionist journals, especially those published in the United Kingdom, upheld the work's didactic purpose for a European audience distant from American slavery. The Cork *Examiner* on 22 October 1845 asserted that the *Narrative* "gives an insight into the slave system in America, which cannot elsewhere be obtained in so concise and interesting a form." Similarly, *Chamber's Edinburgh Journal* published a review of the *Narrative* on 24 January 1846 in which the author declared that it would "help considerably to disseminate correct ideas respecting slavery and its attendant evils. Some of the passages present a dismal picture of what is endured by the negro race in the slave-holding states of the union." The review in England's Newcastle *Guardian* looked upon the *Narrative* primarily as a revelation about American religion and as a corrective to many previously published accounts of American slavery.[46]

Writers for nonabolitionist journals tended to be more skeptical than the abolitionist reviewers and were anxious to determine the credibility of Douglass's account. Generally assuming "that Frederick Douglass is what he professes," the London *Spectator* reviewer thought it "improbable" that Douglass fought with a slaveholder or learned to read in the manner he described in the *Narrative*. Doubt about Douglass's authorship lingered until the end and the reviewer concluded: "If this narrative is really true in its basis, and untouched by any one save Douglass himself, it is a singular book, and he is a more singular man. Even if it is of the nature of the true stories of De Foe, it is curious as a picture of slavery, and worth reading."[47]

Most critics had fewer doubts about Douglass's credibility than the *Spectator* reviewer. The Boston *Transcript,* for example, contended that the *Narrative* "bears throughout the indelible marks of truth." The Boston *Courier* asserted that the book contained "many descriptions of scenes at the South, which, if true, bear sufficient witness against the 'peculiar institution,' to make every honest man to wish its downfall soon, and by almost any means. And there seems to be no reason for believing that more than the

---

45. Massachusetts Anti-Slavery Society, *Fourteenth Annual Report* (Boston, 1846), 44; *NASS,* 12 June 1845.

46. Cork *Examiner,* 22 October 1845; *Chamber's Edinburgh Journal,* new ser., 5 : 56 (24 January 1846); Newcastle *Guardian,* 11 July 1846. See also: *New York Evangelist,* 26 June 1845; *Christian Freeman,* 29 May 1845.

47. Quoted in *Littell's Living Age,* 8 : 65 (10 January 1846).

truth is told." In November 1845, the *British Friend* declared that "Truth seems stamped on every page of this narrative."[48]

For a few critics, the prefatory letters enhanced the credibility of Douglass's autobiography. The London *League* referred, for instance, to the book's being "certified by highly respectable persons" as "authentic." William Howitt, reviewing the first Irish edition of the book for the London *Atlas,* commented on Douglass's authenticating prefaces because readers might well ask, "Who is this FREDERICK DOUGLASS? And what guarantee have we that he is what he represents himself to be? In answer to this, we have only to say that his book is prefaced by two admirable letters from the well-known champions of American freedom, WILLIAM LLOYD GARRISON and WENDELL PHILLIPS, bearing the highest testimonies to his character and to his services in the abolition cause."[49]

Other critics distrusted the letters. The most extreme reaction came from the *Religious Spectator* reviewer, who felt their endorsement of the book was reason enough not to read it: "We might possibly have laid it aside without reading it, from perceiving that it was published under the patronage of several individuals, whose course on the subject of slavery we have never regarded as either politic or right." The New York *Tribune* found Phillips's letter to be neutral but Garrison's remarks counterproductive. The *Tribune* was highly critical of the "noble and generous" Garrison and contended that the tone of his comments made Douglass's seem "very just and temperate" in contrast. Beyond this, the *Tribune* argued the prefatory comments did little to authenticate Douglass's account. Phillips, at least, did not invalidate the account. By contrast, Garrison's comments were, the *Tribune* charged, "in his usual over emphatic style . . . he has indulged in violent invective and denunciation till he has spoiled the temper of his mind. Like a man who has been in the habit of screaming himself hoarse to make the deaf hear, he can no longer pitch his voice on a key agreeable to common ears."[50]

Many commented on Douglass's use of personal and place names. The Bristol *Mercury* asserted that Douglass had done much to remove doubt about his identity in the book by "giving the names of the masters under

---

48. *Courier* and *Transcript* quoted in *Narrative* (Dublin, 1846), cxxi; *Lib.,* 6 June 1845; *British Friend,* 3 : 191 (December 1845). See also *Lib.,* 26 December 1845.

49. Quoted in *Lib.,* 28 November 1845; *Narrative* (Dublin, 1846), cxxx–cxxxi. See also: *British Friend,* 3 : 191 (December 1845).

50. *Religious Spectator,* n.d., as quoted in *PaF,* 31 July 1845, *NASS,* 7 August 1845; New York *Tribune,* 10 June 1845.

whom he had lived, and dates and events which would at once prove the correctness of his account." Specificity represented a major part of the *Tribune*'s reason for accepting the validity of the *Narrative:* "He has had the courage to name the persons, times and places, thus exposing himself to obvious danger, and setting the seal on his deep convictions as to the religious need of speaking the whole truth."[51]

But most critics looked beyond specificity for additional evidence to show that Douglass had written his autobiography and that it was a faithful account of his life. Ironically, they found confirmation of Douglass's written words in his spoken words. A thoughtful and very skeptical reviewer for the *Religious Spectator,* upon being given a copy of the book, initially cast it aside because it had been published by the American Anti-Slavery Society. With such an imprimatur on the book, he doubted that Douglass had either written it or was a fugitive slave until he learned "upon good authority, that his lectures are characterized by as able reasoning, as genuine wit, and as bold and stirring appeals, as we almost ever find in connexion with the highest intellectual culture."[52]

Skeptical critics in the United Kingdom often delayed the publication of reviews of the *Narrative* until they had an opportunity to hear Douglass speak. In his speeches they found proof that he had written his autobiography. Typical of such critics was the Irish abolitionist Isaac Nelson, who declared in January 1846:

> I looked forward with much interest and some incredulity to a meeting with the author of this unique piece of autobiography, doubting whether any man reared a slave, and so recently escaped from bonds, could, under the circumstances, produce such a work. My meeting with Frederick Douglass dispelled my doubts; he is indeed an extraordinary man—the type of a class—such an intellectual phenomenon as only appears at times in the republic of letters. I have had opportunities of observing his mind in several attitudes, and applied to various subjects during his stay in Belfast, and I take leave to say that not only do I consider him adequate to the task of writing such a book as the one before us, but also of achieving more Herculean feats.[53]

51. Bristol *Mercury,* 6 January 1846, as quoted in *NASS,* 5 March 1846; New York *Tribune,* 10 June 1845.

52. Quoted in *PaF,* 31 July 1845, *NASS,* 7 August 1845. See also: *New York Evangelist,* 26 June 1845.

53. Quoted in *Narrative* (Dublin, 1846), cxxxii.

A number of reviewers found it impossible to separate Douglass the antislavery orator from Douglass the autobiographer. Identifying Douglass as an escaped slave and "itinerant lecturer" of the American Anti-Slavery Society, a reviewer for the London *Spectator* declared that Douglass, "having a natural force and fluency of language, and dealing with things within his own experience, . . . appears to have spoken with so much acceptance as to have been stimulated to commit to paper the autobiographical portion of his addresses." The New York *Tribune* reacted in a similar fashion in an 1845 review. Douglass, the *Tribune* reported, "is said to be an excellent speaker—can speak from a thorough personal experience—and has upon the audience, beside, the influence of a strong character and uncommon talents. In the book before us he has put into the story of his life the thoughts, the feelings and the adventures that have been so affecting through the living voice; nor are they less so from the printed page."[54]

Some of the most significant reviews concentrated on Douglass's revelations about the development of his interior character. The *British Friend* in its November 1845 assessment of the style and content of the "plain, but eloquent narrative" declared: "In reading it, one sees before him the fearful tossings and heavings of an immortal soul, herded with beasts, and compelled to grope about, feeling after God among reptiles. The reader feels himself in communion with immortality—sunk to a thing—with the image of God turned into a brute." Similarly, the review in an issue of the Newcastle *Guardian* noted the revelations about Douglass's character contained in "his simple yet spirit-stirring narration" of his life and especially "the risings of noble and generous feelings of his soul, and of the exertions which he made for the acquisition of knowledge, despite the almost insuperable obstacles which were thrown in his way." Abolitionist Ralph Varian, writing in the December 1845 issue of the *British Friend,* asserted that the book was "a revelation of the wondrous power which a highly gifted nature possesses, to triumph over brute force, and circumstances the most disheartening."[55]

The work's plainness of style suggested an absence of guile and thus advanced its credibility for the critics. The Lynn, Massachusetts, *Pioneer* argued that the *Narrative* was "evidently drawn with a nice eye, and the coloring is chaste and subdued, rather than extravagant or overwrought.

54. Quoted in *Littell's Living Age,* 8 : 64–65 (10 January 1846); New York *Tribune, 10* June 1845.

55. *British Friend,* 3 : 174 (November 1845), 3 : 191 (December 1845); Newcastle *Guardian,* 11 July 1846. See also *Lib.,* 26 December 1845.

Thrilling as it is, and full of the most burning eloquence, it is yet simple and unimpassioned. Its eloquence is the eloquence of truth, and so is as simple and touching as the impulses of childhood." In his January 1846 review of the *Narrative,* the Reverend Isaac Nelson of Belfast, Ireland, informed his compatriots: "I regard the narrative of FREDERICK DOUGLASS as a literary wonder. The incidents of his life are of such a kind as to hold the reader spell-bound, while they are related in a style simple, perspicuous, and eloquent." Similarly, while viewing the *Narrative* as a "curiosity" focused too heavily on the "incredible brutality" of some individuals, the London *League*'s reviewer concluded: "But even as a literary production, this book possesses no ordinary claims. The author, though uneducated, or rather self-educated, displays great natural powers: he utters his thoughts always lucidly, and often with a polished and vigorous eloquence." The New York *Tribune* was less reserved in its praise of the style of the book than the *League*. In its long critique, the *Tribune* asserted: "Considered merely as a narrative, we have never read one more simple, true, coherent, and warm with genuine feeling. It is an excellent piece of writing."[56]

The pathos and metaphorical flights in the *Narrative* elicited comments from several reviewers. Douglass's autobiography was, they argued, "affecting," "touching," "unspeakably affecting" and filled with passages demonstrating "simple pathos," "deep pathos," or "pathos and sublimity." Wilson Armistead, reviewing the book in 1848, asserted that "the narrative of Douglass contains many affecting incidents, many passages of great eloquence and power." "A.M.," a *Liberator* correspondent, illustrated most fully the pathetic elements of the *Narrative* when she wrote from Albany, New York: "I have wept over the pages of Dickens' 'Oliver Twist'—I have moistened with my tears whole chapters of Eugene Sue's mysteries of Paris—but Douglass's history of the wrongs of the American Slave, brought, not tears—no, tears refused me their comfort—its horrible truths crowded in such quick succession, and entered so deep into the chambers of my soul, as to entirely close the relief valve. . . . I groaned in the agony of my spirit." According to the critics, the passages demonstrating Douglass's masterful use of pathos included those describing his relationship with his mother, the songs of the slaves, his acquisition of an education, and the treatment of aged slaves. The most frequent comments on the use of meta-

---

56. Lynn (Mass.) *Pioneer,* n.d., as quoted in *Lib.,* 30 May 1845; London *League,* n.d., as quoted in *Lib.,* 28 November 1845; Isaac Nelson, as quoted in *Narrative* (Dublin, 1846), cxxxii; New York *Tribune,* 10 June 1845.

phors in the *Narrative* centered on Douglass's apostrophe to freedom as he watched ships in the Chesapeake Bay.[57]

The reception accorded the *Narrative* in the South ironically verified its details and lent authority to it. The American Anti-Slavery Society apparently exhausted every means to push the book in Maryland and was relatively successful. The early reactions of Marylanders to the *Narrative* boosted sales because they testified to its credibility. For example, the editor of a Philadelphia newspaper, the *Elevator,* while reviewing Douglass's "exceedingly interesting" autobiography, reported that on a trip to Maryland he encountered several blacks who knew Douglass "by his assumed as well as by his real name, and related to us many interesting incidents about their former companion."[58]

More direct testimony validating the *Narrative* came from the pens of white Marylanders personally acquainted with slavery on the Eastern Shore and Douglass's owners. This valuable testimony began when a white resident of Baltimore reported in September 1845 that Douglass's *Narrative* "is now circulating and being read in this city, and five hundred copies are still wanted here. They would be read with avidity, and do much good." Signing his letter "A Citizen of Maryland," the writer then assessed the credibility of Douglass's account: "I have made some inquiry, and have reason to believe his statements are true. Col. Edward Lloyd's relatives are my relatives! Let this suffice for the present." Another white native of Maryland and acquaintance of the Lloyds read Douglass's account in the spring of 1846 and wrote "from my knowledge of slavery as it really exists . . . I am fully prepared to bear a decided testimony to the truth of all his assertions, with regard to the discipline upon the plantations of Maryland, as well as his descriptions of cruelty and murder."[59]

Unfavorable southern responses to the *Narrative,* however, far outstripped the favorable ones over the next several years. Whether it was true or false, most southern whites felt that the *Narrative* was an incendiary document inciting slaves to rebel. As late as the spring of 1849 a grand jury in Grayson County, Virginia, indicted Jarvis C. Bacon for "feloniously and knowingly circulating" the *Narrative* because the jurors felt the book was

---

57. Wilson Armistead, *A Tribute for the Negro* (Manchester, Eng., 1848), 455; *Lib.,* 6 June 1845. See also *NASS,* 12 June 1845; New York *Tribune,* 10 June 1845; (London) *People's Journal,* 2 : 302–305 (1847).

58. Philadelphia *Elevator,* n.d., as quoted in *Lib.,* 15 August 1845.

59. Ibid., 26 September 1845, 15 May 1846.

"intended to cause slaves to rebel and make insurrection, and denying the right of property of masters in their slaves."[60]

However much Douglass may have sympathized with Jarvis Bacon, he first had to confront the persistent challenge of A. C. C. Thompson of Delaware. Apparently prompted by Douglass's former owner Thomas Auld, Thompson wrote a long review essay of the *Narrative* for the *Delaware Republican*. Describing Douglass's autobiography variously as "dirty," "false," "infamous libel," and a "ridiculous publication," Thompson contended that it was filled with "glaring falsehoods" and declared "the whole to be a budget of falsehoods from beginning to end." While refuting Douglass's claim that slave children were customarily separated from their mothers in Maryland, Thompson concentrated on correcting the *Narrative*'s unflattering characterization of Edward Lloyd, Aaron Anthony, Giles Hicks, Austin Gore, Thomas Lambdin, Edward Covey, and Thomas Auld. From what he knew of these men and Douglass when he was a slave, Thompson concluded that Douglass did not write the book, which, he argued, bore "the glaring impress of falsehood on every page."[61]

This was just the challenge Douglass had been awaiting. Writing to Thompson from England in 1846, Douglass thanked him profusely for proving that he had been a slave and that the people he wrote about were not fictitious. To Thompson's charge that he had maligned good masters and Christian men with charitable feelings, Douglass restated his complaints concerning his treatment and observed, "The cowskin makes as deep a gash in my flesh, when wielded by a professed saint, as it does when wielded by an open sinner." The chief focus of Douglass's response was, however, on Thompson's "triumphant vindication of the truth" of this *Narrative:* "your testimony is direct and perfect—just what I have long wanted . . . you . . . brush away the miserable insinuation of my northern pro-slavery enemies, that I have used fictitious not real names." Douglass promised to add Thompson's letter as an appendix to the second Irish edition of his *Narrative*.[62]

Thompson launched a second and more systematic attack on Douglass's autobiography after some northern journalists expressed doubts about the *Delaware Republican* review. As the basis for his second attack, Thompson collected letters from Thomas Auld, James Dawson, Dr. A. C. C.

---

60. Ibid., 18 May 1849.

61. Wilmington *Delaware Republican*, n.d., as quoted in *NASS*, 25 December 1845.

62. *Lib.*, 27 February 1846.

Thompson, L. Dodson, and Thomas Graham denying the validity of Douglass's autobiography. The central focus of the letters was the character of Thomas Auld. Auld's neighbors and acquaintances contended that Douglass's portrayal of Auld was "a base and villainous fabrication," "basely false," and "palpably untrue." A number of Thompson's witnesses claimed that Auld's "conduct to his servants was more like an indulgent father than a master." Auld himself denied that he had ever flogged Douglass and claimed that Douglass had suppressed information about his promise that "when he was 25 years old I would emancipate him; . . . He does not say one word about this in his Narrative, as it would not have answered to have mentioned so much truth." Thompson argued that the testimony of Auld and his neighbors demonstrated that "the assertions of this negro Douglass are nothing more than gross misrepresentations."[63]

On 6 February 1846, when Douglass wrote the preface to the second Irish edition of his autobiography, he kept his promise to Thompson. In spite of the confident tone of his earlier response to Thompson, Douglass nevertheless repeated in his preface sections of the report of his farewell meeting in Lynn, Massachusetts, and the resolutions passed at that meeting testifying to his fugitive status. He also reprinted the declaration of a committee of the Hibernian Anti-Slavery Society that Douglass "has long been known to us by reputation, and is now introduced to us by letters from some of the most distinguished and faithful friends of the Anti-Slavery cause in the United States."

Douglass's central focus in the four-page preface, however, was Thompson. Conceding that the two naturally "differ in our details," Douglass began his references to Thompson by declaring: "He agrees with me at least in the important fact, that I am what I proclaim myself to be, an ungrateful fugitive from the 'patriarchal institutions' of the Slave States; and he certifies that many of the heroes of my Narrative are still living and doing well, as 'honored and worthy members of the Methodist Episcopal Church.'" The Thompson-Douglass exchange maintained interest in the *Narrative* for years after its publication. Douglass fueled the fires by repeatedly referring to it in his speeches, letters, and editorials.[64]

What concerned Douglass most, however, about Thompson's charges was the allegation that he had misrepresented the character of his master Thomas Auld. Since Auld had specifically denied that Douglass's portrayal

---

63. Ibid., 20 February 1846.
64. *Narrative* (Dublin, 1846), ii–vi; Blassingame, *Douglass Papers,* 1 : 200–201.

of him was accurate, Douglass concentrated more and more on Auld in his speeches and writings. With consummate skill, Douglass transformed Auld, in the public mind, into the archetypal vindictive slaveholder desperate to recapture and punish his former slave. Speaking in London in May 1846, Douglass gave a characteristic presentation when he said that his master, after trying unsuccessfully to refute the *Narrative,* had transferred title in him to his brother, who "resolves that if ever I touch American soil, I shall be instantly reduced to a state of slavery. However, it is not to a state of slavery that they wish now to have me reduced. They have a feeling of revenge to gratify."[65]

Thomas Auld's actions after Douglass arrived in England highlighted and exaggerated the danger the fugitive slave faced. By giving the impression that Douglass would be immediately reenslaved if he returned to the United States, Auld created greater sympathy for Douglass in the United Kingdom that eventually led abolitionists there to raise money to purchase the fugitive so they could manumit him. Long before the inauguration of this manumission effort, however, Douglass began a literary and oratorical campaign to neutralize Thomas Auld's assault on the credibility of his *Narrative*. Even in responding to attacks from third parties, Douglass tried, whenever possible, to allude to Auld's letter to Thompson. The earliest opportunity Douglass had for a full response to Auld came in 1846, when an American in the United Kingdom declared that Douglass lied about slavery in his speeches. Writing a response from Glasgow in April 1846, Douglass concentrated on Auld and contended that Auld felt so keenly Douglass's "exposures" and "severe goadings" that his "old master is in a state of mind quite favorable to an attempt at re-capture . . . to feed his revenge." According to Douglass, Auld told "a positive lie," when he swore "he never struck me, or told any one else to do so." Recalling an occasion when Auld beat him "until he wearied himself," Douglass declared: "My memory in such matters, is better than his."[66]

Two years later Douglass began using Auld's denial of the validity of the *Narrative* in an attempt to goad his former master into a public debate. He inaugurated the campaign by writing his first public letter to his master on 3 September 1848, the anniversary of his escape from slavery. Receiving no reply from Auld, Douglass then reprinted his response of 1846 to A. C. C. Thompson in the 13 October 1848 issue of the *North Star*. Then, on 3

65. Blassingame, *Douglass Papers,* 1 : 252.

66. *Lib.,* 15 May 1846; Benjamin Quarles, *Frederick Douglass* (Washington, D.C., 1948), 51.

September 1849, Douglass wrote his second letter to Auld. Although other fugitive slaves wrote public letters to their masters, few tried to use their correspondence as Douglass did to shore up the credibility of their auto-biographies. Douglass, for example, began his second "friendly epistle" to Auld by denying that he would "wilfully malign the character even of a slaveholder" and asserted: "I can say, with a clear conscience, in all that I have ever written or spoken respecting yourself, I have tried to remember that, though I am beyond your power and control, I am still accountable to our common Father and Judge,—in the sight of whom I believe that I stand acquitted of all intentional misrepresentation against you. Of course, I have said many hard things respecting yourself; but all has been based upon what I knew of you at the time I was a slave in your family."[67]

Three other critics agreed, in part, with the claims of Thomas Auld and A. C. C. Thompson. The most important of such reviews of the *Narrative* appeared in July 1849 when the Reverend Ephraim Peabody included it in his thirty-two-page *Christian Examiner* essay, "Narratives of Fugitive Slaves." Peabody's review of the autobiographies of Henry Watson, Lewis and Milton Clarke, William Wells Brown, Josiah Henson, and Douglass was important for two reasons. First, Peabody was one of the few ante-bellum critics to concentrate on black autobiographies as literature. Second, Frederick Douglass published a response to Peabody's essay. In his oft-quoted opening paragraph, Peabody declared: "AMERICA has the mournful honor of adding a new department to the literature of civiliza-tion,—the autobiographies of escaped slaves." Viewing such works as "remarkable as being pictures of slavery by the slave" revealing the black's "native love of freedom" and sense of poetry and romance, they contained, Peabody asserted, adventures comparable to the *Iliad* and the *Odyssey*.[68]

Peabody was most impressed with the autobiography of Josiah Henson and spent fourteen pages summarizing it because, he asserted, his readers would "be interested in the efforts of one who, without noise or pretension, without bitterness towards the whites, without extravagant claims in behalf of the blacks, has patiently, wisely, and devotedly given himself to the improvement of the large body of his wretched countrymen amongst whom his lot has been cast." Writing approvingly of Henson's attempt to purchase his freedom, his religious convictions, his "fidelity," "freedom from exag-

67. *NS,* 8 September, 13 October 1848, 7 September 1849; *Lib.,* 14 September 1849; Blassingame, *Slave Testimony,* 48–57, 114–15.
68. (Boston) *Christian Examiner,* 47 : 61–62 (July 1849).

geration," "absence of personal bitterness," and "commiseration for all classes," Peabody declared that Henson's narrative presented "the best picture of the evils incident to slave life on the plantations which can be found."[69]

All of the other autobiographies, and especially Douglass's, suffered in comparison to Henson's. Indeed, from Peabody's perspective, beside Henson's account, the other autobiographies

> possess no especial interest beyond what must belong to the life of almost any fugitive slave. They are records of degradation on the part of both blacks and whites,—of suffering and wrong and moral corruption. They give, doubtless, a just idea of what slavery is to the slave. But, on the other hand, while we have no reason to question the truth of particular facts representing individuals, we have no doubt that they convey an altogether erroneous idea of the general character of the masters. The best qualities of the master are likely to appear anywhere rather than in his connection with the slave. And except it be an easy kindness, the slave is in no position to estimate aright the virtues of one who, towards himself, appears simply as a power whom he cannot resist. They stand in such utterly false relations to each other, that their whole intercourse must necessarily be vitiated, and the worst qualities of each, and these almost exclusively, must be perpetually forced on the attention of the other. But human society could not long exist were the great body of slaveholders like those whom these narratives describe.[70]

Peabody admitted that he was personally acquainted with Douglass and that his narrative "contains the life of a superior man." He then shifted to a critique of Douglass's speaking style. Peabody took special umbrage at Douglass's "severity of judgement and a one-sidedness of view," his "seeing only the evils of slavery," and his "violence and extravagance of expression." Although Peabody acknowledged "the sympathy which his narrative excites, and our respect for the force of character he has shown in rising from the depths of bondage," he let his critical remarks stand in hopes that they would lead Douglass to follow a wiser course.[71]

Douglass responded to Peabody in an editorial in the *North Star* on 3 August 1849. Contending that because Peabody was a northern minister he was "ill qualified" to write his essay, Douglass argued that, contrary to

69. Ibid., 80, 83, 93.
70. Ibid., 69–70.
71. Ibid., 74–75.

Peabody's claims, there were few truly antislavery masters. Northerners had, for too long, been deceived by southern words. Douglass conceded that "slaveholders frequently speak of slavery as an evil . . . in the presence of persons from the North," but rarely in front of slaves, and concluded that "if we judge the slaveholder by his words, it will be difficult to convict him of unkindness to his slaves, or to charge him with the desire to continue the relation of slavery; but the unmistakable language of conduct leaves no doubt of his guilt in both these points. To detest slavery in words, and to cling to it in practice, is a display of hypocrisy that should deceive no one." Rejecting Peabody's advice about the style and content of his lectures, Douglass then turned to his criticisms of the slave autobiographies. In the process he defended the honesty of his portrait of slaveholders:

> Speaking of the Narratives, Mr. Peabody admits, "they give a just idea of what slavery is to the slave," but adds, "they convey an altogether erroneous idea of the character of the masters." Here we think Mr. Peabody's logic at fault. What slavery is to the slave, the slaveholder is to the slave; and the character of the slaveholder may be fairly inferred from his treatment of the slave. It is not by the courtesy and hospitality which slaveholders extend to Northern clergymen and travellers, whose good opinions they think desirable, that we are to learn their true characters. Here they have an end to attain. But it is their conduct towards those over whom they have unlimited power, by which they are to be tried and adjudged. In this relation they act freely and without restraint; in the other case they act from necessity.[72]

Support for, and popularization of, the views Douglass expressed in his *Narrative* and responses to Thompson and Peabody came from Harriet Beecher Stowe. The publication of Stowe's *Uncle Tom's Cabin* in 1852 led to renewed interest in all slave autobiographies, and especially those of Josiah Henson, Lewis Clarke, and Douglass. When reviewers questioned "whether the representations of 'Uncle Tom's Cabin' are a fair representation of slavery as it at present exists," Stowe published in 1853 *The Key to Uncle Tom's Cabin,* which, she claimed, was the factual base for the novel. The *Key* contained a collection of "real incidents,—of actions really performed, of words and expressions really uttered." To prove that George Harris, the intelligent mulatto character, was not overdrawn in her novel, Stowe quoted extracts from the autobiographies of Lewis and Milton

72. *NS,* 3 August 1849.

Clarke, Josiah Henson, and Frederick Douglass because their accounts, she contended, were "related by those who know slavery by the best of all tests—experience; and they are given by men who have earned a character in freedom which makes their word as good as the word of any man living." The central incident that Stowe focused on in Douglass's *Narrative* was his description of his acquisition of an education, which she argued was "a most interesting and affecting parallel" to George's teaching himself to read and write.[73]

Stowe's defense and use of Douglass's *Narrative* and other black autobiographies prompted the *Key*'s critics to comment specifically on the slave testimony section and to publish their reflections on slave autobiographies and Douglass's account. For reviewers in southern newspapers and magazines, the *Key* sometimes led to extended criticism of a body of literature they had previously ignored. The critic in the July 1853 issue of the *Southern Quarterly Review,* for example, found little that was credible in slave autobiographies:

> The runaway narratives are, no doubt, pure inventions of the cunning fugitives, to work upon the charities and sympathies of those who are simple enough to receive their statements as truthful. . . . Such tales of torture of the whites, such pictures of sorrow by the meek and sensitive blacks, would draw tears from eyes of stone. . . . These narratives are now pretty much stereotyped. The runaways have learned their part, and they go through it, on the one key, with great dexterity, and with daily improvement on the music; so that the horrors of poor Frederick Douglass, himself, have been greatly surpassed by later sufferers, who have set up as rivals for Northern favour.[74]

Although there is no evidence that Douglass responded to the essay in the *Southern Quarterly Review,* he did react to similar criticisms of Harriet Beecher Stowe's works in *Graham's Magazine.* The dispute arose over some general comments made by the editor in the course of reviewing *Uncle Tom's Cabin.* He included his severe criticisms of recent writings on slavery in an essay entitled "Black Letters; or Uncle Tom-Foolery in Literature." George Graham complained that the bookshelves "groan under the weight of Sambo's woes, done up in covers! . . . We hate this niggerism, and hope it may be done away with." Graham admonished writers to "turn

73. Harriet Beecher Stowe, *A Key to Uncle Tom's Cabin; Presenting the Original Facts and Documents Upon Which the Story Is Founded* (Boston, 1853), 5, 16, 19.

74. *Southern Quarterly Review,* 24 : 232–33 (July 1853).

to something worthier than these negro subjects" and expressed his displeasure over the literary "incursion of blacks." After a scathing attack on *Uncle Tom's Cabin,* Graham refused to review "the other black books—those literary nigritudes—those little tadpoles of the press—sable bodies and stirring tales."[75]

Douglass replied by classing Graham among the "Northern cringers to the slave power" and arguing that it was an "ungenerous and ungentlemanly attack (*'miscalled a Review'*)." Graham's attack on Stowe was, however, understandable: "Recrimination is the favorite artillery of the defenders and abettors of the slave system." Graham accepted Douglass's challenge by attacking him specifically in the March issue of his magazine. Graham contended that although he respected Douglass, "we hate the present negro literature—especially that of Fred.'s, which by abusing the white, is intended to elevate the black man." Arguing that Graham indicted himself, Douglass reprinted Graham's March editorial without comment.[76]

Among antebellum critics of Douglass's *Narrative,* George Graham was in a distinct minority of those claiming that the book had little literary merit. Along with A. C. C. Thompson, Ephraim Peabody, Thomas Auld, and the *Southern Quarterly Review,* Graham felt that the book exaggerated the faults of southern whites, contained more invention than truth, or had not been written by Douglass. Contrary to these views, the overwhelming majority of antebellum critics found much to praise in the *Narrative*.

Blazoned, scrutinized, celebrated, excoriated, Frederick Douglass by the early 1850s was fixed in the American public's mind as a real person who had earlier passed through the mill of slavery on the Eastern Shore of Maryland. Subjected to the tough test of credibility leveled against nineteenth-century autobiographers, he had almost singlehandedly restored vigor to the slave narratives as key weapons in the antislavery crusade. But Douglass also established that his tremendous gift as a writer was not limited to political instruments. Douglass proved himself a master of one of the most American of literary genres—the salvational autobiography.

Embracing the tradition of Puritan conversion narratives, Indian captivity narratives, and especially the secularized yet deeply moral autobiographies best represented by Benjamin Franklin, Douglass so crafted his work that his positive relationship with them all was unmistakable as he, too, encountered and renounced the snares of the world and stayed to an

75. *Graham's Magazine,* 42 : 209–14 (January 1853), 42 : 365 (March 1853).
76. *FDP,* 25 February, 4 March 1853.

ever clearer pursuit of moral responsibility, wisdom, and freedom. However black, enslaved, and seemingly other, his affecting and lucid prose argued for oneness with Franklin and his racial brethren. By jeopardizing his very security as a fugitive in order to rebuild the credibility of the American slave narrative, none so dramatically as Douglass integrated both the horror and the great quest of the African-American experience into this deep stream of American autobiography. He advanced and extended that tradition and is rightfully designated one of its greatest practitioners.

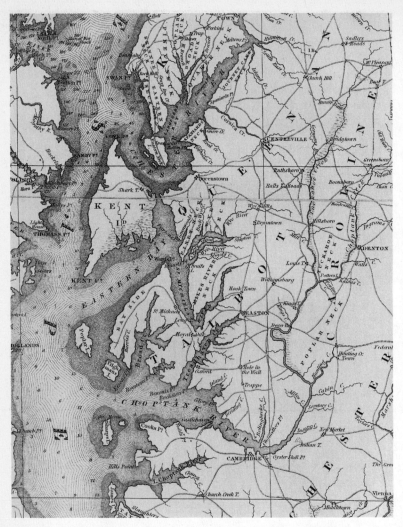

The Maryland Eastern Shore at the time of Douglass's boyhood. Source: Fielding Lucas, Jr., *The State of Maryland. Detail of the Eastern Shore.* (Baltimore, 1840)

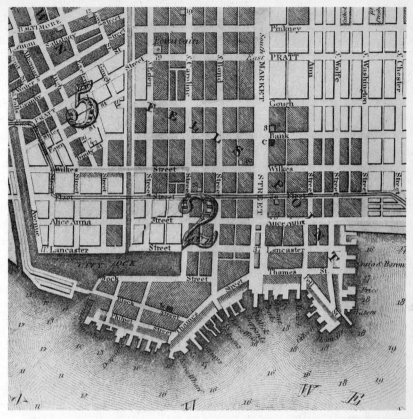

Baltimore's Fells Point Neighborhood at the time of Douglass's residence in the 1820s and 1830s. Source: Fielding Lucas, Jr., Plan of the City of Baltimore (detail). (Baltimore, 1836)

NARRATIVE

OF THE

LIFE

OF

FREDERICK DOUGLASS,

AN

AMERICAN SLAVE.

WRITTEN BY HIMSELF.

BOSTON:

PUBLISHED AT THE ANTI-SLAVERY OFFICE,

No. 25 CORNHILL.

1845.

Title page of *Narrative of the Life of Frederick Douglass, an American Slave* (Boston: Published at the Anti-Slavery Office, 1845).

NARRATIVE

OF THE

LIFE

OF

FREDERICK DOUGLASS,

AN

AMERICAN SLAVE.

———————

WRITTEN BY HIMSELF.

———————

BOSTON:

PUBLISHED AT THE ANTI-SLAVERY OFFICE,

No. 25 CORNHILL.

1845.

PREFACE.

In the month of August, 1841, I attended an anti-slavery convention in Nantucket, at which it was my happiness to become acquainted with FREDERICK DOUGLASS, the writer of the following Narrative. He was a stranger to nearly every member of that body; but, having recently made his escape from the southern prison-house of bondage, and feeling his curiosity excited to ascertain the principles and measures of the abolitionists,—of whom he had heard a somewhat vague description while he was a slave,— he was induced to give his attendance, on the occasion alluded to, though at that time a resident in New Bedford.

Fortunate, most fortunate occurrence!—fortunate for the millions of his manacled brethren, yet panting for deliverance from their awful thraldom!—fortunate for the cause of negro emancipation, and of universal liberty!—fortunate for the land of his birth, which he has already done so much to save and bless!—fortunate for a large circle of friends and acquaintances, whose sympathy and affection he has strongly secured by the many sufferings he has endured, by his virtuous traits of character, by his ever-abiding remembrance of those who are in bonds, as being bound with them!—fortunate for the multitudes, in various parts of our republic, whose minds he has enlightened on the subject of slavery, and who have been melted to tears by his pathos, or roused to virtuous indignation by his stirring eloquence against the enslavers of men!—fortunate for himself, as it at once brought him into the field of public usefulness, "gave the world assurance of a MAN," quickened the slumbering energies of his soul, and consecrated him to the great work of breaking the rod of the oppressor, and letting the oppressed go free!

I shall never forget his first speech at the convention—the extraordinary emotion it excited in my own mind—the powerful impression it created upon a crowded auditory, completely taken by surprise—the applause which followed from the beginning to the end of his felicitous remarks. I think I never hated slavery so intensely as at that moment; certainly, my perception of the enormous outrage which is inflicted by it, on the godlike nature of its victims, was rendered far more clear than ever. There stood one, in physical proportion and stature commanding and exact—in intellect richly endowed—in natural eloquence a prodigy—in soul manifestly "created but a little lower than the angels"—yet a slave, ay, a fugitive slave,— trembling for his safety, hardly daring to believe that on the American soil,

3

a single white person could be found who would befriend him at all hazards, for the love of God and humanity! Capable of high attainments as an intellectual and moral being—needing nothing but a comparatively small amount of cultivation to make him an ornament to society and a blessing to his race—by the law of the land, by the voice of the people, by the terms of the slave code, he was only a piece of property, a beast of burden, a chattel personal, nevertheless!

A beloved friend from New Bedford prevailed on Mr. DOUGLASS to address the convention. He came forward to the platform with a hesitancy and embarrassment, necessarily the attendants of a sensitive mind in such a novel position. After apologizing for his ignorance, and reminding the audience that slavery was a poor school for the human intellect and heart, he proceeded to narrate some of the facts in his own history as a slave, and in the course of his speech gave utterance to many noble thoughts and thrilling reflections. As soon as he had taken his seat, filled with hope and admiration, I rose, and declared that PATRICK HENRY, of revolutionary fame, never made a speech more eloquent in the cause of liberty, than the one we had just listened to from the lips of that hunted fugitive. So I believed at that time—such is my belief now. I reminded the audience of the peril which surrounded this self-emancipated young man at the North,—even in Massachusetts, on the soil of the Pilgrim Fathers, among the descendants of revolutionary sires; and I appealed to them, whether they would ever allow him to be carried back into slavery,—law or no law, constitution or no constitution. The response was unanimous and in thunder-tones—"NO!" "Will you succor and protect him as a brother-man—a resident of the old Bay State?" "YES!" shouted the whole mass, with an energy so startling, that the ruthless tyrants south of Mason and Dixon's line might almost have heard the mighty burst of feeling, and recognized it as the pledge of an invincible determination, on the part of those who gave it, never to betray him that wanders, but to hide the outcast, and firmly to abide the consequences.

It was at once deeply impressed upon my mind, that, if Mr. DOUGLASS could be persuaded to consecrate his time and talents to the promotion of the anti-slavery enterprise, a powerful impetus would be given to it, and a stunning blow at the same time inflicted on northern prejudice against a colored complexion. I therefore endeavored to instil hope and courage into his mind, in order that he might dare to engage in a vocation so anomalous and responsible for a person in his situation; and I was seconded in this effort by warm-hearted friends, especially by the late General Agent of the

Massachusetts Anti-Slavery Society, Mr. JOHN A. COLLINS, whose judgment in this instance entirely coincided with my own. At first, he could give no encouragement; with unfeigned diffidence, he expressed his conviction that he was not adequate to the performance of so great a task; the path marked out was wholly an untrodden one; he was sincerely apprehensive that he should do more harm than good. After much deliberation, however, he consented to make a trial; and ever since that period, he has acted as a lecturing agent, under the auspices either of the American or the Massachusetts Anti-Slavery Society. In labors he has been most abundant; and his success in combating prejudice, in gaining proselytes, in agitating the public mind, has far surpassed the most sanguine expectations that were raised at the commencement of his brilliant career. He has borne himself with gentleness and meekness, yet with true manliness of character. As a public speaker, he excels in pathos, wit, comparison, imitation, strength of reasoning, and fluency of language. There is in him that union of head and heart, which is indispensable to an enlightenment of the heads and a winning of the hearts of others. May his strength continue to be equal to his day! May he continue to "grow in grace, and in the knowledge of God," that he may be increasingly serviceable in the cause of bleeding humanity, whether at home or abroad!

It is certainly a very remarkable fact, that one of the most efficient advocates of the slave population, now before the public, is a fugitive slave, in the person of FREDERICK DOUGLASS; and that the free colored population of the United States are as ably represented by one of their own number, in the person of CHARLES LENOX REMOND, whose eloquent appeals have extorted the highest applause of multitudes on both sides of the Atlantic. Let the calumniators of the colored race despise themselves for their baseness and illiberality of spirit, and henceforth cease to talk of the natural inferiority of those who require nothing but time and opportunity to attain to the highest point of human excellence.

It may, perhaps, be fairly questioned, whether any other portion of the population of the earth could have endured the privations, sufferings and horrors of slavery, without having become more degraded in the scale of humanity than the slaves of African descent. Nothing has been left undone to cripple their intellects, darken their minds, debase their moral nature, obliterate all traces of their relationship to mankind; and yet how wonderfully they have sustained the mighty load of a most frightful bondage, under which they have been groaning for centuries! To illustrate the effect of slavery on the white man,—to show that he has no powers of endurance, in

such a condition, superior to those of his black brother,—DANIEL O'CON-
NELL, the distinguished advocate of universal emancipation, and the
mightiest champion of prostrate but not conquered Ireland, relates the
following anecdote in a speech delivered by him in the Conciliation Hall,
Dublin, before the Loyal National Repeal Association, March 31, 1845.
"No matter," said Mr. O'CONNELL, "under what specious term it may
disguise itself, slavery is still hideous. *It has a natural, an inevitable tendency to brutalize every noble faculty of man.* An American sailor, who was
cast away on the shore of Africa, where he was kept in slavery for three
years, was, at the expiration of that period, found to be imbruted and
stultified—he had lost all reasoning power; and having forgotten his native
language, could only utter some savage gibberish between Arabic and
English, which nobody could understand, and which even he himself found
difficulty in pronouncing. So much for the humanizing influence of THE
DOMESTIC INSTITUTION!" Admitting this to have been an extraordinary case
of mental deterioration, it proves at least that the white slave can sink as low
in the scale of humanity as the black one.

Mr. DOUGLASS has very properly chosen to write his own Narrative, in
his own style, and according to the best of his ability, rather than to employ
some one else. It is, therefore, entirely his own production; and, considering
how long and dark was the career he had to run as a slave,—how few have
been his opportunities to improve his mind since he broke his iron fetters,—
it is, in my judgment, highly creditable to his head and heart. He who can
peruse it without a tearful eye, a heaving breast, an afflicted spirit,—
without being filled with an unutterable abhorrence of slavery and all its
abettors, and animated with a determination to seek the immediate overthrow of that execrable system,—without trembling for the fate of this
country in the hands of a righteous God, who is ever on the side of the
oppressed, and whose arm is not shortened that it cannot save,—must have
a flinty heart, and be qualified to act the part of a trafficker "in slaves and the
souls of men." I am confident that it is essentially true in all its statements;
that nothing has been set down in malice, nothing exaggerated, nothing
drawn from the imagination; that it comes short of the reality, rather than
overstates a single fact in regard to SLAVERY AS IT IS. The experience of
FREDERICK DOUGLASS, as a slave, was not a peculiar one; his lot was not
especially a hard one; his case may be regarded as a very fair specimen of
the treatment of slaves in Maryland, in which State it is conceded that they
are better fed and less cruelly treated than in Georgia, Alabama, or Louisiana. Many have suffered incomparably more, while very few on the planta-

tions have suffered less, than himself. Yet how deplorable was his situation! what terrible chastisements were inflicted upon his person! what still more shocking outrages were perpetrated upon his mind! with all his noble powers and sublime aspirations, how like a brute was he treated, even by those professing to have the same mind in them that was in Christ Jesus! to what dreadful liabilities was he continually subjected! how destitute of friendly counsel and aid, even in his greatest extremities! how heavy was the midnight of woe which shrouded in blackness the last ray of hope, and filled the future with terror and gloom! what longings after freedom took possession of his breast, and how his misery augmented, in proportion as he grew reflective and intelligent,—thus demonstrating that a happy slave is an extinct man! how he thought, reasoned, felt, under the lash of the driver, with the chains upon his limbs! what perils he encountered in his endeavors to escape from his horrible doom! and how signal have been his deliverance and preservation in the midst of a nation of pitiless enemies!

This Narrative contains many affecting incidents, many passages of great eloquence and power; but I think the most thrilling one of them all is the description DOUGLASS gives of his feelings, as he stood soliloquizing respecting his fate, and the chances of his one day being a freeman, on the banks of the Chesapeake Bay—viewing the receding vessels as they flew with their white wings before the breeze, and apostrophizing them as animated by the living spirit of freedom. Who can read that passage, and be insensible to its pathos and sublimity? Compressed into it is a whole Alexandrian library of thought, feeling, and sentiment—all that can, all that need be urged, in the form of expostulation, entreaty, rebuke, against that crime of crimes,—making man the property of his fellow-man! O, how accursed is that system, which entombs the godlike mind of man, defaces the divine image, reduces those who by creation were crowned with glory and honor to a level with four-footed beasts, and exalts the dealer in human flesh above all that is called God! Why should its existence be prolonged one hour? Is it not evil, only evil, and that continually? What does its presence imply but the absence of all fear of God, all regard for man, on the part of the people of the United States? Heaven speed its eternal overthrow!

So profoundly ignorant of the nature of slavery are many persons, that they are stubbornly incredulous whenever they read or listen to any recital of the cruelties which are daily inflicted on its victims. They do not deny that the slaves are held as property; but that terrible fact seems to convey to their minds no idea of injustice, exposure to outrage, or savage barbarity. Tell them of cruel scourgings, of mutilations and brandings, of scenes of pollution and blood, of the banishment of all light and knowledge, and they affect to be greatly indignant at such enormous exaggerations, such whole-sale misstatements, such abominable libels on the character of the southern planters! As if all these direful outrages were not the natural results of slavery! As if it were less cruel to reduce a human being to the condition of a thing, than to give him a severe flagellation, or to deprive him of necessary food and clothing! As if whips, chains, thumb-screws, paddles, blood-hounds, overseers, drivers, patrols, were not all indispensable to keep the slaves down, and to give protection to their ruthless oppressors! As if, when the marriage institution is abolished, concubinage, adultery, and incest, must not necessarily abound; when all the rights of humanity are annihi-lated, any barrier remains to protect the victim from the fury of the spoiler; when absolute power is assumed over life and liberty, it will not be wielded with destructive sway! Skeptics of this character abound in society. In some few instances, their incredulity arises from a want of reflection; but, gener-ally, it indicates a hatred of the light, a desire to shield slavery from the assaults of its foes, a contempt of the colored race, whether bond or free. Such will try to discredit the shocking tales of slaveholding cruelty which are recorded in this truthful Narrative; but they will labor in vain. Mr. DOUGLASS has frankly disclosed the place of his birth, the names of those who claimed ownership in his body and soul, and the names also of those who committed the crimes which he has alleged against them. His state-ments, therefore, may easily be disproved, if they are untrue.

In the course of his Narrative, he relates two instances of murderous cruelty,—in one of which a planter deliberately shot a slave belonging to a neighboring plantation, who had unintentionally gotten within his lordly domain in quest of fish; and in the other, an overseer blew out the brains of a slave who had fled to a stream of water to escape a bloody scourging. Mr. DOUGLASS states that in neither of these instances was any thing done by way of legal arrest or judicial investigation. The Baltimore American, of March 17, 1845, relates a similar case of atrocity, perpetrated with similar impunity—as follows:—"*Shooting a Slave.*—We learn, upon the authority of a letter from Charles county, Maryland, received by a gentleman of this city, that a young man, named Matthews, a nephew of General Matthews, and whose father, it is believed, holds an office at Washington, killed one of the slaves upon his father's farm by shooting him. The letter states that young Matthews had been left in charge of the farm; that he gave an order to the servant, which was disobeyed, when he proceeded to the house, *ob-tained a gun, and, returning, shot the servant.* He immediately, the letter continues, fled to his father's residence, where he still remains unmolested."—Let it never be forgotten, that no slaveholder or overseer can be convicted of any outrage perpetrated on the person of a slave, however diabolical it may be, on the testimony of colored witnesses, whether bond or free. By the slave code, they are adjudged to be as incompetent to testify against a white man, as though they were indeed a part of the brute creation. Hence, there is no legal protection in fact, whatever there may be in form, for the slave population; and any amount of cruelty may be inflicted on them with impunity. Is it possible for the human mind to conceive of a more horrible state of society?

The effect of a religious profession on the conduct of southern masters is vividly described in the following Narrative, and shown to be any thing but salutary. In the nature of the case, it must be in the highest degree pernicious. The testimony of Mr. DOUGLASS, on this point, is sustained by a cloud of witnesses, whose veracity is unimpeachable. "A slaveholder's profession of Christianity is a palpable imposture. He is a felon of the highest grade. He is a man-stealer. It is of no importance what you put in the other scale."

Reader! are you with the man-stealers in sympathy and purpose, or on the side of their down-trodden victims? If with the former, then are you the foe of God and man. If with the latter, what are you prepared to do and dare in their behalf? Be faithful, be vigilant, be untiring in your efforts to break every yoke, and let the oppressed go free. Come what may—cost what it may—inscribe on the banner which you unfurl to the breeze, as your religious and political motto—"NO COMPROMISE WITH SLAVERY! NO UNION WITH SLAVEHOLDERS!"

WM. LLOYD GARRISON.

BOSTON, *May* 1, 1845.

LETTER
FROM WENDELL PHILLIPS, ESQ.

———————————

BOSTON, *April* 22, 1845.

My Dear Friend:

YOU remember the old fable of "The Man and the Lion," where the lion complained that he should not be so misrepresented "when the lions wrote history."

I am glad the time has come when the "lions write history." We have been left long enough to gather the character of slavery from the involuntary evidence of the masters. One might, indeed, rest sufficiently satisfied with what, it is evident, must be, in general, the results of such a relation, without seeking farther to find whether they have followed in every instance. Indeed, those who stare at the half-peck of corn a week, and love to count the lashes on the slave's back, are seldom the "stuff" out of which reformers and abolitionists are to be made. I remember that, in 1838, many were waiting for the results of the West India experiment, before they could come into our ranks. Those "results" have come long ago; but, alas! few of that number have come with them, as converts. A man must be disposed to judge of emancipation by other tests than whether it has increased the produce of sugar,—and to hate slavery for other reasons than because it starves men and whips women,—before he is ready to lay the first stone of his anti-slavery life.

I was glad to learn, in your story, how early the most neglected of God's children waken to a sense of their rights, and of the injustice done them. Experience is a keen teacher; and long before you had mastered your A B C, or knew where the "white sails" of the Chesapeake were bound, you began, I see, to gauge the wretchedness of the slave, not by his hunger and want, not by his lashes and toil, but by the cruel and blighting death which gathers over his soul.

In connection with this, there is one circumstance which makes your recollections peculiarly valuable, and renders your early insight the more remarkable. You come from that part of the country where we are told slavery appears with its fairest features. Let us hear, then, what it is at its best estate—gaze on its bright side, if it has one; and then imagination may task her powers to add dark lines to the picture, as she travels southward to that (for the colored man) Valley of the Shadow of Death, where the Mississippi sweeps along.

Again, we have known you long, and can put the most entire confidence in your truth, candor, and sincerity. Every one who has heard you speak has felt, and, I am confident, every one who reads your book will feel, persuaded that you give them a fair specimen of the whole truth. No one-sided portrait,—no wholesale complaints,—but strict justice done, whenever individual kindliness has neutralized, for a moment, the deadly system with which it was strangely allied. You have been with us, too, some years, and can fairly compare the twilight of rights, which your race enjoy at the North, with that "noon of night" under which they labor south of Mason and Dixon's line. Tell us whether, after all, the half-free colored man of Massachusetts is worse off than the pampered slave of the rice swamps!

In reading your life, no one can say that we have unfairly picked out some rare specimens of cruelty. We know that the bitter drops, which even you have drained from the cup, are no incidental aggravations, no individual ills, but such as must mingle always and necessarily in the lot of every slave. They are the essential ingredients, not the occasional results, of the system.

After all, I shall read your book with trembling for you. Some years ago, when you were beginning to tell me your real name and birthplace, you may remember I stopped you, and preferred to remain ignorant of all. With the exception of a vague description, so I continued, till the other day, when you read me your memoirs. I hardly knew, at the time, whether to thank you or not for the sight of them, when I reflected that it was still dangerous, in Massachusetts, for honest men to tell their names! They say the fathers, in 1776, signed the Declaration of Independence with the halter about their necks. You, too, publish your declaration of freedom with danger compassing you around. In all the broad lands which the Constitution of the United States overshadows, there is no single spot,—however narrow or desolate,—where a fugitive slave can plant himself and say, "I am safe." The whole armory of Northern Law has no shield for you. I am free to say that, in your place, I should throw the MS. into the fire.

You, perhaps, may tell your story in safety, endeared as you are to so many warm hearts by rare gifts, and a still rarer devotion of them to the service of others. But it will be owing only to your labors, and the fearless efforts of those who, trampling the laws and Constitution of the country under their feet, are determined that they will "hide the outcast," and that their hearths shall be, spite of the law, an asylum for the oppressed, if, some time or other, the humblest may stand in our streets, and bear witness in safety against the cruelties of which he has been the victim.

Yet it is sad to think, that these very throbbing hearts which welcome your story, and form your best safeguard in telling it, are all beating contrary to the "statute in such case made and provided." Go on, my dear friend, till you, and those who, like you, have been saved, so as by fire, from the dark prison-house, shall stereotype these free, illegal pulses into statutes; and New England, cutting loose from a blood-stained Union, shall glory in being the house of refuge for the oppressed;—till we no longer merely "*hide* the outcast," or make a merit of standing idly by while he is hunted in our midst; but, consecrating anew the soil of the Pilgrims as an asylum for the oppressed, proclaim our *welcome* to the slave so loudly, that the tones shall reach every hut in the Carolinas, and make the broken-hearted bondman leap up at the thought of old Massachusetts.

God speed the day!

Till then, and ever,

Yours truly,

WENDELL PHILLIPS.

FREDERICK DOUGLASS.

NARRATIVE
OF THE
LIFE OF FREDERICK DOUGLASS.

CHAPTER I.

I was born in Tuckahoe, near Hillsborough, and about twelve miles from Easton, in Talbot county, Maryland. I have no accurate knowledge of my age, never having seen any authentic record containing it. By far the larger part of the slaves know as little of their ages as horses know of theirs, and it is the wish of most masters within my knowledge to keep their slaves thus ignorant. I do not remember to have ever met a slave who could tell his birthday. They seldom come nearer to it than planting-time, harvest-time, cherry-time, spring-time, or fall-time. A want of information concerning my own was a source of unhappiness to me even during childhood. The white children could tell their ages. I could not tell why I ought to be deprived of the same privilege. I was not allowed to make any inquiries of my master concerning it. He deemed all such inquiries on the part of a slave improper and impertinent, and evidence of a restless spirit. The nearest estimate I can give makes me now between twenty-seven and twenty-eight years of age. I come to this, from hearing my master say, some time during 1835, I was about seventeen years old.

My mother was named Harriet Bailey. She was the daughter of Isaac and Betsey Bailey, both colored, and quite dark. My mother was of a darker complexion than either my grandmother or grandfather.

My father was a white man. He was admitted to be such by all I ever heard speak of my parentage. The opinion was also whispered that my master was my father; but of the correctness of this opinion, I know nothing; the means of knowing was withheld from me. My mother and I were separated when I was but an infant—before I knew her as my mother. It is a common custom, in the part of Maryland from which I ran away, to part children from their mothers at a very early age. Frequently, before the child has reached its twelfth month, its mother is taken from it, and hired out on some farm a considerable distance off, and the child is placed under the care of an old woman, too old for field labor. For what this separation is done, I do not know, unless it be to hinder the development of the child's affection toward its mother, and to blunt and destroy the natural affection of the mother for the child. This is the inevitable result.

I never saw my mother, to know her as such, more than four or five times in my life; and each of these times was very short in duration, and at night. She was hired by a Mr. Stewart, who lived about twelve miles from my home. She made her journeys to see me in the night, travelling the whole distance on foot, after the performance of her day's work. She was a field hand, and a whipping is the penalty of not being in the field at sunrise, unless a slave has special permission from his or her master to the contrary—a permission which they seldom get, and one that gives to him that gives it the proud name of being a kind master. I do not recollect ever seeing my mother by the light of day. She was with me in the night. She would lie down with me, and get me to sleep, but long before I waked she was gone. Very little communication ever took place between us. Death soon ended what little we could have while she lived, and with it her hardships and suffering. She died when I was about seven years old, on one of my master's farms, near Lee's Mill. I was not allowed to be present during her illness, at her death, or burial. She was gone long before I knew any thing about it. Never having enjoyed, to any considerable extent, her soothing presence, her tender and watchful care, I received the tidings of her death with much the same emotions I should have probably felt at the death of a stranger.

Called thus suddenly away, she left me without the slightest intimation of who my father was. The whisper that my master was my father, may or may not be true; and, true or false, it is of but little consequence to my purpose whilst the fact remains, in all its glaring odiousness, that slaveholders have ordained, and by law established, that the children of slave women shall in all cases follow the condition of their mothers; and this is done too obviously to administer to their own lusts, and make a gratification of their wicked desires profitable as well as pleasurable; for by this cunning arrangement, the slaveholder, in cases not a few, sustains to his slaves the double relation of master and father.

I know of such cases; and it is worthy of remark that such slaves invariably suffer greater hardships, and have more to contend with, than others. They are, in the first place, a constant offence to their mistress. She is ever disposed to find fault with them; they can seldom do any thing to please her; she is never better pleased than when she sees them under the lash, especially when she suspects her husband of showing to his mulatto children favors which he withholds from his black slaves. The master is frequently compelled to sell this class of his slaves, out of deference to the feelings of his white wife; and, cruel as the deed may strike any one to be, for a man to sell his own children to human flesh-mongers, it is often the dictate of humanity for him to do so; for, unless he does this, he must not only whip them himself, but must stand by and see one white son tie up his brother, of but few shades darker complexion than himself, and ply the gory lash to his naked back; and if he lisp one word of disapproval, it is set down to his parental partiality, and only makes a bad matter worse, both for himself and the slave whom he would protect and defend.

Every year brings with it multitudes of this class of slaves. It was doubtless in consequence of a knowledge of this fact, that one great states-man of the south predicted the downfall of slavery by the inevitable laws of population. Whether this prophecy is ever fulfilled or not, it is nevertheless plain that a very different-looking class of people are springing up at the south, and are now held in slavery, from those originally brought to this country from Africa; and if their increase will do no other good, it will do away the force of the argument, that God cursed Ham, and therefore Ameri-can slavery is right. If the lineal descendants of Ham are alone to be scripturally enslaved, it is certain that slavery at the south must soon be-come unscriptural; for thousands are ushered into the world, annually, who, like myself, owe their existence to white fathers, and those fathers most frequently their own masters.

I have had two masters. My first master's name was Anthony. I do not remember his first name. He was generally called Captain Anthony— a title which, I presume, he acquired by sailing a craft on the Chesapeake Bay. He was not considered a rich slaveholder. He owned two or three farms, and about thirty slaves. His farms and slaves were under the care of an overseer. The overseer's name was Plummer. Mr. Plummer was a miserable drunkard, a profane swearer, and a savage monster. He always went armed with a cowskin and a heavy cudgel. I have known him to cut and slash the women's heads so horribly, that even master would be en-raged at his cruelty, and would threaten to whip him if he did not mind himself. Master, however, was not a humane slaveholder. It required ex-traordinary barbarity on the part of an overseer to affect him. He was a cruel man, hardened by a long life of slaveholding. He would at times seem to take great pleasure in whipping a slave. I have often been awak-ened at the dawn of day by the most heart-rending shrieks of an own aunt of mine, whom he used to tie up to a joist, and whip upon her naked back till she was literally covered with blood. No words, no tears, no prayers, from his gory victim, seemed to move his iron heart from its bloody pur-pose. The louder she screamed, the harder he whipped; and where the blood ran fastest, there he whipped longest. He would whip her to make her scream, and whip her to make her hush; and not until overcome by fatigue, would he cease to swing the blood-clotted cowskin. I remember the first time I ever witnessed this horrible exhibition. I was quite a child, but I well remember it. I never shall forget it whilst I remember any thing. It was the first of a long series of such outrages, of which I was doomed to be a witness and a participant. It struck me with awful force. It was the blood-stained gate, the entrance to the hell of slavery, through which I was about to pass. It was a most terrible spectacle. I wish I could commit to paper the feelings with which I beheld it.

This occurrence took place very soon after I went to live with my old master, and under the following circumstances. Aunt Hester went out one night,—where or for what I do not know,—and happened to be absent when my master desired her presence. He had ordered her not to go out evenings, and warned her that she must never let him catch her in company with a young man, who was paying attention to her belonging to Colonel Lloyd. The young man's name was Ned Roberts, generally called Lloyd's Ned. Why master was so careful of her, may be safely left to conjecture. She was a woman of noble form, and of graceful proportions, having very few equals, and fewer superiors, in personal appearance, among the colored or white women of our neighborhood.

Aunt Hester had not only disobeyed his orders in going out, but had been found in company with Lloyd's Ned; which circumstance, I found, from what he said while whipping her, was the chief offence. Had he been a man of pure morals himself, he might have been thought interested in protecting the innocence of my aunt; but those who knew him will not suspect him of any such virtue. Before he commenced whipping Aunt Hester, he took her into the kitchen, and stripped her from neck to waist, leaving her neck, shoulders, and back, entirely naked. He then told her to cross her hands, calling her at the same time a d——d b——h. After crossing her hands, he tied them with a strong rope, and led her to a stool under a large hook in the joist, put in for the purpose. He made her get upon the stool, and tied her hands to the hook. She now stood fair for his infernal purpose. Her arms were stretched up at their full length, so that she stood upon the ends of her toes. He then said to her, "Now, you d——d b——h, I'll learn you how to disobey my orders!" and after rolling up his sleeves, he commenced to lay on the heavy cowskin, and soon the warm, red blood (amid heart-rending shrieks from her, and horrid oaths from him) came dripping to the floor. I was so terrified and horror-stricken at the sight, that I hid myself in a closet, and dared not venture out till long after the bloody transaction was over. I expected it would be my turn next. It was all new to me. I had never seen any thing like it before. I had always lived with my grandmother on the outskirts of the plantation, where she was put to raise the children of the younger women. I had therefore been, until now, out of the way of the bloody scenes that often occurred on the plantation.

CHAPTER II.

MY master's family consisted of two sons, Andrew and Richard; one daughter, Lucretia, and her husband, Captain Thomas Auld. They lived in one house, upon the home plantation of Colonel Edward Lloyd. My master was Colonel Lloyd's clerk and superintendent. He was what might be called the overseer of the overseers. I spent two years of childhood on this plantation in my old master's family. It was here that I witnessed the bloody transaction recorded in the first chapter; and as I received my first impressions of slavery on this plantation, I will give some description of it, and of slavery as it there existed. The plantation is about twelve miles north of Easton, in Talbot county, and is situated on the border of Miles River. The principal products raised upon it were tobacco, corn, and wheat. These were raised in great abundance; so that, with the products of this and the other farms belonging to him, he was able to keep in almost constant employment a large sloop, in carrying them to market at Baltimore. This sloop was named Sally Lloyd, in honor of one of the colonel's daughters. My master's son-in-law, Captain Auld, was master of the vessel; she was otherwise manned by the colonel's own slaves. Their names were Peter, Isaac, Rich, and Jake. These were esteemed very highly by the other slaves, and looked upon as the privileged ones of the plantation; for it was no small affair, in the eyes of the slaves, to be allowed to see Baltimore.

Colonel Lloyd kept from three to four hundred slaves on his home plantation, and owned a large number more on the neighboring farms belonging to him. The names of the farms nearest to the home plantation were Wye Town and New Design. "Wye Town" was under the overseership of a man named Noah Willis. New Design was under the overseership of a Mr. Townsend. The overseers of these, and all the rest of the farms, numbering over twenty, received advice and direction from the managers of the home plantation. This was the great business place. It was the seat of government for the whole twenty farms. All disputes among the overseers were settled here. If a slave was convicted of any high misdemeanor, became unmanageable, or evinced a determination to run away, he was brought immediately here, severely whipped, put on board the sloop, carried to Baltimore, and sold to Austin Woolfolk, or some other slave-trader, as a warning to the slaves remaining.

Here, too, the slaves of all the other farms received their monthly allowance of food, and their yearly clothing. The men and women slaves received, as their monthly allowance of food, eight pounds of pork, or its equivalent in fish, and one bushel of corn meal. Their yearly clothing consisted of two coarse linen shirts, one pair of linen trousers, like the shirts, one jacket, one pair of trousers for winter, made of coarse negro cloth, one pair of stockings, and one pair of shoes; the whole of which could not have cost more than seven dollars. The allowance of the slave children was given to their mothers, or the old women having the care of them. The children unable to work in the field had neither shoes, stockings, jackets, nor trousers, given to them; their clothing consisted of two coarse linen shirts per year. When these failed them, they went naked until the next allowance-day. Children from seven to ten years old, of both sexes, almost naked, might be seen at all seasons of the year.

There were no beds given the slaves, unless one coarse blanket be considered such, and none but the men and women had these. This, however, is not considered a very great privation. They find less difficulty from the want of beds, than from the want of time to sleep; for when their day's work in the field is done, the most of them having their washing, mending, and cooking to do, and having few or none of the ordinary facilities for doing either of these, very many of their sleeping hours are consumed in preparing for the field the coming day; and when this is done, old and young, male and female, married and single, drop down side by side, on one common bed,—the cold, damp floor,—each covering himself or herself with their miserable blankets; and here they sleep till they are summoned to the field by the driver's horn. At the sound of this, all must rise, and be off to the field. There must be no halting; every one must be at his or her post; and woe betides them who hear not this morning summons to the field; for if they are not awakened by the sense of hearing, they are by the sense of feeling: no age nor sex finds any favor. Mr. Severe, the overseer, used to stand by the door of the quarter, armed with a large hickory stick and heavy cowskin, ready to whip any one who was so unfortunate as not to hear, or, from any other cause, was prevented from being ready to start for the field at the sound of the horn.

Mr. Severe was rightly named: he was a cruel man. I have seen him whip a woman, causing the blood to run half an hour at the time; and this, too, in the midst of her crying children, pleading for their mother's release. He seemed to take pleasure in manifesting his fiendish barbarity. Added to his cruelty, he was a profane swearer. It was enough to chill the blood and stiffen the hair of an ordinary man to hear him talk. Scarce a sentence escaped him but what was commenced or concluded by some horrid oath. The field was the place to witness his cruelty and profanity. His presence made it both the field of blood and blasphemy. From the rising till the going down of the sun, he was cursing, raving, cutting, and slashing among the slaves of the field, in the most frightful manner. His career was short. He died very soon after I went to Colonel Lloyd's; and he died as he lived, uttering, with his dying groans, bitter curses and horrid oaths. His death was regarded by the slaves as the result of a merciful Providence.

Mr. Severe's place was filled by a Mr. Hopkins. He was a very different man. He was less cruel, less profane, and made less noise, than Mr. Severe. His course was characterized by no extraordinary demonstrations of cruelty. He whipped, but seemed to take no pleasure in it. He was called by the slaves a good overseer.

The home plantation of Colonel Lloyd wore the appearance of a country village. All the mechanical operations for all the farms were performed here. The shoemaking and mending, the blacksmithing, cartwrighting, coopering, weaving, and grain-grinding, were all performed by the slaves on the home plantation. The whole place wore a business-like aspect very unlike the neighboring farms. The number of houses, too, conspired to give it advantage over the neighboring farms. It was called by the slaves the *Great House Farm*. Few privileges were esteemed higher, by the slaves of the out-farms, than that of being selected to do errands at the Great House Farm. It was associated in their minds with greatness. A representative could not be prouder of his election to a seat in the American Congress, than a slave on one of the out-farms would be of his election to do errands at the Great House Farm. They regarded it as evidence of great confidence reposed in them by their overseers; and it was on this account, as well as a constant desire to be out of the field from under the driver's lash, that they esteemed it a high privilege, one worth careful living for. He was called the smartest and most trusty fellow, who had this honor conferred upon him the most frequently. The competitors for this office sought as diligently to please their overseers, as the office-seekers in the political parties seek to please and deceive the people. The same traits of character might be seen in Colonel Lloyd's slaves, as are seen in the slaves of the political parties.

The slaves selected to go to the Great House Farm, for the monthly allowance for themselves and their fellow-slaves, were peculiarly enthusiastic. While on their way, they would make the dense old woods, for miles around, reverberate with their wild songs, revealing at once the highest joy and the deepest sadness. They would compose and sing as they went along, consulting neither time nor tune. The thought that came up, came out—if not in the word, in the sound;—and as frequently in the one as in the other. They would sometimes sing the most pathetic sentiment in the most rapturous tone, and the most rapturous sentiment in the most pathetic tone. Into all of their songs they would manage to weave something of the Great House Farm. Especially would they do this, when leaving home. They would then sing most exultingly the following words:—

"I am going away to the Great House Farm!
O, yea! O, yea! O!"

This they would sing, as a chorus, to words which to many would seem unmeaning jargon, but which, nevertheless, were full of meaning to themselves. I have sometimes thought that the mere hearing of those songs would do more to impress some minds with the horrible character of slavery, than the reading of whole volumes of philosophy on the subject could do.

I did not, when a slave, understand the deep meaning of those rude and apparently incoherent songs. I was myself within the circle; so that I neither saw nor heard as those without might see and hear. They told a tale of woe which was then altogether beyond my feeble comprehension; they were tones loud, long, and deep; they breathed the prayer and complaint of souls boiling over with the bitterest anguish. Every tone was a testimony against slavery, and a prayer to God for deliverance from chains. The hearing of those wild notes always depressed my spirit, and filled me with ineffable sadness. I have frequently found myself in tears while hearing them. The mere recurrence to those songs, even now, afflicts me; and while I am writing these lines, an expression of feeling has already found its way down my cheek. To those songs I trace my first glimmering conception of the dehumanizing character of slavery. I can never get rid of that conception. Those songs still follow me, to deepen my hatred of slavery, and quicken my sympathies for my brethren in bonds. If any one wishes to be impressed with the soul-killing effects of slavery, let him go to Colonel Lloyd's plantation, and, on allowance-day, place himself in the deep pine woods, and there let him, in silence, analyze the sounds that shall pass through the chambers of his soul,—and if he is not thus impressed, it will only be because "there is no flesh in his obdurate heart."

I have often been utterly astonished, since I came to the north, to find persons who could speak of the singing, among slaves, as evidence of their contentment and happiness. It is impossible to conceive of a greater mistake. Slaves sing most when they are most unhappy. The songs of the slave represent the sorrows of his heart; and he is relieved by them, only as an aching heart is relieved by its tears. At least, such is my experience. I have often sung to drown my sorrow, but seldom to express my happiness. Crying for joy, and singing for joy, were alike uncommon to me while in the jaws of slavery. The singing of a man cast away upon a desolate island might be as appropriately considered as evidence of contentment and happiness, as the singing of a slave; the songs of the one and of the other are prompted by the same emotion.

CHAPTER III.

COLONEL LLOYD kept a large and finely cultivated garden, which afforded almost constant employment for four men, besides the chief gardener, (Mr. M'Durmond.) This garden was probably the greatest attraction of the place. During the summer months, people came from far and near—from Baltimore, Easton, and Annapolis—to see it. It abounded in fruits of almost every description, from the hardy apple of the north to the delicate orange of the south. This garden was not the least source of trouble on the plantation. Its excellent fruit was quite a temptation to the hungry swarms of boys, as well as the older slaves, belonging to the colonel, few of whom had the virtue to resist it. Scarcely a day passed, during the summer, but that some slave had to take the lash for stealing fruit. The colonel had to resort to all kinds of stratagems to keep his slaves out of the garden. The last and most successful one was that of tarring his fence all around; after which, if a slave was caught with any tar upon his person, it was deemed sufficient proof that he had either been into the garden, or had tried to get in. In either case, he was severely whipped by the chief gardener. This plan worked well; the slaves became as fearful of tar as of the lash. They seemed to realize the impossibility of touching *tar* without being defiled.

The colonel also kept a splendid riding equipage. His stable and carriage-house presented the appearance of some of our large city livery establishments. His horses were of the finest form and noblest blood. His carriage-house contained three splendid coaches, three or four gigs, besides dearborns and barouches of the most fashionable style.

This establishment was under the care of two slaves—Old Barney and Young Barney—father and son. To attend to this establishment was their sole work. But it was by no means an easy employment; for in nothing was Colonel Lloyd more particular than in the management of his horses. The slightest inattention to these was unpardonable, and was visited upon those, under whose care they were placed, with the severest punishment; no excuse could shield them, if the colonel only suspected any want of attention to his horses—a supposition which he frequently indulged, and one which, of course, made the office of Old and Young Barney a very trying one. They never knew when they were safe from punishment. They were frequently whipped when least deserving, and escaped whipping when most deserving it. Every thing depended upon the looks of the horses, and the state of Colonel Lloyd's own mind when his horses were brought to him for use. If a horse did not move fast enough, or hold his head high enough, it was owing to some fault of his keepers. It was painful to stand near the stable-door, and hear the various complaints against the keepers when a horse was taken out for use. "This horse has not had proper attention. He has not been sufficiently rubbed and curried, or he has not been properly fed; his food was too wet or too dry; he got it too soon or too late; he was too hot or too cold; he had too much hay, and not enough of grain; or he had too much grain, and not enough of hay; instead of Old Barney's attending to the horse, he had very improperly left it to his son." To all these complaints, no matter how unjust, the slave must answer never a word. Colonel Lloyd could not brook any contradiction from a slave. When he spoke, a slave must stand, listen, and tremble; and such was literally the case. I have seen Colonel Lloyd make Old Barney, a man between fifty and sixty years of age, uncover his bald head, kneel down upon the cold, damp ground, and receive upon his naked and toil-worn shoulders more than thirty lashes at the time. Colonel Lloyd had three sons—Edward, Murray, and Daniel,— and three sons-in-law, Mr. Winder, Mr. Nicholson, and Mr. Lowndes. All of these lived at the Great House Farm, and enjoyed the luxury of whipping the servants when they pleased, from Old Barney down to William Wilkes, the coach-driver. I have seen Winder make one of the house-servants stand off from him a suitable distance to be touched with the end of his whip, and at every stroke raise great ridges upon his back.

To describe the wealth of Colonel Lloyd would be almost equal to describing the riches of Job. He kept from ten to fifteen house-servants. He was said to own a thousand slaves, and I think this estimate quite within the truth. Colonel Lloyd owned so many that he did not know them when he saw them; nor did all the slaves of the out-farms know him. It is reported of him, that, while riding along the road one day, he met a colored man, and addressed him in the usual manner of speaking to colored people on the public highways of the south: "Well, boy, whom do you belong to?" "To Colonel Lloyd," replied the slave. "Well, does the colonel treat you well?" "No, sir," was the ready reply. "What, does he work you too hard?" "Yes, sir." "Well, don't he give you enough to eat?" "Yes, sir, he gives me enough, such as it is."

The colonel, after ascertaining whom the slave belonged to, rode on; the man also went on about his business, not dreaming that he had been conversing with his master. He thought, said, and heard nothing more of the matter, until two or three weeks afterwards. The poor man was then informed by his overseer that, for having found fault with his master, he was now to be sold to a Georgia trader. He was immediately chained and handcuffed; and thus, without a moment's warning, he was snatched away, and forever sundered, from his family and friends, by a hand more unrelenting than death. This is the penalty of telling the truth, of telling the simple truth, in answer to a series of plain questions.

It is partly in consequence of such facts, that slaves, when inquired of as to their condition and the character of their masters, almost universally say they are contented, and that their masters are kind. The slaveholders have been known to send in spies among their slaves, to ascertain their views and feelings in regard to their condition. The frequency of this has had the effect to establish among the slaves the maxim, that a still tongue makes a wise head. They suppress the truth rather than take the consequences of telling it, and in so doing prove themselves a part of the human family. If they have any thing to say of their masters, it is generally in their masters' favor, especially when speaking to an untried man. I have been frequently asked, when a slave, if I had a kind master, and do not remember ever to have given a negative answer; nor did I, in pursuing this course, consider myself as uttering what was absolutely false; for I always measured the kindness of my master by the standard of kindness set up among slaveholders around us. Moreover, slaves are like other people, and imbibe prejudices quite common to others. They think their own better than that of others. Many, under the influence of this prejudice, think their own masters are better than the masters of other slaves; and this, too, in some cases, when the very reverse is true. Indeed, it is not uncommon for slaves even to fall out and quarrel among themselves about the relative goodness of their masters, each contending for the superior goodness of his own over that of the others. At the very same time, they mutually execrate their masters when viewed separately. It was so on our plantation. When Colonel Lloyd's slaves met the slaves of Jacob Jepson, they seldom parted without a quarrel about their masters; Colonel Lloyd's slaves contending that he was the richest, and Mr. Jepson's slaves that he was the smartest, and most of a man. Colonel Lloyd's slaves would boast his ability to buy and sell Jacob Jepson. Mr. Jepson's slaves would boast his ability to whip Colonel Lloyd. These quarrels would almost always end in a fight between the parties, and those that whipped were supposed to have gained the point at issue. They seemed to think that the greatness of their masters was transferable to themselves. It was considered as being bad enough to be a slave; but to be a poor man's slave was deemed a disgrace indeed!

CHAPTER IV.

MR. HOPKINS remained but a short time in the office of overseer. Why his career was so short, I do not know, but suppose he lacked the necessary severity to suit Colonel Lloyd. Mr. Hopkins was succeeded by Mr. Austin Gore, a man possessing, in an eminent degree, all those traits of character indispensable to what is called a first-rate overseer. Mr. Gore had served Colonel Lloyd, in the capacity of overseer, upon one of the out-farms, and had shown himself worthy of the high station of overseer upon the home or Great House Farm.

Mr. Gore was proud, ambitious, and persevering. He was artful, cruel, and obdurate. He was just the man for such a place, and it was just the place for such a man. It afforded scope for the full exercise of all his powers, and he seemed to be perfectly at home in it. He was one of those who could torture the slightest look, word, or gesture, on the part of the slave, into impudence, and would treat it accordingly. There must be no answering back to him; no explanation was allowed a slave, showing himself to have been wrongfully accused. Mr. Gore acted fully up to the maxim laid down by slaveholders,—"It is better that a dozen slaves suffer under the lash, than that the overseer should be convicted, in the presence of the slaves, of having been at fault." No matter how innocent a slave might be—it availed him nothing, when accused by Mr. Gore of any misdemeanor. To be accused was to be convicted, and to be convicted was to be punished; the one always following the other with immutable certainty. To escape punishment was to escape accusation; and few slaves had the fortune to do either, under the overseership of Mr. Gore. He was just proud enough to demand the most debasing homage of the slave, and quite servile enough to crouch, himself, at the feet of the master. He was ambitious enough to be contented with nothing short of the highest rank of overseers, and persevering enough to reach the height of his ambition. He was cruel enough to inflict the severest punishment, artful enough to descend to the lowest trickery, and obdurate enough to be insensible to the voice of a reproving conscience. He was, of all the overseers, the most dreaded by the slaves. His presence was painful; his eye flashed confusion; and seldom was his sharp, shrill voice heard, without producing horror and trembling in their ranks.

Mr. Gore was a grave man, and, though a young man, he indulged in no jokes, said no funny words, seldom smiled. His words were in perfect keeping with his looks, and his looks were in perfect keeping with his words. Overseers will sometimes indulge in a witty word, even with the slaves; not so with Mr. Gore. He spoke but to command, and commanded but to be obeyed; he dealt sparingly with his words, and bountifully with his whip, never using the former where the latter would answer as well. When he whipped, he seemed to do so from a sense of duty, and feared no consequences. He did nothing reluctantly, no matter how disagreeable; always at his post, never inconsistent. He never promised but to fulfil. He was, in a word, a man of the most inflexible firmness and stone-like coolness.

His savage barbarity was equalled only by the consummate coolness with which he committed the grossest and most savage deeds upon the slaves under his charge. Mr. Gore once undertook to whip one of Colonel Lloyd's slaves, by the name of Demby. He had given Demby but few stripes, when, to get rid of the scourging, he ran and plunged himself into a creek, and stood there at the depth of his shoulders, refusing to come out. Mr. Gore told him that he would give him three calls, and that, if he did not come out at the third call, he would shoot him. The first call was given. Demby made no response, but stood his ground. The second and third calls were given with the same result. Mr. Gore then, without consultation or deliberation with any one, not even giving Demby an additional call, raised his musket to his face, taking deadly aim at his standing victim, and in an instant poor Demby was no more. His mangled body sank out of sight, and blood and brains marked the water where he had stood.

A thrill of horror flashed through every soul upon the plantation, excepting Mr. Gore. He alone seemed cool and collected. He was asked by

Colonel Lloyd and my old master, why he resorted to this extraordinary expedient. His reply was, (as well as I can remember,) that Demby had become unmanageable. He was setting a dangerous example to the other slaves,—one which, if suffered to pass without some such demonstration on his part, would finally lead to the total subversion of all rule and order upon the plantation. He argued that if one slave refused to be corrected, and escaped with his life, the other slaves would soon copy the example; the result of which would be, the freedom of the slaves, and the enslavement of the whites. Mr. Gore's defence was satisfactory. He was continued in his station as overseer upon the home plantation. His fame as an overseer went abroad. His horrid crime was not even submitted to judicial investigation. It was committed in the presence of slaves, and they of course could neither institute a suit, nor testify against him; and thus the guilty perpetrator of one of the bloodiest and most foul murders goes unwhipped of justice, and uncensured by the community in which he lives. Mr. Gore lived in St. Michael's, Talbot county, Maryland, when I left there; and if he is still alive, he very probably lives there now; and if so, he is now, as he was then, as highly esteemed and as much respected as though his guilty soul had not been stained with his brother's blood.

I speak advisedly when I say this,—that killing a slave, or any colored person, in Talbot county, Maryland, is not treated as a crime, either by the courts or the community. Mr. Thomas Lanman, of St. Michael's, killed two slaves, one of whom he killed with a hatchet, by knocking his brains out. He used to boast of the commission of the awful and bloody deed. I have heard him do so laughingly, saying, among other things, that he was the only benefactor of his country in the company, and that when others would do as much as he had done, we should be relieved of "the d——d niggers."

The wife of Mr. Giles Hicks, living but a short distance from where I used to live, murdered my wife's cousin, a young girl between fifteen and sixteen years of age, mangling her person in the most horrible manner, breaking her nose and breastbone with a stick, so that the poor girl expired in a few hours afterward. She was immediately buried, but had not been in her untimely grave but a few hours before she was taken up and examined by the coroner, who decided that she had come to her death by severe beating. The offence for which this girl was thus murdered was this:—She had been set that night to mind Mrs. Hicks' baby, and during the night she fell asleep, and the baby cried. She, having lost her rest for several nights previous, did not hear the crying. They were both in the room with Mrs. Hicks. Mrs. Hicks, finding the girl slow to move, jumped from her bed, seized an oak stick of wood by the fireplace, and with it broke the girl's nose and breastbone, and thus ended her life. I will not say that this most horrid murder produced no sensation in the community. It did produce sensation, but not enough to bring the murderess to punishment. There was a warrant issued for her arrest, but it was never served. Thus she escaped not only punishment, but even the pain of being arraigned before a court for her horrid crime.

Whilst I am detailing bloody deeds which took place during my stay on Colonel Lloyd's plantation, I will briefly narrate another, which occurred about the same time as the murder of Demby by Mr. Gore.

Colonel Lloyd's slaves were in the habit of spending a part of their nights and Sundays in fishing for oysters, and in this way made up the deficiency of their scanty allowance. An old man belonging to Colonel Lloyd, while thus engaged, happened to get beyond the limits of Colonel Lloyd's, and on the premises of Mr. Beal Bondly. At this trespass, Mr. Bondly took offence, and with his musket came down to the shore, and blew its deadly contents into the poor old man.

Mr. Bondly came over to see Colonel Lloyd the next day, whether to pay him for his property, or to justify himself in what he had done, I know not. At any rate, this whole fiendish transaction was soon hushed up. There was very little said about it at all, and nothing done. It was a common saying, even among little white boys, that it was worth a half-cent to kill a "nigger," and a half-cent to bury one.

CHAPTER V.

As to my own treatment while I lived on Colonel Lloyd's plantation, it was very similar to that of the other slave children. I was not old enough to work in the field, and there being little else than field work to do, I had a great deal of leisure time. The most I had to do was to drive up the cows at evening, keep the fowls out of the garden, keep the front yard clean, and run of errands for my old master's daughter, Mrs. Lucretia Auld. The most of my leisure time I spent in helping Master Daniel Lloyd in finding his birds, after he had shot them. My connection with Master Daniel was of some advantage to me. He became quite attached to me, and was a sort of protector of me. He would not allow the older boys to impose upon me, and would divide his cakes with me.

I was seldom whipped by my old master, and suffered little from any thing else than hunger and cold. I suffered much from hunger, but much more from cold. In hottest summer and coldest winter, I was kept almost naked—no shoes, no stockings, no jacket, no trousers, nothing on but a coarse tow linen shirt, reaching only to my knees. I had no bed. I must have perished with cold, but that, the coldest nights, I used to steal a bag which was used for carrying corn to the mill. I would crawl into this bag, and there sleep on the cold, damp, clay floor, with my head in and feet out. My feet have been so cracked with the frost, that the pen with which I am writing might be laid in the gashes.

We were not regularly allowanced. Our food was coarse corn meal boiled. This was called *mush*. It was put into a large wooden tray or trough, and set down upon the ground. The children were then called, like so many pigs, and like so many pigs they would come and devour the mush; some with oyster-shells, others with pieces of shingle, some with naked hands, and none with spoons. He that ate fastest got most; he that was strongest secured the best place; and few left the trough satisfied.

I was probably seven or eight years old when I left Colonel Lloyd's plantation. I left it with joy. I shall never forget the ecstasy with which I received the intelligence that my old master (Anthony) had determined to let me go to Baltimore, to live with Mr. Hugh Auld, brother to my old master's son-in-law, Captain Thomas Auld. I received this information about three days before my departure. They were three of the happiest days I ever enjoyed. I spent the most part of all these three days in the creek, washing off the plantation scurf, and preparing myself for my departure.

The pride of appearance which this would indicate was not my own. I spent the time in washing, not so much because I wished to, but because Mrs. Lucretia had told me I must get all the dead skin off my feet and knees before I could go to Baltimore; for the people in Baltimore were very cleanly, and would laugh at me if I looked dirty. Besides, she was going to give me a pair of trousers, which I should not put on unless I got all the dirt off me. The thought of owning a pair of trousers was great indeed! It was almost a sufficient motive, not only to make me take off what would be called by pig-drovers the mange, but the skin itself. I went at it in good earnest, working for the first time with the hope of reward.

The ties that ordinarily bind children to their homes were all suspended in my case. I found no severe trial in my departure. My home was charm-less; it was not home to me; on parting from it, I could not feel that I was leaving any thing which I could have enjoyed by staying. My mother was dead, my grandmother lived far off, so that I seldom saw her. I had two sisters and one brother, that lived in the same house with me; but the early separation of us from our mother had well nigh blotted the fact of our relationship from our memories. I looked for home elsewhere, and was confident of finding none which I should relish less than the one which I was leaving. If, however, I found in my new home hardship, hunger, whipping, and nakedness, I had the consolation that I should not have escaped any one of them by staying. Having already had more than a taste of them in the house of my old master, and having endured them there, I very naturally inferred my ability to endure them elsewhere, and especially at Baltimore; for I had something of the feeling about Baltimore that is expressed in the proverb, that "being hanged in England is preferable to dying a natural death in Ireland." I had the strongest desire to see Baltimore. Cousin Tom, though not fluent in speech, had inspired me with that desire by his eloquent description of the place. I could never point out any thing at the Great House, no matter how beautiful or powerful, but that he had seen something at Baltimore far exceeding, both in beauty and strength, the object which I pointed out to him. Even the Great House itself, with all its pictures, was far inferior to many buildings in Baltimore. So strong was my desire, that I thought a gratification of it would fully compensate for whatever loss of comfort I should sustain by the exchange. I left without a regret, and with the highest hopes of future happiness.

We sailed out of Miles River for Baltimore on a Saturday morning. I remember only the day of the week, for at that time I had no knowledge of the days of the month, nor the months of the year. On setting sail, I walked aft, and gave to Colonel Lloyd's plantation what I hoped would be the last look. I then placed myself in the bows of the sloop, and there spent the remainder of the day in looking ahead, interesting myself in what was in the distance rather than in things near by or behind.

In the afternoon of that day, we reached Annapolis, the capital of the State. We stopped but a few moments, so that I had no time to go on shore. It was the first large town that I had ever seen, and though it would look small compared with some of our New England factory villages, I thought it a wonderful place for its size—more imposing even than the Great House Farm!

We arrived at Baltimore early on Sunday morning, landing at Smith's Wharf, not far from Bowley's Wharf. We had on board the sloop a large flock of sheep; and after aiding in driving them to the slaughter-house of Mr. Curtis on Loudon Slater's Hill, I was conducted by Rich, one of the hands belonging on board of the sloop, to my new home in Alliciana Street, near Mr. Gardner's ship-yard, on Fell's Point.

'Mr. and Mrs. Auld were both at home, and met me at the door with their little son Thomas, to take care of whom I had been given. And here I saw what I had never seen before; it was a white face beaming with the most kindly emotions; it was the face of my new mistress, Sophia Auld. I wish I could describe the rapture that flashed through my soul as I beheld it. It was a new and strange sight to me, brightening up my pathway with the light of happiness. Little Thomas was told, there was his Freddy,—and I was told to take care of little Thomas; and thus I entered upon the duties of my new home with the most cheering prospect ahead.

I look upon my departure from Colonel Lloyd's plantation as one of the most interesting events of my life. It is possible, and even quite probable, that but for the mere circumstance of being removed from that plantation to Baltimore, I should have to-day, instead of being here seated by my own table, in the enjoyment of freedom and the happiness of home, writing this Narrative, been confined in the galling chains of slavery. Going to live at Baltimore laid the foundation, and opened the gateway, to all my subsequent prosperity. I have ever regarded it as the first plain manifestation of that kind Providence which has ever since attended me, and marked my life with so many favors. I regarded the selection of myself as being somewhat remarkable. There were a number of slave children that might have been sent from the plantation to Baltimore. There were those younger, those older, and those of the same age. I was chosen from among them all, and was the first, last, and only choice.

I may be deemed superstitious, and even egotistical, in regarding this event as a special interposition of divine Providence in my favor. But I should be false to the earliest sentiments of my soul, if I suppressed the opinion. I prefer to be true to myself, even at the hazard of incurring the ridicule of others, rather than to be false, and incur my own abhorrence. From my earliest recollection, I date the entertainment of a deep conviction that slavery would not always be able to hold me within its foul embrace; and in the darkest hours of my career in slavery, this living word of faith and spirit of hope departed not from me, but remained like ministering angels to cheer me through the gloom. This good spirit was from God, and to him I offer thanksgiving and praise.

CHAPTER VI.

My new mistress proved to be all she appeared when I first met her at the door,—a woman of the kindest heart and finest feelings. She had never had a slave under her control previously to myself, and prior to her marriage she had been dependent upon her own industry for a living. She was by trade a weaver; and by constant application to her business, she had been in a good degree preserved from the blighting and dehumanizing effects of slavery. I was utterly astonished at her goodness. I scarcely knew how to behave towards her. She was entirely unlike any other white woman I had ever seen. I could not approach her as I was accustomed to approach other white ladies. My early instruction was all out of place. The crouching servility, usually so acceptable a quality in a slave, did not answer when manifested towards her. Her favor was not gained by it; she seemed to be disturbed by it. She did not deem it impudent or unmannerly for a slave to look her in the face. The meanest slave was put fully at ease in her presence, and none left without feeling better for having seen her. Her face was made of heavenly smiles, and her voice of tranquil music.

But, alas! this kind heart had but a short time to remain such. The fatal poison of irresponsible power was already in her hands, and gradually commenced its infernal work. That cheerful eye, under the influence of slavery, eventually became red with rage; that voice, made all of sweet accord, changed to one of harsh and horrid discord; and that angelic face gave place to that of a demon. Thus is slavery the enemy of both the slave and the slaveholder.

Very soon after I went to live with Mr. and Mrs. Auld, she very kindly commenced to teach me the A, B, C. After I had learned this, she assisted me in learning to spell words of three or four letters. Just at this point of my progress, Mr. Auld found out what was going on, and at once forbade Mrs. Auld to instruct me further, telling her, among other things, that it was unlawful, as well as unsafe, to teach a slave to read. To use his own words, further, he said, "If you give a nigger an inch, he will take an ell. A nigger should know nothing but to obey his master—to do as he is told to do. Learning would *spoil* the best nigger in the world. Now," said he, "if you teach that nigger (speaking of myself) how to read, there would be no keeping him. It would forever unfit him to be a slave. He would at once become unmanageable, and of no value to his master. As to himself, it could do him no good, but a great deal of harm. It would make him discontented and unhappy." These words sank deep into my heart, stirred up sentiments within that lay slumbering, and called into existence an entirely new train of thought. It was a new and special revelation, explaining dark and myste-rious things, with which my youthful understanding had struggled, but struggled in vain. I now understood what had been to me a most perplexing difficulty—to wit, the white man's power to enslave the black man. It was a grand achievement, and I prized it highly. From that moment, I understood the pathway from slavery to freedom. It was just what I wanted, and I got it at a time when I the least expected it. Whilst I was saddened by the thought of losing the aid of my kind mistress, I was gladdened by the invaluable instruction which, by the merest accident, I had gained from my master. Though conscious of the difficulty of learning without a teacher, I set out with high hope, and a fixed purpose, at whatever cost of trouble, to learn how to read. The very decided manner with which he spoke, and strove to impress his wife with the evil consequences of giving me instruction, served to convince me that he was deeply sensible of the truths he was uttering. It gave me the best assurance that I might rely with the utmost confidence on the results which, he said, would flow from teaching me to read. What he most dreaded, that I most desired. What he most loved, that I most hated. That which to him was a great evil, to be carefully shunned, was to me a great good, to be diligently sought; and the argument which he so warmly urged, against my learning to read, only served to inspire me with a desire and determination to learn. In learning to read, I owe almost as much to the bitter opposition of my master, as to the kindly aid of my mistress. I acknowledge the benefit of both.

I had resided but a short time in Baltimore before I observed a marked difference, in the treatment of slaves, from that which I had witnessed in the country. A city slave is almost a freeman, compared with a slave on the plantation. He is much better fed and clothed, and enjoys privileges altogether unknown to the slave on the plantation. There is a vestige of decency, a sense of shame, that does much to curb and check those outbreaks of atrocious cruelty so commonly enacted upon the plantation. He is a desperate slaveholder, who will shock the humanity of his non-slaveholding neighbors with the cries of his lacerated slave. Few are willing to incur the odium attaching to the reputation of being a cruel master; and above all things, they would not be known as not giving a slave enough to eat. Every city slaveholder is anxious to have it known of him, that he feeds his slaves well; and it is due to them to say, that most of them do give their slaves enough to eat. There are, however, some painful exceptions to this rule. Directly opposite to us, on Philpot Street, lived Mr. Thomas Hamilton. He owned two slaves. Their names were Henrietta and Mary. Henrietta was about twenty-two years of age, Mary was about fourteen; and of all the mangled and emaciated creatures I ever looked upon, these two were the most so. His heart must be harder than stone, that could look at these unmoved. The head, neck, and shoulders of Mary were literally cut to pieces. I have frequently felt her head, and found it nearly covered with festering sores, caused by the lash of her cruel mistress. I do not know that her master ever whipped her, but I have been an eye-witness to the cruelty of Mrs. Hamilton. I used to be in Mr. Hamilton's house nearly every day. Mrs. Hamilton used to sit in a large chair in the middle of the room, with a heavy cowskin always by her side, and scarce an hour passed during the day but was marked by the blood of one of these slaves. The girls seldom passed her without her saying, "Move faster, you *black gip!*" at the same time giving them a blow with the cowskin over the head or shoulders, often drawing the blood. She would then say, "Take that, you *black gip!*"— continuing, "If you don't move faster, I'll move you!" Added to the cruel lashings to which these slaves were subjected, they were kept nearly half-starved. They seldom knew what it was to eat a full meal. I have seen Mary contending with the pigs for the offal thrown into the street. So much was Mary kicked and cut to pieces, that she was oftener called *"pecked"* than by her name.

CHAPTER VII.

I LIVED in Master Hugh's family about seven years. During this time, I succeeded in learning to read and write. In accomplishing this, I was compelled to resort to various stratagems. I had no regular teacher. My mistress, who had kindly commenced to instruct me, had, in compliance with the advice and direction of her husband, not only ceased to instruct, but had set her face against my being instructed by any one else. It is due, however, to my mistress to say of her, that she did not adopt this course of treatment immediately. She at first lacked the depravity indispensable to shutting me up in mental darkness. It was at least necessary for her to have some training in the exercise of irresponsible power, to make her equal to the task of treating me as though I were a brute.

My mistress was, as I have said, a kind and tender-hearted woman; and in the simplicity of her soul she commenced, when I first went to live with her, to treat me as she supposed one human being ought to treat another. In entering upon the duties of a slaveholder, she did not seem to perceive that I sustained to her the relation of a mere chattel, and that for her to treat me as a human being was not only wrong, but dangerously so. Slavery proved as injurious to her as it did to me. When I went there, she was a pious, warm, and tender-hearted woman. There was no sorrow or suffering for which she had not a tear. She had bread for the hungry, clothes for the naked, and comfort for every mourner that came within her reach. Slavery soon proved its ability to divest her of these heavenly qualities. Under its influence, the tender heart became stone, and the lamb-like disposition gave way to one of tiger-like fierceness. The first step in her downward course was in her ceasing to instruct me. She now commenced to practise her husband's precepts. She finally became even more violent in her opposition than her husband himself. She was not satisfied with simply doing as well as he had commanded; she seemed anxious to do better. Nothing seemed to make her more angry than to see me with a newspaper. She seemed to think that here lay the danger. I have had her rush at me with a face made all up of fury, and snatch from me a newspaper, in a manner that fully revealed her apprehension. She was an apt woman; and a little experience soon demonstrated, to her satisfaction, that education and slavery were incompatible with each other.

From this time I was most narrowly watched. If I was in a separate room any considerable length of time, I was sure to be suspected of having a book, and was at once called to give an account of myself. All this, however, was too late. The first step had been taken. Mistress, in teaching me the alphabet, had given me the *inch,* and no precaution could prevent me from taking the *ell.*

The plan which I adopted, and the one by which I was most successful, was that of making friends of all the little white boys whom I met in the street. As many of these as I could, I converted into teachers. With their kindly aid, obtained at different times and in different places, I finally succeeded in learning to read. When I was sent of errands, I always took my book with me, and by going one part of my errand quickly, I found time to get a lesson before my return. I used also to carry bread with me, enough of which was always in the house, and to which I was always welcome; for I was much better off in this regard than many of the poor white children in the neighborhood. This bread I used to bestow on the hungry little urchins, who, in return, would give me the more valuable bread of knowledge. I am strongly tempted to give the names of two or three of those little boys, as a testimonial of the gratitude and affection I bear them; but prudence forbids;—not that it would injure me, but it might embarrass them; for it is almost an unpardonable offence to teach slaves to read in this Christian country. It is enough to say of the dear little fellows, that they lived on Philpot Street, very near Durgin and Bailey's ship-yard. I used to talk this matter of slavery over with them. I would sometimes say to them, I wished I could be as free as they would be when they got to be men. "You will be free as soon as you are twenty-one, *but I am a slave for life!* Have not I as good a right to be free as you have?" These words used to trouble them; they would express for me the liveliest sympathy, and console me with the hope that something would occur by which I might be free.

I was now about twelve years old, and the thought of being *a slave for life* began to bear heavily upon my heart. Just about this time, I got hold of a book entitled "The Columbian Orator." Every opportunity I got, I used to read this book. Among much of other interesting matter, I found in it a dialogue between a master and his slave. The slave was represented as having run away from his master three times. The dialogue represented the conversation which took place between them, when the slave was retaken the third time. In this dialogue, the whole argument in behalf of slavery was brought forward by the master, all of which was disposed of by the slave. The slave was made to say some very smart as well as impressive things in reply to his master—things which had the desired though unexpected effect; for the conversation resulted in the voluntary emancipation of the slave on the part of the master.

In the same book, I met with one of Sheridan's mighty speeches on and in behalf of Catholic emancipation. These were choice documents to me. I read them over and over again with unabated interest. They gave tongue to interesting thoughts of my own soul, which had frequently flashed through my mind, and died away for want of utterance. The moral which I gained from the dialogue was the power of truth over the conscience of even a slaveholder. What I got from Sheridan was a bold denunciation of slavery, and a powerful vindication of human rights. The reading of these documents enabled me to utter my thoughts, and to meet the arguments brought forward to sustain slavery; but while they relieved me of one difficulty, they brought on another even more painful than the one of which I was relieved. The more I read, the more I was led to abhor and detest my enslavers. I could regard them in no other light than a band of successful robbers, who had left their homes, and gone to Africa, and stolen us from our homes, and in a strange land reduced us to slavery. I loathed them as being the meanest as well as the most wicked of men. As I read and contemplated the subject, behold! that very discontentment which Master Hugh had predicted would follow my learning to read had already come, to torment and sting my soul to unutterable anguish. As I writhed under it, I would at times feel that learning to read had been a curse rather than a blessing. It had given me a view of my wretched condition, without the remedy. It opened my eyes to the horrible pit, but to no ladder upon which to get out. In moments of agony, I envied my fellow-slaves for their stupidity. I have often wished myself a beast. I preferred the condition of the meanest reptile to my own. Any thing, no matter what, to get rid of thinking! It was this everlasting thinking of my condition that tormented me. There was no getting rid of it. It was pressed upon me by every object within sight or hearing, animate or inanimate. The silver trump of freedom had roused my soul to eternal wakefulness. Freedom now appeared, to disappear no more forever. It was heard in every sound, and seen in every thing. It was ever present to torment me with a sense of my wretched condition. I saw nothing without seeing it, I heard nothing without hearing it, and felt nothing without feeling it. It looked from every star, it smiled in every calm, breathed in every wind, and moved in every storm.

I often found myself regretting my own existence, and wished myself dead; and but for the hope of being free, I have no doubt but that I should have killed myself, or done something for which I should have been killed. While in this state of mind, I was eager to hear any one speak of slavery. I was a ready listener. Every little while, I could hear something about the abolitionists. It was some time before I found what the word meant. It was always used in such connections as to make it an interesting word to me. If a slave ran away and succeeded in getting clear, or if a slave killed his master, set fire to a barn, or did any thing very wrong in the mind of a slaveholder, it was spoken of as the fruit of *abolition*. Hearing the word in this connection very often, I set about learning what it meant. The dictionary afforded me little or no help. I found it was "the act of abolishing;" but then I did not know what was to be abolished. Here I was perplexed. I did not dare to ask any one about its meaning, for I was satisfied that it was something they wanted me to know very little about. After a patient waiting, I got one of our city papers, containing an account of the number of petitions from the north, praying for the abolition of slavery in the District of Columbia, and of the slave trade between the States. From this time I understood the words *abolition* and *abolitionist,* and always drew near when that word was spoken, expecting to hear something of importance to myself and fellow-slaves. The light broke in upon me by degrees. I went one day down on the wharf of Mr. Waters; and seeing two Irishmen unloading a scow of stone, I went, unasked, and helped them. When we had finished, one of them came to me and asked me if I were a slave. I told him I was. He asked, "Are ye a slave for life?" I told him that I was. The good Irishman seemed to be deeply affected by the statement. He said to the other that it was a pity so fine a little fellow as myself should be a slave for life. He said it was a shame to hold me. They both advised me to run away to the north; that I should find friends there, and that I should be free. I pretended not to be interested in what they said, and treated them as if I did not understand them; for I feared they might be treacherous. White men have been known to encourage slaves to escape, and then, to get the reward, catch them and return them to their masters. I was afraid that these seemingly good men might use me so; but I nevertheless remembered their advice, and from that time I resolved to run away. I looked forward to a time at which it would be safe for me to escape. I was too young to think of doing so immediately; besides, I wished to learn how to write, as I might have occasion to write my own pass. I consoled myself with the hope that I should one day find a good chance. Meanwhile, I would learn to write.

The idea as to how I might learn to write was suggested to me by being in Durgin and Bailey's ship-yard, and frequently seeing the ship carpenters, after hewing, and getting a piece of timber ready for use, write on the timber the name of that part of the ship for which it was intended. When a piece of timber was intended for the larboard side, it would be marked thus—"L." When a piece was for the starboard side, it would be marked thus—"S." A piece for the larboard side forward, would be marked thus—"L.F." When a piece was for starboard side forward, it would be marked thus—"S.F." For larboard aft, it would be marked thus—"L.A." For starboard aft, it would be marked thus—"S.A." I soon learned the names of these letters, and for what they were intended when placed upon a piece of timber in the ship-yard. I immediately commenced copying them, and in a short time was able to make the four letters named. After that, when I met with any boy who I knew could write, I would tell him I could write as well as he. The next word would be, "I don't believe you. Let me see you try it." I would then make the letters which I had been so fortunate as to learn, and ask him to beat that. In this way I got a good many lessons in writing, which it is quite possible I should never have gotten in any other way. During this time, my copy-book was the board fence, brick wall, and pavement; my pen and ink was a lump of chalk. With these, I learned mainly how to write. I then commenced and continued copying the italics in Webster's Spelling Book, until I could make them all without looking on the book. By this time, my little Master Thomas had gone to school, and learned how to write, and had written over a number of copy-books. These had been brought home, and shown to some of our near neighbors, and then laid aside. My mistress used to go to class meeting at the Wilk Street meeting-house every Monday afternoon, and leave me to take care of the house. When left thus, I used to spend the time in writing in the spaces left in Master Thomas's copy-book, copying what he had written. I continued to do this until I could write a hand very similar to that of Master Thomas. Thus, after a long, tedious effort for years, I finally succeeded in learning how to write.

CHAPTER VIII.

IN a very short time after I went to live at Baltimore, my old master's youngest son, Richard, died; and in about three years and six months after his death, my old master, Captain Anthony, died, leaving only his son, Andrew, and daughter, Lucretia, to share his estate. He died while on a visit to see his daughter at Hillsborough. Cut off thus unexpectedly, he left no will as to the disposal of his property. It was therefore necessary to have a valuation of the property, that it might be equally divided between Mrs. Lucretia and Master Andrew. I was immediately sent for, to be valued with the other property. Here again my feelings rose up in detestation of slavery. I had now a new conception of my degraded condition. Prior to this, I had become, if not insensible to my lot, at least partly so. I left Baltimore with a young heart overborne with sadness, and a soul full of apprehension. I took passage with Captain Rowe, in the schooner Wild Cat, and, after a sail of about twenty-four hours, I found myself near the place of my birth. I had now been absent from it almost, if not quite, five years. I, however, remembered the place very well. I was only about five years old when I left it, to go and live with my old master on Colonel Lloyd's plantation; so that I was now between ten and eleven years old.

We were all ranked together at the valuation. Men and women, old and young, married and single, were ranked with horses, sheep, and swine. There were horses and men, cattle and women, pigs and children, all holding the same rank in the scale of being, and all were subjected to the same narrow examination. Silvery-headed age and sprightly youth, maids and matrons, had to undergo the same indelicate inspection. At this moment, I saw more clearly than ever the brutalizing effects of slavery upon both slave and slaveholder.

After the valuation, then came the division. I have no language to express the high excitement and deep anxiety which were felt among us poor slaves during this time. Our fate for life was now to be decided. We had no more voice in that decision than the brutes among whom we were ranked. A single word from the white men was enough—against all our wishes, prayers, and entreaties—to sunder forever the dearest friends, dearest kindred, and strongest ties known to human beings. In addition to the pain of separation, there was the horrid dread of falling into the hands of Master Andrew. He was known to us all as being a most cruel wretch,—a common drunkard, who had, by his reckless mismanagement and profligate dissipation, already wasted a large portion of his father's property. We all felt that we might as well be sold at once to the Georgia traders, as to pass into his hands; for we knew that that would be our inevitable condition,—a condition held by us all in the utmost horror and dread.

I suffered more anxiety than most of my fellow-slaves. I had known what it was to be kindly treated; they had known nothing of the kind. They had seen little or nothing of the world. They were in very deed men and women of sorrow, and acquainted with grief. Their backs had been made familiar with the bloody lash, so that they had become callous; mine was yet tender; for while at Baltimore I got few whippings, and few slaves could boast of a kinder master and mistress than myself; and the thought of passing out of their hands into those of Master Andrew—a man who, but a few days before, to give me a sample of his bloody disposition, took my little brother by the throat, threw him on the ground, and with the heel of his boot stamped upon his head till the blood gushed from his nose and ears— was well calculated to make me anxious as to my fate. After he had committed this savage outrage upon my brother, he turned to me, and said that was the way he meant to serve me one of these days,—meaning, I suppose, when I came into his possession.

Thanks to a kind Providence, I fell to the portion of Mrs. Lucretia, and was sent immediately back to Baltimore, to live again in the family of Master Hugh. Their joy at my return equalled their sorrow at my departure. It was a glad day to me. I had escaped a fate worse than lion's jaws. I was absent from Baltimore, for the purpose of valuation and division, just about one month, and it seemed to have been six.

Very soon after my return to Baltimore, my mistress, Lucretia, died, leaving her husband and one child, Amanda; and in a very short time after her death, Master Andrew died. Now all the property of my old master, slaves included, was in the hands of strangers,—strangers who had nothing to do with accumulating it. Not a slave was left free. All remained slaves, from the youngest to the oldest. If any one thing in my experience, more than another, served to deepen my conviction of the infernal character of slavery, and to fill me with unutterable loathing of slaveholders, it was their base ingratitude to my poor old grandmother. She had served my old master faithfully from youth to old age. She had been the source of all his wealth; she had peopled his plantation with slaves; she had become a great grandmother in his service. She had rocked him in infancy, attended him in childhood, served him through life, and at his death wiped from his icy brow the cold death-sweat, and closed his eyes forever. She was nevertheless left a slave—a slave for life—a slave in the hands of strangers; and in their hands she saw her children, her grandchildren, and her great-grandchildren, divided, like so many sheep, without being gratified with the small privilege of a single word, as to their or her own destiny. And, to cap the climax of their base ingratitude and fiendish barbarity, my grandmother, who was now very old, having outlived my old master and all his children, having seen the beginning and end of all of them, and her present owners finding she was of but little value, her frame already racked with the pains of old age, and complete helplessness fast stealing over her once active limbs, they took her to the woods, built her a little hut, put up a little mud-chimney, and then made her welcome to the privilege of supporting herself there in perfect loneliness; thus virtually turning her out to die! If my poor old grandmother now lives, she lives to suffer in utter loneliness; she lives to remember and mourn over the loss of children, the loss of grandchildren, and the loss of great-grandchildren. They are, in the language of the slave's poet, Whittier,—

> "Gone, gone, sold and gone
> To the rice swamp dank and lone,
> Where the slave-whip ceaseless swings,
> Where the noisome insect stings,
> Where the fever-demon strews
> Poison with the falling dews,
> Where the sickly sunbeams glare
> Through the hot and misty air:—
>> Gone, gone, sold and gone
>> To the rice swamp dank and lone,
>> From Virginia's hills and waters—
>> Woe is me, my stolen daughters!"

The hearth is desolate. The children, the unconscious children, who once sang and danced in her presence, are gone. She gropes her way, in the darkness of age, for a drink of water. Instead of the voices of her children, she hears by day the moans of the dove, and by night the screams of the hideous owl. All is gloom. The grave is at the door. And now, when weighed down by the pains and aches of old age, when the head inclines to the feet, when the beginning and ending of human existence meet, and helpless infancy and painful old age combine together—at this time, this most needful time, the time for the exercise of that tenderness and affection which children only can exercise towards a declining parent—my poor old grandmother, the devoted mother of twelve children, is left all alone, in yonder little hut, before a few dim embers. She stands—she sits—she staggers—she falls—she groans—she dies—and there are none of her children or grandchildren present, to wipe from her wrinkled brow the cold sweat of death, or to place beneath the sod her fallen remains. Will not a righteous God visit for these things?

In about two years after the death of Mrs. Lucretia, Master Thomas married his second wife. Her name was Rowena Hamilton. She was the eldest daughter of Mr. William Hamilton. Master now lived in St. Michael's. Not long after his marriage, a misunderstanding took place between himself and Master Hugh; and as a means of punishing his brother, he took me from him to live with himself at St. Michael's. Here I underwent another most painful separation. It, however, was not so severe as the one I dreaded at the division of property; for, during this interval, a great change had taken place in Master Hugh and his once kind and affectionate wife. The influence of brandy upon him, and of slavery upon her, had effected a disastrous change in the characters of both; so that, as far as they were concerned, I thought I had little to lose by the change. But it was not to them that I was attached. It was to those little Baltimore boys that I felt the strongest attachment. I had received many good lessons from them, and was still receiving them, and the thought of leaving them was painful indeed. I was leaving, too, without the hope of ever being allowed to return. Master Thomas had said he would never let me return again. The barrier betwixt himself and his brother he considered impassable.

I then had to regret that I did not at least make the attempt to carry out my resolution to run away; for the chances of success are tenfold greater from the city than from the country.

I sailed from Baltimore for St. Michael's in the sloop Amanda, Captain Edward Dodson. On my passage, I paid particular attention to the direction which the steamboats took to go to Philadelphia. I found, instead of going down, on reaching North Point they went up the bay, in a north-easterly direction. I deemed this knowledge of the utmost importance. My determination to run away was again revived. I resolved to wait only so long as the

offering of a favorable opportunity. When that came, I was determined to
be off.

CHAPTER IX.

I HAVE now reached a period of my life when I can give dates. I left
Baltimore, and went to live with Master Thomas Auld, at St. Michael's, in
March, 1832. It was now more than seven years since I lived with him in the
family of my old master, on Colonel Lloyd's plantation. We of course were
now almost entire strangers to each other. He was to me a new master, and I
to him a new slave. I was ignorant of his temper and disposition; he was
equally so of mine. A very short time, however, brought us into full acquaintance with each other. I was made acquainted with his wife not less
than with himself. They were well matched, being equally mean and cruel. I
was now, for the first time during a space of more than seven years, made to
feel the painful gnawings of hunger—a something which I had not experienced before since I left Colonel Lloyd's plantation. It went hard enough
with me then, when I could look back to no period at which I had enjoyed a
sufficiency. It was tenfold harder after living in Master Hugh's family,
where I had always had enough to eat, and of that which was good. I have
said Master Thomas was a mean man. He was so. Not to give a slave
enough to eat, is regarded as the most aggravated development of meanness
even among slaveholders. The rule is, no matter how coarse the food, only
let there be enough of it. This is the theory; and in the part of Maryland from
which I came, it is the general practice,—though there are many exceptions. Master Thomas gave us enough of neither coarse nor fine food. There
were four slaves of us in the kitchen—my sister Eliza, my aunt Priscilla,
Henny, and myself; and we were allowed less than half of a bushel of corn-
meal per week, and very little else, either in the shape of meat or vegetables.
It was not enough for us to subsist upon. We were therefore reduced to the
wretched necessity of living at the expense of our neighbors. This we did by
begging and stealing, whichever came handy in the time of need, the one
being considered as legitimate as the other. A great many times have we
poor creatures been nearly perishing with hunger, when food in abundance
lay mouldering in the safe and smoke-house, and our pious mistress was
aware of the fact; and yet that mistress and her husband would kneel every
morning, and pray that God would bless them in basket and store!

Bad as all slaveholders are, we seldom meet one destitute of every
element of character commanding respect. My master was one of this rare

sort. I do not know of one single noble act ever performed by him. The leading trait in his character was meanness; and if there were any other element in his nature, it was made subject to this. He was mean; and, like most other mean men, he lacked the ability to conceal his meanness. Captain Auld was not born a slaveholder. He had been a poor man, master only of a Bay craft. He came into possession of all his slaves by marriage; and of all men, adopted slaveholders are the worst. He was cruel, but cowardly. He commanded without firmness. In the enforcement of his rules, he was at times rigid, and at times lax. At times, he spoke to his slaves with the firmness of Napoleon and the fury of a demon; at other times, he might well be mistaken for an inquirer who had lost his way. He did nothing of himself. He might have passed for a lion, but for his ears. In all things noble which he attempted, his own meanness shone most conspicuous. His airs, words, and actions, were the airs, words, and actions of born slaveholders, and, being assumed, were awkward enough. He was not even a good imitator. He possessed all the disposition to deceive, but wanted the power. Having no resources within himself, he was compelled to be the copyist of many, and being such, he was forever the victim of inconsistency; and of consequence he was an object of contempt, and was held as such even by his slaves. The luxury of having slaves of his own to wait upon him was something new and unprepared for. He was a slaveholder without the ability to hold slaves. He found himself incapable of managing his slaves either by force, fear, or fraud. We seldom called him "master;" we generally called him "Captain Auld," and were hardly disposed to title him at all. I doubt not that our conduct had much to do with making him appear awkward, and of consequence fretful. Our want of reverence for him must have perplexed him greatly. He wished to have us call him master, but lacked the firmness necessary to command us to do so. His wife used to insist upon our calling him so, but to no purpose. In August, 1832, my master attended a Methodist camp-meeting held in the Bay-side, Talbot county, and there experienced religion. I indulged a faint hope that his conversion would lead him to emancipate his slaves, and that, if he did not do this, it would, at any rate, make him more kind and humane. I was disappointed in both these respects. It neither made him to be humane to his slaves, nor to emancipate them. If it had any effect on his character, it made him more cruel and hateful in all his ways; for I believe him to have been a much worse man after his conversion than before. Prior to his conversion, he relied upon his own depravity to shield and sustain him in his savage barbarity; but after his conversion, he found religious sanction and support for his slaveholding cruelty. He made the greatest pretensions to piety. His house was the house of prayer. He prayed morning, noon, and night. He very soon distinguished himself among his brethren, and was soon made a class-leader and exhorter. His activity in revivals was great, and he proved himself an instrument in the hands of the church in converting many souls. His house was the preachers' home. They used to take great pleasure in coming there to put up; for while he starved us, he stuffed them. We have had three or four preachers there at a time. The names of those who used to come most frequently while I lived there, were Mr. Storks, Mr. Ewery, Mr. Humphry, and Mr. Hickey. I have also seen Mr. George Cookman at our house. We slaves loved Mr. Cookman. We believed him to be a good man. We thought him instrumental in getting Mr. Samuel Harrison, a very rich slaveholder, to emancipate his slaves; and by some means got the impression that he was laboring to effect the emancipation of all the slaves. When he was at our house, we were sure to be called in to prayers. When the others were there, we were sometimes called in and sometimes not. Mr. Cookman took more notice of us than either of the other ministers. He could not come among us without betraying his sympathy for us, and, stupid as we were, we had the sagacity to see it.

While I lived with my master in St. Michael's, there was a white young man, a Mr. Wilson, who proposed to keep a Sabbath school for the instruction of such slaves as might be disposed to learn to read the New Testament. We met but three times, when Mr. West and Mr. Fairbanks, both class-leaders, with many others, came upon us with sticks and other missiles, drove us off, and forbade us to meet again. Thus ended our little Sabbath school in the pious town of St. Michael's.

I have said my master found religious sanction for his cruelty. As an example, I will state one of many facts going to prove the charge. I have seen him tie up a lame young woman, and whip her with a heavy cowskin upon her naked shoulders, causing the warm red blood to drip; and, in justification of the bloody deed, he would quote this passage of Scripture— "He that knoweth his master's will, and doeth it not, shall be beaten with many stripes."

Master would keep this lacerated young woman tied up in this horrid situation four or five hours at a time. I have known him to tie her up early in the morning, and whip her before breakfast; leave her, go to his store, return at dinner, and whip her again, cutting her in the places already made raw with his cruel lash. The secret of master's cruelty toward "Henny" is found in the fact of her being almost helpless. When quite a child, she fell into the fire, and burned herself horribly. Her hands were so burnt that she never got the use of them. She could do very little but bear heavy burdens. She was to master a bill of expense; and as he was a mean man, she was a constant offence to him. He seemed desirous of getting the poor girl out of existence. He gave her away once to his sister; but, being a poor gift, she was not disposed to keep her. Finally, my benevolent master, to use his own words, "set her adrift to take care of herself." Here was a recently-converted man, holding on upon the mother, and at the same time turning out her helpless child, to starve and die! Master Thomas was one of the many pious slave-holders who hold slaves for the very charitable purpose of taking care of them.

My master and myself had quite a number of differences. He found me unsuitable to his purpose. My city life, he said, had had a very pernicious effect upon me. It had almost ruined me for every good purpose, and fitted me for every thing which was bad. One of my greatest faults was that of letting his horse run away, and go down to his father-in-law's farm, which was about five miles from St. Michael's. I would then have to go after it. My reason for this kind of carelessness, or carefulness, was, that I could always get something to eat when I went there. Master William Hamilton, my master's father-in-law, always gave his slaves enough to eat. I never left there hungry, no matter how great the need of my speedy return. Master Thomas at length said he would stand it no longer. I had lived with him nine months, during which time he had given me a number of severe whippings, all to no good purpose. He resolved to put me out, as he said, to be broken; and, for this purpose, he let me for one year to a man named Edward Covey. Mr. Covey was a poor man, a farm-renter. He rented the place upon which he lived, as also the hands with which he tilled it. Mr. Covey had acquired a very high reputation for breaking young slaves, and this reputation was of immense value to him. It enabled him to get his farm tilled with much less expense to himself than he could have had it done without such a reputation. Some slaveholders thought it not much loss to allow Mr. Covey to have their slaves one year, for the sake of the training to which they were subjected, without any other compensation. He could hire young help with great ease, in consequence of this reputation. Added to the natural good qualities of Mr. Covey, he was a professor of religion—a pious soul—a member and a class-leader in the Methodist church. All of this added weight to his reputation as a "nigger-breaker." I was aware of all the facts, having been made acquainted with them by a young man who had lived there. I nevertheless made the change gladly; for I was sure of getting enough to eat, which is not the smallest consideration to a hungry man.

_____

CHAPTER X.

I LEFT Master Thomas's house, and went to live with Mr. Covey, on the 1st of January, 1833. I was now, for the first time in my life, a field hand. In my new employment, I found myself even more awkward than a country boy appeared to be in a large city. I had been at my new home but one week before Mr. Covey gave me a very severe whipping, cutting my back, causing the blood to run, and raising ridges on my flesh as large as my little finger. The details of this affair are as follows: Mr. Covey sent me, very early in the morning of one of our coldest days in the month of January, to the woods, to get a load of wood. He gave me a team of unbroken oxen. He told me which was the in-hand ox, and which the off-hand one. He then tied the end of a large rope around the horns of the in-hand ox, and gave me the other end of it, and told me, if the oxen started to run, that I must hold on upon the rope. I had never driven oxen before, and of course I was very awkward. I, however, succeeded in getting to the edge of the woods with little difficulty; but I had got a very few rods into the woods, when the oxen took fright, and started full tilt, carrying the cart against trees, and over stumps, in the most frightful manner. I expected every moment that my brains would be dashed out against the trees. After running thus for a considerable distance, they finally upset the cart, dashing it with great force against a tree, and threw themselves into a dense thicket. How I escaped death, I do not know. There I was, entirely alone, in a thick wood, in a place new to me. My cart was upset and shattered, my oxen were entangled among the young trees, and there was none to help me. After a long spell of effort, I succeeded in getting my cart righted, my oxen disentangled, and again yoked to the cart. I now proceeded with my team to the place where I had, the day before, been chopping wood, and loaded my cart pretty heavily, thinking in this way to tame my oxen. I then proceeded on my way home. I had now consumed one half of the day. I got out of the woods safely, and now felt out of danger. I stopped my oxen to open the gate; and just as I did so, before I could get hold of my ox-rope, the oxen again started, rushed through the gate, catching it between the wheel and the body of the cart, tearing it to pieces, and coming within a few inches of crushing me against the gate-post. Thus twice, in one short day, I escaped death by the merest chance. On my return, I told Mr. Covey what had happened, and how it happened. He ordered me to return to the woods again immediately. I did so, and he followed on after me. Just as I got into the woods, he came up and told me to stop my cart, and that he would teach me how to trifle away my time, and break gates. He then went to a large gum-tree, and with his axe cut three large switches, and, after trimming them up neatly with his pocket-knife, he ordered me to take off my clothes. I made him no answer, but stood with my clothes on. He repeated his order. I still made him no answer, nor did I move to strip myself. Upon this he rushed at me with the fierceness of a tiger, tore off my clothes, and lashed me till he had worn out his switches, cutting me so savagely as to leave the marks visible for a long time after. This whipping was the first of a number just like it, and for similar offences.

I lived with Mr. Covey one year. During the first six months, of that year, scarce a week passed without his whipping me. I was seldom free from a sore back. My awkwardness was almost always his excuse for whipping me. We were worked fully up to the point of endurance. Long before day we were up, our horses fed, and by the first approach of day we were off to the field with our hoes and ploughing teams. Mr. Covey gave us enough to eat, but scarce time to eat it. We were often less than five minutes taking our meals. We were often in the field from the first approach of day till its last lingering ray had left us; and at saving-fodder time, midnight often caught us in the field binding blades.

Covey would be out with us. The way he used to stand it, was this. He would spend the most of his afternoons in bed. He would then come out fresh in the evening, ready to urge us on with his word, example, and frequently with the whip. Mr. Covey was one of the few slaveholders who could and did work with his hands. He was a hard-working man. He knew by himself just what a man or a boy could do. There was no deceiving him. His work went on in his absence almost as well as in his presence; and he had the faculty of making us feel that he was ever present with us. This he did by surprising us. He seldom approached the spot where we were at work openly, if he could do it secretly. He always aimed at taking us by surprise. Such was his cunning, that we used to call him, among ourselves, "the snake." When we were at work in the cornfield, he would sometimes crawl on his hands and knees to avoid detection, and all at once he would rise nearly in our midst, and scream out, "Ha, ha! Come, come! Dash on, dash on!" This being his mode of attack, it was never safe to stop a single minute. His comings were like a thief in the night. He appeared to us as being ever at hand. He was under every tree, behind every stump, in every bush, and at every window, on the plantation. He would sometimes mount his horse, as if bound to St. Michael's, a distance of seven miles, and in half an hour afterwards you would see him coiled up in the corner of the wood-fence, watching every motion of the slaves. He would, for this purpose, leave his horse tied up in the woods. Again, he would sometimes walk up to us, and give us orders as though he was upon the point of starting on a long journey, turn his back upon us, and make as though he was going to the house to get ready; and, before he would get half way thither, he would turn short and crawl into a fence-corner, or behind some tree, and there watch us till the going down of the sun.

Mr. Covey's *forte* consisted in his power to deceive. His life was devoted to planning and perpetrating the grossest deceptions. Every thing he possessed in the shape of learning or religion, he made conform to his disposition to deceive. He seemed to think himself equal to deceiving the Almighty. He would make a short prayer in the morning, and a long prayer at night; and, strange as it may seem, few men would at times appear more devotional than he. The exercises of his family devotions were always commenced with singing; and, as he was a very poor singer himself, the duty of raising the hymn generally came upon me. He would read his hymn, and nod at me to commence. I would at times do so; at others, I would not. My non-compliance would almost always produce much confusion. To show himself independent of me, he would start and stagger through with his hymn in the most discordant manner. In this state of mind, he prayed with more than ordinary spirit. Poor man! such was his disposition, and success at deceiving, I do verily believe that he sometimes deceived himself into the solemn belief, that he was a sincere worshipper of the most high God; and this, too, at a time when he may be said to have been guilty of compelling his woman slave to commit the sin of adultery. The facts in the case are these: Mr. Covey was a poor man; he was just commencing in life; he was only able to buy one slave; and, shocking as is the fact, he bought her, as he said, for *a breeder*. This woman was named Caroline. Mr. Covey bought her from Mr. Thomas Lowe, about six miles from St. Michael's. She was a large, able-bodied woman, about twenty years old. She had already given birth to one child, which proved her to be just what he wanted. After buying her, he hired a married man of Mr. Samuel Harrison, to live with him one year; and him he used to fasten up with her every night! The result was, that, at the end of the year, the miserable woman gave birth to twins. At this result Mr. Covey seemed to be highly pleased, both with the man and the wretched woman. Such was his joy, and that of his wife, that nothing they could do for Caroline during her confinement was too good, or too hard, to be done. The children were regarded as being quite an addition to his wealth.

If at any one time of my life more than another, I was made to drink the bitterest dregs of slavery, that time was during the first six months of my stay with Mr. Covey. We were worked in all weathers. It was never too hot or too cold; it could never rain, blow, hail, or snow, too hard for us to work in the field. Work, work, work, was scarcely more the order of the day than of the night. The longest days were too short for him, and the shortest nights too long for him. I was somewhat unmanageable when I first went there, but a few months of this discipline tamed me. Mr. Covey succeeded in breaking me. I was broken in body, soul, and spirit. My natural elasticity was crushed, my intellect languished, the disposition to read departed, the cheerful spark that lingered about my eye died; the dark night of slavery closed in upon me; and behold a man transformed into a brute!

Sunday was my only leisure time. I spent this in a sort of beast-like stupor, between sleep and wake, under some large tree. At times I would rise up, a flash of energetic freedom would dart through my soul, accompanied with a faint beam of hope, that flickered for a moment, and then vanished. I sank down again, mourning over my wretched condition. I was sometimes prompted to take my life, and that of Covey, but was prevented by a combination of hope and fear. My sufferings on this plantation seem now like a dream rather than a stern reality.

Our house stood within a few rods of the Chesapeake Bay, whose broad bosom was ever white with sails from every quarter of the habitable globe. Those beautiful vessels, robed in purest white, so delightful to the eye of freemen, were to me so many shrouded ghosts, to terrify and torment me with thoughts of my wretched condition. I have often, in the deep stillness of a summer's Sabbath, stood all alone upon the lofty banks of that noble bay, and traced, with saddened heart and tearful eye, the countless number of sails moving off to the mighty ocean. The sight of these always affected me powerfully. My thoughts would compel utterance; and there, with no audience but the Almighty, I would pour out my soul's complaint, in my rude way, with an apostrophe to the moving multitude of ships:—

"You are loosed from your moorings, and are free; I am fast in my chains, and am a slave! You move merrily before the gentle gale, and I sadly before the bloody whip! You are freedom's swift-winged angels, that fly round the world; I am confined in bands of iron! O that I were free! O, that I were on one of your gallant decks, and under your protecting wing! Alas! betwixt me and you, the turbid waters roll. Go on, go on. O that I could also go! Could I but swim! If I could fly! O, why was I born a man, of whom to make a brute! The glad ship is gone; she hides in the dim distance. I am left in the hottest hell of unending slavery. O God, save me! God, deliver me! Let me be free! Is there any God? Why am I a slave? I will run away. I will not stand it. Get caught, or get clear, I'll try it. I had as well die with ague as the fever. I have only one life to lose. I had as well be killed running as die standing. Only think of it; one hundred miles straight north, and I am free! Try it? Yes! God helping me, I will. It cannot be that I shall live and die a slave. I will take to the water. This very bay shall yet bear me into freedom. The steamboats steered in a north-east course from North Point. I will do the same; and when I get to the head of the bay, I will turn my canoe adrift, and walk straight through Delaware into Pennsylvania. When I get there, I shall not be required to have a pass; I can travel without being disturbed. Let but the first opportunity offer, and, come what will, I am off. Meanwhile, I will try to bear up under the yoke. I am not the only slave in the world. Why should I fret? I can bear as much as any of them. Besides, I am but a boy, and all boys are bound to some one. It may be that my misery in slavery will only increase my happiness when I get free. There is a better day coming."

Thus I used to think, and thus I used to speak to myself; goaded almost to madness at one moment, and at the next reconciling myself to my wretched lot.

I have already intimated that my condition was much worse, during the first six months of my stay at Mr. Covey's, than in the last six. The circumstances leading to the change in Mr. Covey's course toward me form an epoch in my humble history. You have seen how a man was made a slave; you shall see how a slave was made a man. On one of the hottest days of the month of August, 1833, Bill Smith, William Hughes, a slave named Eli, and myself, were engaged in fanning wheat. Hughes was clearing the fanned wheat from before the fan, Eli was turning, Smith was feeding, and I was carrying wheat to the fan. The work was simple, requiring strength rather than intellect; yet, to one entirely unused to such work, it came very hard. About three o'clock of that day, I broke down; my strength failed me; I was seized with a violent aching of the head, attended with extreme dizziness; I trembled in every limb. Finding what was coming, I nerved myself up, feeling it would never do to stop work. I stood as long as I could stagger to the hopper with grain. When I could stand no longer, I fell, and felt as if held down by some immense weight. The fan of course stopped; every one had his own work to do; and no one could do the work of the other, and have his own go on at the same time.

Mr. Covey was at the house, about one hundred yards from the tread-ing-yard where we were fanning. On hearing the fan stop, he left imme-diately, and came to the spot where we were. He hastily inquired what the matter was. Bill answered that I was sick, and there was no one to bring wheat to the fan. I had by this time crawled away under the side of the post and rail-fence by which the yard was enclosed, hoping to find relief by getting out of the sun. He then asked where I was. He was told by one of the hands. He came to the spot, and, after looking at me awhile, asked me what was the matter. I told him as well as I could, for I scarce had strength to speak. He then gave me a savage kick in the side, and told me to get up. I tried to do so, but fell back in the attempt. He gave me another kick, and again told me to rise. I again tried, and succeeded in gaining my feet; but, stooping to get to the tub with which I was feeding the fan, I again staggered and fell. While down in this situation, Mr. Covey took up the hickory slat with which Hughes had been striking off the half-bushel measure, and with it gave me a heavy blow upon the head, making a large wound, and the blood ran freely; and with this again told me to get up. I made no effort to comply, having now made up my mind to let him do his worst. In a short time after receiving this blow, my head grew better. Mr. Covey had now left me to my fate. At this moment I resolved, for the first time, to go to my master, enter a complaint, and ask his protection. In order to do this, I must that afternoon walk seven miles; and this, under the circumstances, was truly a severe undertaking. I was exceedingly feeble; made so as much by the kicks and blows which I received, as by the severe fit of sickness to which I had been subjected. I, however, watched my chance, while Covey was looking in an opposite direction, and started for St. Michael's. I suc-ceeded in getting a considerable distance on my way to the woods, when Covey discovered me, and called after me to come back, threatening what he would do if I did not come. I disregarded both his calls and his threats, and made my way to the woods as fast as my feeble state would allow; and thinking I might be overhauled by him if I kept the road, I walked through the woods, keeping far enough from the road to avoid detection, and near enough to prevent losing my way. I had not gone far before my little strength again failed me. I could go no farther. I fell down, and lay for a considerable time. The blood was yet oozing from the wound on my head. For a time I thought I should bleed to death; and think now that I should have done so, but that the blood so matted my hair as to stop the wound. After lying there about three quarters of an hour, I nerved myself up again, and started on my way, through bogs and briers, barefooted and bareheaded, tearing my feet sometimes at nearly every step; and after a journey of about seven miles, occupying some five hours to perform it, I arrived at master's store. I then presented an appearance enough to affect any but a heart of iron. From the crown of my head to my feet, I was covered with blood. My hair was all clotted with dust and blood; my shirt was stiff with blood. My legs and feet were torn in sundry places with briers and thorns, and were also covered with blood. I suppose I looked like a man who had escaped a den of wild beasts, and barely escaped them. In this state I appeared before my master, humbly entreating him to interpose his authority for my protection. I told him all the circumstances as well as I could, and it seemed, as I spoke, at times to affect him. He would then walk the floor, and seek to justify Covey by saying he expected I deserved it. He asked me what I wanted. I told him, to let me get a new home; that as sure as I lived with Mr. Covey again, I should live with but to die with him; that Covey would surely kill me; he was in a fair way for it. Master Thomas ridiculed the idea that there was any danger of Mr. Covey's killing me, and said that he knew Mr. Covey; that he was a good man, and that he could not think of taking me from him; that, should he do so, he would lose the whole year's wages; that I belonged to Mr. Covey for one year, and that I must go back to him, come what might; and that I must not trouble him with any more stories, or that he would himself *get hold of me*. After threatening me thus, he gave me a very large dose of salts, telling me that I might remain in St. Michael's that night, (it being quite late,) but that I must be off back to Mr. Covey's early in the morning; and that if I did not, he would *get hold of me,* which meant that he would whip me. I remained all night, and, according to his orders, I started off to Covey's in the morning, (Saturday morning,) wearied in body and broken in spirit. I got no supper that night, or breakfast that morning. I reached Covey's about nine o'clock; and just as I was getting over the fence that divided Mrs. Kemp's fields from ours, out ran Covey with his cowskin, to give me another whipping. Before he could reach me, I succeeded in getting to the cornfield; and as the corn was very high, it afforded me the means of hiding. He seemed very angry, and searched for me a long time. My behavior was altogether unaccountable. He finally gave up the chase, thinking, I suppose, that I must come home for something to eat; he would give himself no further trouble in looking for me. I spent that day mostly in the woods, having the alternative before me,—to go home and be whipped to death, or stay in the woods and be starved to death. That night, I fell in with Sandy Jenkins, a slave with whom I was somewhat acquainted. Sandy had a free wife who lived about four miles from Mr. Covey's; and it being Saturday, he was on his way to see her. I told him my circumstances, and he very kindly invited me to go home with him. I went home with him, and talked this whole matter over, and got his advice as to what course it was best for me to pursue. I found Sandy an old adviser. He told me, with great solemnity, I must go back to Covey; but that before I went, I must go with him into another part of the woods, where there was a certain *root,* which, if I would take some of it with me, carrying it *always on my right side,* would render it impossible for Mr. Covey, or any other white man, to whip me. He said he had carried it for years; and since he had done so, he had never received a blow, and never expected to while he carried it. I at first rejected the idea, that the simple carrying of a root in my pocket would have any such effect as he had said, and was not disposed to take it; but Sandy impressed the necessity with much earnestness, telling me it could do no harm, if it did no good. To please him, I at length took the root, and, according to his direction, carried it upon my right side. This was Sunday morning. I immediately started for home; and upon entering the yard gate, out came Mr. Covey on his way to meeting. He spoke to me very kindly, bade me drive the pigs from a lot near by, and passed on towards the church. Now, this singular conduct of Mr. Covey really made me begin to think that there was something in the *root* which Sandy had given me; and had it been on any other day than Sunday, I could have attributed the conduct to no other cause than the influence of that root; and as it was, I was half inclined to think the *root* to be something more than I at first had taken it to be. All went well till Monday morning. On this morning, the virtue of the *root* was fully tested. Long before daylight, I was called to go and rub, curry, and feed, the horses. I obeyed, and was glad to obey. But whilst thus engaged, whilst in the act of throwing down some blades from the loft, Mr. Covey entered the stable with a long rope; and just as I was half out of the loft, he caught hold of my legs, and was about tying me. As soon as I found what he was up to, I gave a sudden spring, and as I did so, he holding to my legs, I was brought sprawling on the stable floor. Mr. Covey seemed now to think he had me, and could do what he pleased; but at this moment—from whence came the spirit I don't know—I resolved to fight; and, suiting my action to the resolution, I seized Covey hard by the throat; and as I did so, I rose. He held on to me, and I to him. My resistance was so entirely unexpected, that Covey seemed taken all aback. He trembled like a leaf. This gave me assurance, and I held him uneasy, causing the blood to run where I touched him with the ends of my fingers. Mr. Covey soon called out to Hughes for help. Hughes came, and, while Covey held me, attempted to tie my right hand. While he was in the act of doing so, I watched my chance, and gave him a heavy kick close under the ribs. This kick fairly sickened Hughes, so that he left me in the hands of Mr. Covey. This kick had the effect of not only weakening Hughes, but Covey also. When he saw Hughes bending over with pain, his courage quailed. He asked me if I meant to persist in my resistance. I told him I did, come what might; that he had used me like a brute for six months, and that I was determined to be used so no longer. With that, he strove to drag me to a stick that was lying just out of the stable door. He meant to knock me down. But just as he was leaning over to get the stick, I seized him with both hands by his collar, and brought him by a sudden snatch to the ground. By this time, Bill came. Covey called upon him for assistance. Bill wanted to know what he could do. Covey said, "Take hold of him, take hold of him!" Bill said his master hired him out to work, and not to help to whip me; so he left Covey and myself to fight our own battle out. We were at it for nearly two hours. Covey at length let me go, puffing and blowing at a great rate, saying that if I had not resisted, he would not have whipped me half so much. The truth was, that he had not whipped me at all. I considered him as getting entirely the worst end of the bargain; for he had drawn no blood from me, but I had from him. The whole six months afterwards, that I spent with Mr. Covey, he never laid the weight of his finger upon me in anger. He would occasionally say, he didn't want to get hold of me again. "No," thought I, "you need not; for you will come off worse than you did before."

This battle with Mr. Covey was the turning-point in my career as a slave. It rekindled the few expiring embers of freedom, and revived within me a sense of my own manhood. It recalled the departed self-confidence, and inspired me again with a determination to be free. The gratification afforded by the triumph was a full compensation for whatever else might follow, even death itself. He only can understand the deep satisfaction which I experienced, who has himself repelled by force the bloody arm of slavery. I felt as I never felt before. It was a glorious resurrection, from the tomb of slavery, to the heaven of freedom. My long-crushed spirit rose, cowardice departed, bold defiance took its place; and I now resolved that, however long I might remain a slave in form, the day had passed forever when I could be a slave in fact. I did not hesitate to let it be known of me, that the white man who expected to succeed in whipping, must also succeed in killing me.

From this time I was never again what might be called fairly whipped, though I remained a slave four years afterwards. I had several fights, but was never whipped.

It was for a long time a matter of surprise to me why Mr. Covey did not immediately have me taken by the constable to the whipping-post, and there regularly whipped for the crime of raising my hand against a white man in defence of myself. And the only explanation I can now think of does not entirely satisfy me; but such as it is, I will give it. Mr. Covey enjoyed the most unbounded reputation for being a first-rate overseer and negro-breaker. It was of considerable importance to him. That reputation was at stake; and had he sent me—a boy about sixteen years old—to the public whipping-post, his reputation would have been lost; so, to save his reputation, he suffered me to go unpunished.

My term of actual service to Mr. Edward Covey ended on Christmas day, 1833. The days between Christmas and New Year's day are allowed as holidays; and, accordingly, we were not required to perform any labor, more than to feed and take care of the stock. This time we regarded as our own, by the grace of our masters; and we therefore used or abused it nearly as we pleased. Those of us who had families at a distance, were generally allowed to spend the whole six days in their society. This time, however, was spent in various ways. The sober, staid, thinking and industrious ones of our number would employ themselves in making corn-brooms, mats, horse-collars, and baskets; and another class of us would spend the time in hunting opossums, hares, and coons. But by far the larger part engaged in such sports and merriments as ball playing, wrestling, running foot-races, fiddling, dancing, and drinking whisky; and this latter mode of spending the time was by far the most agreeable to the feelings of our masters. A slave who would work during the holidays was considered by our masters as scarcely deserving them. He was regarded as one who rejected the favor of his master. It was deemed a disgrace not to get drunk at Christmas; and he was regarded as lazy indeed, who had not provided himself with the necessary means, during the year, to get whisky enough to last him through Christmas.

From what I know of the effect of these holidays upon the slave, I believe them to be among the most effective means in the hands of the slaveholder in keeping down the spirit of insurrection. Were the slaveholders at once to abandon this practice, I have not the slightest doubt it would lead to an immediate insurrection among the slaves. These holidays serve as conductors, or safety-valves, to carry off the rebellious spirit of enslaved humanity. But for these, the slave would be forced up to the wildest desperation; and woe betide the slaveholder, the day he ventures to remove or hinder the operation of those conductors! I warn him that, in such an event, a spirit will go forth in their midst, more to be dreaded than the most appalling earthquake.

The holidays are part and parcel of the gross fraud, wrong, and inhumanity of slavery. They are professedly a custom established by the benevolence of the slaveholders; but I undertake to say, it is the result of selfishness, and one of the grossest frauds committed upon the down-trodden slave. They do not give the slaves this time because they would not like to have their work during its continuance, but because they know it would be unsafe to deprive them of it. This will be seen by the fact, that the slaveholders like to have their slaves spend those days just in such a manner as to make them as glad of their ending as of their beginning. Their object seems to be, to disgust their slaves with freedom, by plunging them into the lowest depths of dissipation. For instance, the slaveholders not only like to see the slave drink of his own accord, but will adopt various plans to make him drunk. One plan is, to make bets on their slaves, as to who can drink the most whisky without getting drunk; and in this way they succeed in getting whole multitudes to drink to excess. Thus, when the slave asks for virtuous freedom, the cunning slaveholder, knowing his ignorance, cheats him with a dose of vicious dissipation, artfully labelled with the name of liberty. The most of us used to drink it down, and the result was just what might be supposed: many of us were led to think that there was little to choose between liberty and slavery. We felt, and very properly too, that we had almost as well be slaves to man as to rum. So, when the holidays ended, we staggered up from the filth of our wallowing, took a long breath, and marched to the field,—feeling, upon the whole, rather glad to go, from what our master had deceived us into a belief was freedom, back to the arms of slavery.

I have said that this mode of treatment is a part of the whole system of fraud and inhumanity of slavery. It is so. The mode here adopted to disgust the slave with freedom, by allowing him to see only the abuse of it, is carried out in other things. For instance, a slave loves molasses; he steals some. His master, in many cases, goes off to town, and buys a large quantity; he returns, takes his whip, and commands the slave to eat the molasses, until the poor fellow is made sick at the very mention of it. The same mode is sometimes adopted to make the slaves refrain from asking for more food than their regular allowance. A slave runs through his allowance, and applies for more. His master is enraged at him; but, not willing to send him off without food, gives him more than is necessary, and compels him to eat it within a given time. Then, if he complains that he cannot eat it, he is said to be satisfied neither full nor fasting, and is whipped for being hard to please! I have an abundance of such illustrations of the same principle, drawn from my own observation, but think the cases I have cited sufficient. The practice is a very common one.

On the first of January, 1834, I left Mr. Covey, and went to live with Mr. William Freeland, who lived about three miles from St. Michael's. I soon found Mr. Freeland a very different man from Mr. Covey. Though not rich, he was what would be called an educated southern gentleman. Mr. Covey, as I have shown, was a well-trained negro-breaker and slave-driver. The former (slaveholder though he was) seemed to possess some regard for honor, some reverence for justice, and some respect for humanity. The latter seemed totally insensible to all such sentiments. Mr. Freeland had many of the faults peculiar to slaveholders, such as being very passionate and fretful; but I must do him the justice to say, that he was exceedingly free from those degrading vices to which Mr. Covey was constantly addicted. The one was open and frank, and we always knew where to find him. The other was a most artful deceiver, and could be understood only by such as were skilful enough to detect his cunningly-devised frauds. Another advantage I gained in my new master was, he made no pretensions to, or profession of, religion; and this, in my opinion, was truly a great advantage. I assert most unhesitatingly, that the religion of the south is a mere covering for the most horrid crimes,—a justifier of the most appalling barbarity,—a sanctifier of the most hateful frauds,—and a dark shelter, under which the darkest, foulest, grossest, and most infernal deeds of slaveholders find the strongest protection. Were I to be again reduced to the chains of slavery, next to that enslavement, I should regard being the slave of a religious master the greatest calamity that could befall me. For of all slaveholders with whom I have ever met, religious slaveholders are the worst. I have ever found them the meanest and basest, the most cruel and cowardly, of all others. It was my unhappy lot not only to belong to a religious slaveholder, but to live in a community of such religionists. Very near Mr. Freeland lived the Rev. Daniel Weeden, and in the same neighborhood lived the Rev. Rigby Hopkins. These were members and ministers in the Reformed Methodist Church. Mr. Weeden owned, among others, a woman slave, whose name I have forgotten. This woman's back, for weeks, was kept literally raw, made so by the lash of this merciless, *religious* wretch. He used to hire hands. His maxim was, Behave well or behave ill, it is the duty of a master occasionally to whip a slave, to remind him of his master's authority. Such was his theory, and such his practice.

Mr. Hopkins was even worse than Mr. Weeden. His chief boast was his ability to manage slaves. The peculiar feature of his government was that of whipping slaves in advance of deserving it. He always managed to have one or more of his slaves to whip every Monday morning. He did this to alarm their fears, and strike terror into those who escaped. His plan was to whip for the smallest offences, to prevent the commission of large ones. Mr. Hopkins could always find some excuse for whipping a slave. It would astonish one, unaccustomed to a slaveholding life, to see with what wonderful ease a slaveholder can find things, of which to make occasion to whip a slave. A mere look, word, or motion,—a mistake, accident, or want of power,—are all matters for which a slave may be whipped at any time. Does a slave look dissatisfied? It is said, he has the devil in him, and it must be whipped out. Does he speak loudly when spoken to by his master? Then he is getting high-minded, and should be taken down a button-hole lower. Does he forget to pull off his hat at the approach of a white person? Then he is wanting in reverence, and should be whipped for it. Does he ever venture to vindicate his conduct, when censured for it? Then he is guilty of impudence,—one of the greatest crimes of which a slave can be guilty. Does he ever venture to suggest a different mode of doing things from that pointed out by his master? He is indeed presumptuous, and getting above himself; and nothing less than a flogging will do for him. Does he, while ploughing, break a plough,—or, while hoeing, break a hoe? It is owing to his carelessness, and for it a slave must always be whipped. Mr. Hopkins could always find something of this sort to justify the use of the lash, and he seldom failed to embrace such opportunities. There was not a man in the whole county, with whom the slaves who had the privilege of getting their own home, would not prefer to live, rather than with this Rev. Mr. Hopkins. And yet there was not a man any where round, who made higher professions of religion, or was more active in revivals,—more attentive to the class, love-feast, prayer and preaching meetings, or more devotional in his family,—who prayed earlier, later, louder, and longer,—than this same reverend slave-driver, Rigby Hopkins.

But to return to Mr. Freeland, and to my experience while in his employment. He, like Mr. Covey, gave us enough to eat; but, unlike Mr. Covey, he also gave us sufficient time to take our meals. He worked us hard, but always between sunrise and sunset. He required a good deal of work to be done, but gave us good tools with which to work. His farm was large, but he employed hands enough to work it, and with ease, compared with many of his neighbors. My treatment, while in his employment, was heavenly, compared with what I experienced at the hands of Mr. Edward Covey.

Mr. Freeland was himself the owner of but two slaves. Their names were Henry Harris and John Harris. The rest of his hands he hired. These consisted of myself, Sandy Jenkins,* and Handy Caldwell. Henry and John were quite intelligent, and in a very little while after I went there, I succeeded in creating in them a strong desire to learn how to read. This desire soon sprang up in the others also. They very soon mustered up some old spelling-books, and nothing would do but that I must keep a Sabbath school. I agreed to do so, and accordingly devoted my Sundays to teaching these my loved fellow-slaves how to read. Neither of them knew his letters when I went there. Some of the slaves of the neighboring farms found what was going on, and also availed themselves of this little opportunity to learn to read. It was understood, among all who came, that there must be as little display about it as possible. It was necessary to keep our religious masters at St. Michael's unacquainted with the fact, that, instead of spending the Sabbath in wrestling, boxing, and drinking whisky, we were trying to learn how to read the will of God; for they had much rather see us engaged in those degrading sports, than to see us behaving like intellectual, moral, and accountable beings. My blood boils as I think of the bloody manner in which Messrs. Wright Fairbanks and Garrison West, both class-leaders, in connection with many others, rushed in upon us with sticks and stones, and broke up our virtuous little Sabbath school, at St. Michael's—all calling themselves Christians! humble followers of the Lord Jesus Christ! But I am again digressing.

I held my Sabbath school at the house of a free colored man, whose name I deem it imprudent to mention; for should it be known, it might embarrass him greatly, though the crime of holding the school was committed ten years ago. I had at one time over forty scholars, and those of the right sort, ardently desiring to learn. They were of all ages, though mostly men and women. I look back to those Sundays with an amount of pleasure not to be expressed. They were great days to my soul. The work of instructing my dear fellow-slaves was the sweetest engagement with which I was ever blessed. We loved each other, and to leave them at the close of the Sabbath was a severe cross indeed. When I think that these precious souls are to-day

* This is the same man who gave me the roots to prevent my being whipped by Mr. Covey. He was "a clever soul." We used frequently to talk about the fight with Covey, and as often as we did so, he would claim my success as the result of the roots which he gave me. This superstition is very common among the more ignorant slaves. A slave seldom dies but that his death is attributed to trickery.

shut up in the prison-house of slavery, my feelings overcome me, and I am almost ready to ask, "Does a righteous God govern the universe? and for what does he hold the thunders in his right hand, if not to smite the oppressor, and deliver the spoiled out of the hand of the spoiler?" These dear souls came not to Sabbath school because it was popular to do so, nor did I teach them because it was reputable to be thus engaged. Every moment they spent in that school, they were liable to be taken up, and given thirty-nine lashes. They came because they wished to learn. Their minds had been starved by their cruel masters. They had been shut up in mental darkness. I taught them, because it was the delight of my soul to be doing something that looked like bettering the condition of my race. I kept up my school nearly the whole year I lived with Mr. Freeland; and, beside my Sabbath school, I devoted three evenings in the week, during the winter, to teaching the slaves at home. And I have the happiness to know, that several of those who came to the Sabbath school learned how to read; and that one, at least, is now free through my agency.

The year passed off smoothly. It seemed only about half as long as the year which preceded it. I went through it without receiving a single blow. I will give Mr. Freeland the credit of being the best master I ever had, *till I became my own master*. For the ease with which I passed the year, I was, however, somewhat indebted to the society of my fellow-slaves. They were noble souls; they not only possessed loving hearts, but brave ones. We were linked and interlinked with each other. I loved them with a love stronger than any thing I have experienced since. It is sometimes said that we slaves do not love and confide in each other. In answer to this assertion, I can say, I never loved any or confided in any people more than my fellow-slaves, and especially those with whom I lived at Mr. Freeland's. I believe we would have died for each other. We never undertook to do any thing, of any importance, without a mutual consultation. We never moved separately. We were one; and as much so by our tempers and dispositions, as by the mutual hardships to which we were necessarily subjected by our condition as slaves.

At the close of the year 1834, Mr. Freeland again hired me of my master, for the year 1835. But, by this time, I began to want to live *upon free land* as well as *with Freeland;* and I was no longer content, therefore, to live with him or any other slaveholder. I began, with the commencement of the year, to prepare myself for a final struggle, which should decide my fate one way or the other. My tendency was upward. I was fast approaching manhood, and year after year had passed, and I was still a slave. These thoughts roused me—I must do something. I therefore resolved that 1835 should not pass without witnessing an attempt, on my part, to secure my liberty. But I was not willing to cherish this determination alone. My fellow-slaves were dear to me. I was anxious to have them participate with me in this, my life-giving determination. I therefore, though with great prudence, commenced early to ascertain their views and feelings in regard to their condition, and to imbue their minds with thoughts of freedom. I bent myself to devising ways and means for our escape, and meanwhile strove, on all fitting occasions, to impress them with the gross fraud and inhumanity of slavery. I went first to Henry, next to John, then to the others. I found, in them all, warm hearts and noble spirits. They were ready to hear, and ready to act when a feasible plan should be proposed. This was what I wanted. I talked to them of our want of manhood, if we submitted to our enslavement without at least one noble effort to be free. We met often, and consulted frequently, and told our hopes and fears, recounted the difficulties, real and imagined, which we should be called on to meet. At times we were almost disposed to give up, and try to content ourselves with our wretched lot; at others, we were firm and un-bending in our determination to go. Whenever we suggested any plan, there was shrinking—the odds were fearful. Our path was beset with the greatest obstacles; and if we succeeded in gaining the end of it, our right to be free was yet questionable—we were yet liable to be returned to bondage. We could see no spot, this side of the ocean, where we could be free. We knew nothing about Canada. Our knowledge of the north did not extend farther than New York; and to go there, and be forever harassed with the frightful liability of being returned to slavery—with the certainty of being treated tenfold worse than before—the thought was truly a horrible one, and one which it was not easy to overcome. The case sometimes stood thus: At every gate through which we were to pass, we saw a watchman—at every ferry a guard—on every bridge a sentinel—and in every wood a patrol. We were hemmed in upon every side. Here were the difficulties, real or imag-ined—the good to be sought, and the evil to be shunned. On the one hand, there stood slavery, a stern reality, glaring frightfully upon us,—its robes already crimsoned with the blood of millions, and even now feasting itself greedily upon our own flesh. On the other hand, away back in the dim distance, under the flickering light of the north star, behind some craggy hill or snow-covered mountain, stood a doubtful freedom—half frozen—beck-oning us to come and share its hospitality. This in itself was sometimes enough to stagger us; but when we permitted ourselves to survey the road, we were frequently appalled. Upon either side we saw grim death, assuming the most horrid shapes. Now it was starvation, causing us to eat our own flesh;—now we were contending with the waves, and were drowned;—now we were overtaken, and torn to pieces by the fangs of the terrible bloodhound. We were stung by scorpions, chased by wild beasts, bitten by snakes, and finally, after having nearly reached the desired spot,—after swimming rivers, encountering wild beasts, sleeping in the woods, suffering hunger and nakedness,—we were overtaken by our pursuers, and, in our resistance, we were shot dead upon the spot! I say, this picture sometimes appalled us, and made us

> "rather bear those ills we had,
> Than fly to others, that we knew not of."

In coming to a fixed determination to run away, we did more than Patrick Henry, when he resolved upon liberty or death. With us it was a doubtful liberty at most, and almost certain death if we failed. For my part, I should prefer death to hopeless bondage.

Sandy, one of our number, gave up the notion, but still encouraged us. Our company then consisted of Henry Harris, John Harris, Henry Bailey, Charles Roberts, and myself. Henry Bailey was my uncle, and belonged to my master. Charles married my aunt: he belonged to my master's father-in-law, Mr. William Hamilton.

The plan we finally concluded upon was, to get a large canoe belonging to Mr. Hamilton, and upon the Saturday night previous to Easter holidays, paddle directly up the Chesapeake Bay. On our arrival at the head of the bay, a distance of seventy or eighty miles from where we lived, it was our purpose to turn our canoe adrift, and follow the guidance of the north star till we got beyond the limits of Maryland. Our reason for taking the water route was, that we were less liable to be suspected as runaways; we hoped to be regarded as fishermen; whereas, if we should take the land route, we should be subjected to interruptions of almost every kind. Any one having a white face, and being so disposed, could stop us, and subject us to examination.

The week before our intended start, I wrote several protections, one for each of us. As well as I can remember, they were in the following words:—

> "THIS is to certify that I, the undersigned, have given the bearer, my servant, full liberty to go to Baltimore, and spend the Easter holidays. Written with mine own hand, &c., 1835.
>
>   "WILLIAM HAMILTON,
>   "Near St. Michael's, in Talbot County, Maryland."

We were not going to Baltimore; but, in going up the bay, we went toward Baltimore, and these protections were only intended to protect us while on the bay.

As the time drew near for our departure, our anxiety became more and more intense. It was truly a matter of life and death with us. The strength of our determination was about to be fully tested. At this time, I was very active in explaining every difficulty, removing every doubt, dispelling every fear, and inspiring all with the firmness indispensable to success in our undertaking; assuring them that half was gained the instant we made the move; we had talked long enough; we were now ready to move; if not now, we never should be; and if we did not intend to move now, we had as well fold our arms, sit down, and acknowledge ourselves fit only to be slaves. This, none of us were prepared to acknowledge. Every man stood firm; and at our last meeting, we pledged ourselves afresh, and in the most solemn manner, that, at the time appointed, we would certainly start in pursuit of freedom. This was in the middle of the week, at the end of which we were to be off. We went, as usual, to our several fields of labor, but with bosoms highly agitated with thoughts of our truly hazardous undertaking. We tried to conceal our feelings as much as possible; and I think we succeeded very well.

After a painful waiting, the Saturday morning, whose night was to witness our departure, came. I hailed it with joy, bring what of sadness it might. Friday night was a sleepless one for me. I probably felt more anxious than the rest, because I was, by common consent, at the head of the whole affair. The responsibility of success or failure lay heavily upon me. The glory of the one, and the confusion of the other, were alike mine. The first two hours of that morning were such as I never experienced before, and hope never to again. Early in the morning, we went, as usual, to the field. We were spreading the manure; and all at once, while thus engaged, I was overwhelmed with an indescribable feeling, in the fulness of which I turned to Sandy, who was near by, and said, "We are betrayed!" "Well," said he, "that thought has this moment struck me." We said no more. I was never more certain of any thing.

The horn was blown as usual, and we went up from the field to the house for breakfast. I went for the form, more than for want of any thing to eat that morning. Just as I got to the house, in looking out at the lane gate, I saw four white men, with two colored men. The white men were on horseback, and the colored ones were walking behind, as if tied. I watched them a few moments till they got up to our lane gate. Here they halted, and tied the colored men to the gate-post. I was not yet certain as to what the matter was. In a few moments, in rode Mr. Hamilton, with a speed betokening great excitement. He came to the door, and inquired if Master William was in. He was told he was at the barn. Mr. Hamilton, without dismounting, rode up to the barn with extraordinary speed. In a few moments, he and Mr. Freeland returned to the house. By this time, the three constables rode up, and in great haste dismounted, tied their horses, and met Master William and Mr. Hamilton returning from the barn; and after talking awhile, they all walked up to the kitchen door. There was no one in the kitchen but myself and John. Henry and Sandy were up at the barn. Mr. Freeland put his head in at the door, and called me by my name, saying, there were some gentlemen at the door who wished to see me. I stepped to the door, and inquired what they wanted. They at once seized me, and, without giving me any satisfaction, tied me—lashing my hands closely together. I insisted upon knowing what the matter was. They at length said, that they had learned I had been in a "scrape," and that I was to be examined before my master; and if their information proved false, I should not be hurt.

In a few moments, they succeeded in tying John. They then turned to Henry, who had by this time returned, and commanded him to cross his hands. "I won't!" said Henry, in a firm tone, indicating his readiness to meet the consequences of his refusal. "Won't you?" said Tom Graham, the constable. "No, I won't!" said Henry, in a still stronger tone. With this, two of the constables pulled out their shining pistols, and swore, by their Creator, that they would make him cross his hands or kill him. Each cocked his pistol, and, with fingers on the trigger, walked up to Henry, saying, at the same time, if he did not cross his hands, they would blow his damned heart out. "Shoot me, shoot me!" said Henry; "you can't kill me but once. Shoot, shoot,—and be damned! *I won't be tied!*" This he said in a tone of loud defiance; and at the same time, with a motion as quick as lightning, he with one single stroke dashed the pistols from the hand of each constable. As he did this, all hands fell upon him, and, after beating him some time, they finally overpowered him, and got him tied.

During the scuffle, I managed, I know not how, to get my pass out, and, without being discovered, put it into the fire. We were all now tied; and just as we were to leave for Easton jail, Betsy Freeland, mother of William Freeland, came to the door with her hands full of biscuits, and divided them between Henry and John. She then delivered herself of a speech, to the following effect:—addressing herself to me, she said, "*You devil! You yellow devil!* it was you that put it into the heads of Henry and John to run away. But for you, you long-legged mulatto devil! Henry nor John would never have thought of such a thing." I made no reply, and was immediately hurried off towards St. Michael's. Just a moment previous to the scuffle with Henry, Mr. Hamilton suggested the propriety of making a search for the protections which he had understood Frederick had written for himself and the rest. But, just at the moment he was about carrying his proposal into effect, his aid was needed in helping to tie Henry; and the excitement attending the scuffle caused them either to forget, or to deem it unsafe, under the circumstances, to search. So we were not yet convicted of the intention to run away.

When we got about half way to St. Michael's, while the constables having us in charge were looking ahead, Henry inquired of me what he should do with his pass. I told him to eat it with his biscuit, and own nothing; and we passed the word around, *"Own nothing;"* and *"Own nothing!"* said we all. Our confidence in each other was unshaken. We were resolved to succeed or fail together, after the calamity had befallen us as much as before. We were now prepared for any thing. We were to be dragged that morning fifteen miles behind horses, and then to be placed in the Easton jail. When we reached St. Michael's, we underwent a sort of examination. We all denied that we ever intended to run away. We did this more to bring out the evidence against us, than from any hope of getting clear of being sold; for, as I have said, we were ready for that. The fact was, we cared but little where we went, so we went together. Our greatest concern was about separation. We dreaded that more than any thing this side of death. We found the evidence against us to be the testimony of one person; our master would not tell who it was; but we came to a unanimous decision among ourselves as to who their informant was. We were sent off to the jail at Easton. When we got there, we were delivered up to the sheriff, Mr. Joseph Graham, and by him placed in jail. Henry, John, and myself, were placed in one room together—Charles, and Henry Bailey, in another. Their object in separating us was to hinder concert.

We had been in jail scarcely twenty minutes, when a swarm of slave traders, and agents for slave traders, flocked into jail to look at us, and to ascertain if we were for sale. Such a set of beings I never saw before! I felt myself surrounded by so many fiends from perdition. A band of pirates never looked more like their father, the devil. They laughed and grinned over us, saying, "Ah, my boys! we have got you, haven't we?" And after taunting us in various ways, they one by one went into an examination of us, with intent to ascertain our value. They would impudently ask us if we would not like to have them for our masters. We would make them no answer, and leave them to find out as best they could. Then they would curse and swear at us, telling us that they could take the devil out of us in a very little while, if we were only in their hands.

While in jail, we found ourselves in much more comfortable quarters than we expected when we went there. We did not get much to eat, nor that which was very good; but we had a good clean room, from the windows of which we could see what was going on in the street, which was very much better than if we had been placed in one of the dark, damp cells. Upon the whole, we got along very well, so far as the jail and its keeper were concerned. Immediately after the holidays were over, contrary to all our expectations, Mr. Hamilton and Mr. Freeland came up to Easton, and took Charles, the two Henrys, and John, out of jail, and carried them home, leaving me alone. I regarded this separation as a final one. It caused me more pain than any thing else in the whole transaction. I was ready for any thing rather than separation. I supposed that they had consulted together, and had decided that, as I was the whole cause of the intention of the others to run away, it was hard to make the innocent suffer with the guilty; and that they had, therefore, concluded to take the others home, and sell me, as a warning to the others that remained. It is due to the noble Henry to say, he seemed almost as reluctant at leaving the prison as at leaving home to come to the prison. But we knew we should, in all probability, be separated, if we were sold; and since he was in their hands, he concluded to go peaceably home.

I was now left to my fate. I was all alone, and within the walls of a stone prison. But a few days before, and I was full of hope. I expected to have been safe in a land of freedom; but now I was covered with gloom, sunk down to the utmost despair. I thought the possibility of freedom was gone. I was kept in this way about one week, at the end of which, Captain Auld, my master, to my surprise and utter astonishment, came up, and took me out, with the intention of sending me, with a gentleman of his acquaintance, into Alabama. But, from some cause or other, he did not send me to Alabama, but concluded to send me back to Baltimore, to live again with his brother Hugh, and to learn a trade.

Thus, after an absence of three years and one month, I was once more permitted to return to my old home at Baltimore. My master sent me away, because there existed against me a very great prejudice in the community, and he feared I might be killed.

In a few weeks after I went to Baltimore, Master Hugh hired me to Mr.

William Gardner, an extensive ship-builder, on Fell's Point. I was put there
to learn how to calk. It, however, proved a very unfavorable place for the
accomplishment of this object. Mr. Gardner was engaged that spring in
building two large man-of-war brigs, professedly for the Mexican government. The vessels were to be launched in the July of that year, and in failure
thereof, Mr. Gardner was to lose a considerable sum; so that when I entered,
all was hurry. There was no time to learn any thing. Every man had to do
that which he knew how to do. In entering the ship-yard, my orders from
Mr. Gardner were, to do whatever the carpenters commanded me to do.
This was placing me at the beck and call of about seventy-five men. I was to
regard all these as masters. Their word was to be my law. My situation was a
most trying one. At times I needed a dozen pair of hands. I was called a
dozen ways in the space of a single minute. Three or four voices would
strike my ear at the same moment. It was—"Fred., come help me to cant
this timber here."—"Fred., come carry this timber yonder."—"Fred., bring
that roller here."—"Fred., go get a fresh can of water."—"Fred., come help
saw off the end of this timber."—"Fred., go quick, and get the crowbar."—
"Fred., hold on the end of this fall."—"Fred., go to the blacksmith's shop,
and get a new punch."—"Hurra, Fred.! run and bring me a cold chisel."—
"I say, Fred., bear a hand, and get up a fire as quick as lightning under that
steam-box."—"Halloo, nigger! come, turn this grindstone."—"Come,
come! move, move! and *bowse* this timber forward."—"I say, darky, blast
your eyes, why don't you heat up some pitch?"—"Halloo! halloo! halloo!"
(Three voices at the same time.) "Come here!—Go there!—Hold on where
you are! Damn you, if you move, I'll knock your brains out!"

This was my school for eight months; and I might have remained there
longer, but for a most horrid fight I had with four of the white apprentices, in
which my left eye was nearly knocked out, and I was horribly mangled in
other respects. The facts in the case were these: Until a very little while after
I went there, white and black ship-carpenters worked side by side, and no
one seemed to see any impropriety in it. All hands seemed to be very well
satisfied. Many of the black carpenters were freemen. Things seemed to be
going on very well. All at once, the white carpenters knocked off, and said
they would not work with free colored workmen. Their reason for this, as
alleged, was, that if free colored carpenters were encouraged, they would
soon take the trade into their own hands, and poor white men would be
thrown out of employment. They therefore felt called upon at once to put a
stop to it. And, taking advantage of Mr. Gardner's necessities, they broke
off, swearing they would work no longer, unless he would discharge his

black carpenters. Now, though this did not extend to me in form, it did reach me in fact. My fellow-apprentices very soon began to feel it degrading to them to work with me. They began to put on airs, and talk about the "niggers" taking the country, saying we all ought to be killed; and, being encouraged by the journeymen, they commenced making my condition as hard as they could, by hectoring me around, and sometimes striking me. I, of course, kept the vow I made after the fight with Mr. Covey, and struck back again, regardless of consequences; and while I kept them from combining, I succeeded very well; for I could whip the whole of them, taking them separately. They, however, at length combined, and came upon me, armed with sticks, stones, and heavy handspikes. One came in front with a half brick. There was one at each side of me, and one behind me. While I was attending to those in front, and on either side, the one behind ran up with the handspike, and struck me a heavy blow upon the head. It stunned me. I fell, and with this they all ran upon me, and fell to beating me with their fists. I let them lay on for a while, gathering strength. In an instant, I gave a sudden surge, and rose to my hands and knees. Just as I did that, one of their number gave me, with his heavy boot, a powerful kick in the left eye. My eyeball seemed to have burst. When they saw my eye closed, and badly swollen, they left me. With this I seized the handspike, and for a time pursued them. But here the carpenters interfered, and I thought I might as well give it up. It was impossible to stand my hand against so many. All this took place in sight of not less than fifty white ship-carpenters, and not one interposed a friendly word; but some cried, "Kill the damned nigger! Kill him! kill him! He struck a white person." I found my only chance for life was in flight. I succeeded in getting away without an additional blow, and barely so; for to strike a white man is death by Lynch law,—and that was the law in Mr. Gardner's ship-yard; nor is there much of any other out of Mr. Gardner's ship-yard, within the bounds of the Slave States.

I went directly home, and told the story of my wrongs to Master Hugh; and I am happy to say of him, irreligious as he was, his conduct was heavenly, compared with that of his brother Thomas under similar circumstances. He listened attentively to my narration of the circumstances leading to the savage outrage, and gave many proofs of his strong indignation at it. The heart of my once overkind mistress was again melted into pity. My puffed-out eye and blood-covered face moved her to tears. She took a chair by me, washed the blood from my face, and, with a mother's tenderness, bound up my head, covering the wounded eye with a lean piece of fresh beef. It was almost compensation for my sufferings to witness, once more, a manifestation of kindness from this, my once affectionate old mistress. Master Hugh was very much enraged. He gave expression to his feelings by pouring out curses upon the heads of those who did the deed. As soon as I got a little the better of my bruises, he took me with him to Esquire Watson's, on Bond Street, to see what could be done about the matter. Mr. Watson inquired who saw the assault committed. Master Hugh told him it was done in Mr. Gardner's ship-yard, at mid-day, where there was a large company of men at work. "As to that," he said, "the deed was done, and there was no question as to who did it." His answer was, he could do nothing in the case, unless some white man would come forward and testify. He could issue no warrant on my word. If I had been killed in the presence of a thousand colored people, their testimony combined would have been insufficient to have arrested one of the murderers. Master Hugh, for once, was compelled to say this state of things was too bad. Of course, it was impossible to get any white man to volunteer his testimony in my behalf, and against the white young men. Even those who may have sympathized with me were not prepared to do this. It required a degree of courage unknown to them to do so; for just at that time, the slightest manifestation of humanity towards a colored person was denounced as abolitionism, and that name subjected its bearer to frightful liabilities. The watchwords of the bloody-minded in that region, and in those days, were, "Damn the abolitionists!" and "Damn the niggers!" There was nothing done, and probably nothing would have been done if I had been killed. Such was, and such remains, the state of things in the Christian city of Baltimore.

Master Hugh, finding he could get no redress, refused to let me go back again to Mr. Gardner. He kept me himself, and his wife dressed my wound till I was again restored to health. He then took me into the ship-yard of which he was foreman, in the employment of Mr. Walter Price. There I was immediately set to calking, and very soon learned the art of using my mallet and irons. In the course of one year from the time I left Mr. Gardner's, I was able to command the highest wages given to the most experienced calkers. I was now of some importance to my master. I was bringing him from six to seven dollars per week. I sometimes brought him nine dollars per week: my wages were a dollar and a half a day. After learning how to calk, I sought my own employment, made my own contracts, and collected the money which I earned. My pathway became much more smooth than before; my condition was now much more comfortable. When I could get no calking to do, I did nothing. During these leisure times, those old notions about freedom would steal over me again. When in Mr. Gardner's employment, I was kept in such a perpetual whirl of excitement, I could think of nothing, scarcely, but my life; and in thinking of my life, I almost forgot my liberty. I have observed this in my experience of slavery,—that whenever my condition was improved, instead of its increasing my contentment, it only increased my desire to be free, and set me to thinking of plans to gain my freedom. I have found that, to make a contented slave, it is necessary to make a thoughtless one. It is necessary to darken his moral and mental vision, and, as far as possible, to annihilate the power of reason. He must be able to detect no inconsistencies in slavery; he must be made to feel that slavery is right; and he can be brought to that only when he ceases to be a man.

I was now getting, as I have said, one dollar and fifty cents per day. I contracted for it; I earned it; it was paid to me; it was rightfully my own; yet, upon each returning Saturday night, I was compelled to deliver every cent of that money to Master Hugh. And why? Not because he earned it,—not because he had any hand in earning it,—not because I owed it to him,—nor because he possessed the slightest shadow of a right to it; but solely because he had the power to compel me to give it up. The right of the grim-visaged pirate upon the high seas is exactly the same.

CHAPTER XI.

I NOW come to that part of my life during which I planned, and finally succeeded in making, my escape from slavery. But before narrating any of the peculiar circumstances, I deem it proper to make known my intention not to state all the facts connected with the transaction. My reasons for pursuing this course may be understood from the following: First, were I to give a minute statement of all the facts, it is not only possible, but quite probable, that others would thereby be involved in the most embarrassing difficulties. Secondly, such a statement would most undoubtedly induce greater vigilance on the part of slaveholders than has existed heretofore among them; which would, of course, be the means of guarding a door whereby some dear brother bondman might escape his galling chains. I deeply regret the necessity that impels me to suppress any thing of importance connected with my experience in slavery. It would afford me great pleasure indeed, as well as materially add to the interest of my narrative, were I at liberty to gratify a curiosity, which I know exists in the minds of many, by an accurate statement of all the facts pertaining to my most fortunate escape. But I must deprive myself of this pleasure, and the curious of the gratification which such a statement would afford. I would allow myself to suffer under the greatest imputations which evil-minded men might suggest, rather than exculpate myself, and thereby run the hazard of closing the slightest avenue by which a brother slave might clear himself of the chains and fetters of slavery.

I have never approved of the very public manner in which some of our western friends have conducted what they call the *underground railroad,* but which, I think, by their open declarations, has been made most emphatically the *upperground railroad.* I honor those good men and women for their noble daring, and applaud them for willingly subjecting themselves to bloody persecution, by openly avowing their participation in the escape of slaves. I, however, can see very little good resulting from such a course, either to themselves or the slaves escaping; while, upon the other hand, I see and feel assured that those open declarations are a positive evil to the slaves remaining, who are seeking to escape. They do nothing towards enlightening the slave, whilst they do much towards enlightening the master. They stimulate him to greater watchfulness, and enhance his power to capture his slave. We owe something to the slaves south of the line as well as to those north of it; and in aiding the latter on their way to freedom, we should be careful to do nothing which would be likely to hinder the former from escaping from slavery. I would keep the merciless slaveholder profoundly ignorant of the means of flight adopted by the slave. I would leave him to imagine himself surrounded by myriads of invisible tormentors, ever ready to snatch from his infernal grasp his trembling prey. Let him be left to feel his way in the dark; let darkness commensurate with his crime hover over him; and let him feel that at every step he takes, in pursuit of the flying bondman, he is running the frightful risk of having his hot brains dashed out by an invisible agency. Let us render the tyrant no aid; let us not hold the light by which he can trace the footprints of our flying brother. But enough of this. I will now proceed to the statement of those facts, connected with my escape, for which I am alone responsible, and for which no one can be made to suffer but myself.

In the early part of the year 1838, I became quite restless. I could see no reason why I should, at the end of each week, pour the reward of my toil into the purse of my master. When I carried to him my weekly wages, he would, after counting the money, look me in the face with a robber-like fierceness, and ask, "Is this all?" He was satisfied with nothing less than the last cent. He would, however, when I made him six dollars, sometimes give me six cents, to encourage me. It had the opposite effect. I regarded it as a sort of admission of my right to the whole. The fact that he gave me any part of my wages was proof, to my mind, that he believed me entitled to the whole of them. I always felt worse for having received any thing; for I feared that the giving me a few cents would ease his conscience, and make him feel himself to be a pretty honorable sort of robber. My discontent grew upon me. I was ever on the look-out for means of escape; and, finding no direct means, I determined to try to hire my time, with a view of getting money with which to make my escape. In the spring of 1838, when Master Thomas came to Baltimore to purchase his spring goods, I got an opportunity, and applied to him to allow me to hire my time. He unhesitatingly refused my request, and told me this was another stratagem by which to escape. He told me I could go nowhere but that he could get me; and that, in the event of my running away, he should spare no pains in his efforts to catch me. He exhorted me to content myself, and be obedient. He told me, if I would be happy, I must lay out no plans for the future. He said, if I behaved myself properly, he would take care of me. Indeed, he advised me to complete thoughtlessness of the future, and taught me to depend solely upon him for happiness. He seemed to see fully the pressing necessity of setting aside my intellectual nature, in order to contentment in slavery. But in spite of him, and even in spite of myself, I continued to think, and to think about the injustice of my enslavement, and the means of escape.

About two months after this, I applied to Master Hugh for the privilege of hiring my time. He was not acquainted with the fact that I had applied to Master Thomas, and had been refused. He too, at first, seemed disposed to refuse; but, after some reflection, he granted me the privilege, and proposed the following terms: I was to be allowed all my time, make all contracts with those for whom I worked, and find my own employment; and, in return for this liberty, I was to pay him three dollars at the end of each week, find myself in calking tools, and in board and clothing. My board was two dollars and a half per week. This, with the wear and tear of clothing and calking tools, made my regular expenses about six dollars per week. This amount I was compelled to make up, or relinquish the privilege of hiring my time. Rain or shine, work or no work, at the end of each week the money must be forthcoming, or I must give up my privilege. This arrangement, it will be perceived, was decidedly in my master's favor. It relieved him of all need of looking after me. His money was sure. He received all the benefits of slaveholding without its evils; while I endured all the evils of a slave, and suffered all the care and anxiety of a freeman. I found it a hard bargain. But, hard as it was, I thought it better than the old mode of getting along. It was a step towards freedom to be allowed to bear the responsibilities of a freeman, and I was determined to hold on upon it. I bent myself to the work of making money. I was ready to work at night as well as day, and by the most untiring perseverance and industry, I made enough to meet my expenses, and lay up a little money every week. I went on thus from May till August. Master Hugh then refused to allow me to hire my time longer. The ground for his refusal was a failure on my part, one Saturday night, to pay him for my week's time. This failure was occasioned by my attending a camp meeting about ten miles from Baltimore. During the week, I had entered into an engagement with a number of young friends to start from Baltimore to the camp ground early Saturday evening; and being detained by my employer, I was unable to go down to Master Hugh's without disappointing the company. I knew that Master Hugh was in no special need of the money that night. I therefore decided to go to camp meeting, and upon my return to pay him the three dollars. I staid at the camp meeting one day longer than I intended when I left. But as soon as I returned, I called upon him to pay him what he considered his due. I found him very angry; he could scarce restrain his wrath. He said he had a great mind to give me a severe whipping. He wished to know how I dared go out of the city without asking his permission. I told him I hired my time, and while I paid him the price which he asked for it, I did not know that I was bound to ask him when and where I should go. This reply troubled him; and, after reflecting a few moments, he turned to me, and said I should hire my time no longer; the next thing he should know of, I would be running away. Upon the same plea, he told me to bring my tools and clothing home forthwith. I did so; but instead of seeking work, as I had been accustomed to do previously to hiring my time, I spent the whole week without the performance of a single stroke of work. I did this in retaliation. Saturday night, he called upon me as usual for my week's wages. I told him I had no wages; I had done no work that week. Here we were upon the point of coming to blows. He raved, and swore his determination to get hold of me. I did not allow myself a single word; but was resolved, if he laid the weight of his hand upon me, it should be blow for blow. He did not strike me, but told me that he would find me in constant employment in future. I thought the matter over during the next day, Sunday, and finally resolved upon the third day of September, as the day upon which I would make a second attempt to secure my freedom. I now had three weeks during which to prepare for my journey. Early on Monday morning, before Master Hugh had time to make any engagement for me, I went out and got employment of Mr. Butler, at his ship-yard near the drawbridge, upon what is called the City Block, thus making it unnecessary for him to seek employment for me. At the end of the week, I brought him between eight and nine dollars. He seemed very well pleased, and asked me why I did not do the same the week before. He little knew what my plans were. My object in working steadily was to remove any suspicion he might entertain of my intent to run away; and in this I succeeded admirably. I suppose he thought I was never better satisfied with my condition than at the very time during which I was planning my escape. The second week passed, and again I carried him my full wages; and so well pleased was he, that he gave me twenty-five cents, (quite a large sum for a slaveholder to give a slave,) and bade me to make good use of it. I told him I would.

Things went on without very smoothly indeed, but within there was trouble. It is impossible for me to describe my feelings as the time of my contemplated start drew near. I had a number of warm-hearted friends in Baltimore,—friends that I loved almost as I did my life,—and the thought of being separated from them forever was painful beyond expression. It is my opinion that thousands would escape from slavery, who now remain, but for the strong cords of affection that bind them to their friends. The thought of leaving my friends was decidedly the most painful thought with which I had to contend. The love of them was my tender point, and shook my decision more than all things else. Besides the pain of separation, the dread and apprehension of a failure exceeded what I had experienced at my first attempt. The appalling defeat I then sustained returned to torment me. I felt assured that, if I failed in this attempt, my case would be a hopeless one—it would seal my fate as a slave forever. I could not hope to get off with any thing less than the severest punishment, and being placed beyond the means of escape. It required no very vivid imagination to depict the most frightful scenes through which I should have to pass, in case I failed. The wretchedness of slavery, and the blessedness of freedom, were perpetually before me. It was life and death to me. But I remained firm, and, according to my resolution, on the third day of September, 1838, I left my chains, and succeeded in reaching New York without the slightest interruption of any kind. How I did so,—what means I adopted,—in what direction I travelled, and by what mode of conveyance,—I must leave unexplained, for the reasons before mentioned.

I have been frequently asked how I felt when I found myself in a free State. I have never been able to answer the question with any satisfaction to myself. It was a moment of the highest excitement I ever experienced. I suppose I felt as one may imagine the unarmed mariner to feel when he is rescued by a friendly man-of-war from the pursuit of a pirate. In writing to a

dear friend, immediately after my arrival at New York, I said I felt like one
who had escaped a den of hungry lions. This state of mind, however, very
soon subsided; and I was again seized with a feeling of great insecurity and
loneliness. I was yet liable to be taken back, and subjected to all the tortures
of slavery. This in itself was enough to damp the ardor of my enthusiasm. But
the loneliness overcame me. There I was in the midst of thousands, and yet a
perfect stranger; without home and without friends, in the midst of thousands of my own brethren—children of a common Father, and yet I dared not
unfold to any one of them my sad condition. I was afraid to speak to any one
for fear of speaking to the wrong one, and thereby falling into the hands of
money-loving kidnappers, whose business it was to lie in wait for the panting
fugitive, as the ferocious beasts of the forest lie in wait for their prey. The
motto which I adopted when I started from slavery was this—"Trust no
man!" I saw in every white man an enemy, and in almost every colored man
cause for distrust. It was a most painful situation; and, to understand it, one
must needs experience it, or imagine himself in similar circumstances. Let
him be a fugitive slave in a strange land—a land given up to be the hunting-
ground for slaveholders—whose inhabitants are legalized kidnappers—
where he is every moment subjected to the terrible liability of being seized
upon by his fellow-men, as the hideous crocodile seizes upon his prey!—I
say, let him place himself in my situation—without home or friends—
without money or credit—wanting shelter, and no one to give it—wanting
bread, and no money to buy it,—and at the same time let him feel that he is
pursued by merciless men-hunters, and in total darkness as to what to do,
where to go, or where to stay,—perfectly helpless both as to the means of
defence and means of escape,—in the midst of plenty, yet suffering the
terrible gnawings of hunger,—in the midst of houses, yet having no
home,—among fellow-men, yet feeling as if in the midst of wild beasts,
whose greediness to swallow up the trembling and half-famished fugitive is
only equalled by that with which the monsters of the deep swallow up the
helpless fish upon which they subsist,—I say, let him be placed in this most
trying situation,—the situation in which I was placed,—then, and not till
then, will he fully appreciate the hardships of, and know how to sympathize
with, the toil-worn and whip-scarred fugitive slave.

Thank Heaven, I remained but a short time in this distressed situation. I
was relieved from it by the humane hand of Mr. DAVID RUGGLES, whose
vigilance, kindness, and perseverance, I shall never forget. I am glad of an
opportunity to express, as far as words can, the love and gratitude I bear
him. Mr. Ruggles is now afflicted with blindness, and is himself in need of

the same kind offices which he was once so forward in the performance of toward others. I had been in New York but a few days, when Mr. Ruggles sought me out, and very kindly took me to his boarding-house at the corner of Church and Lespenard Streets. Mr. Ruggles was then very deeply engaged in the memorable *Darg* case, as well as attending to a number of other fugitive slaves, devising ways and means for their successful escape; and, though watched and hemmed in on almost every side, he seemed to be more than a match for his enemies.

Very soon after I went to Mr. Ruggles, he wished to know of me where I wanted to go; as he deemed it unsafe for me to remain in New York. I told him I was a calker, and should like to go where I could get work. I thought of going to Canada; but he decided against it, and in favor of my going to New Bedford, thinking I should be able to get work there at my trade. At this time, Anna,* my intended wife, came on; for I wrote to her immediately after my arrival at New York, (notwithstanding my homeless, houseless, and helpless condition,) informing her of my successful flight, and wishing her to come on forthwith. In a few days after her arrival, Mr. Ruggles called in the Rev. J. W. C. Pennington, who, in the presence of Mr. Ruggles, Mrs. Michaels, and two or three others, performed the marriage ceremony, and gave us a certificate, of which the following is an exact copy:—

> "THIS may certify, that I joined together in holy matrimony Frederick Johnson† and Anna Murray, as man and wife, in the presence of Mr. David Ruggles and Mrs. Michaels.
>
> "JAMES W. C. PENNINGTON.
> *"New York, Sept.* 15, 1838."

Upon receiving this certificate, and a five-dollar bill from Mr. Ruggles, I shouldered one part of our baggage, and Anna took up the other, and we set out forthwith to take passage on board of the steamboat John W. Richmond for Newport, on our way to New Bedford. Mr. Ruggles gave me letter to a Mr. Shaw in Newport, and told me, in case my money did not serve me to New Bedford, to stop in Newport and obtain further assistance; but upon our arrival at Newport, we were so anxious to get to a place of safety, that, notwithstanding we lacked the necessary money to pay our fare, we decided to take seats in the stage, and promise to pay when we got to New Bedford. We were encouraged to do this by two excellent gentlemen, residents of

---

* She was free.
† I had changed my name from Frederick *Bailey* to that of *Johnson*.

New Bedford, whose names I afterward ascertained to be Joseph Ricketson and Willam C. Taber. They seemed at once to understand our circumstances, and gave us such assurance of their friendliness as put us fully at ease in their presence. It was good indeed to meet with such friends, at such a time. Upon reaching New Bedford, we were directed to the house of Mr. Nathan Johnson, by whom we were kindly received, and hospitably provided for. Both Mr. and Mrs. Johnson took a deep and lively interest in our welfare. They proved themselves quite worthy of the name of abolitionists. When the stage-driver found us unable to pay our fare, he held on upon our baggage as security for the debt. I had but to mention the fact to Mr. Johnson, and he forthwith advanced the money.

We now began to feel a degree of safety, and to prepare ourselves for the duties and responsibilities of a life of freedom. On the morning after our arrival at New Bedford, while at the breakfast-table, the question arose as to what name I should be called by. The name given me by my mother was, "Frederick Augustus Washington Bailey." I, however, had dispensed with the two middle names long before I left Maryland so that I was generally known by the name of "Frederick Bailey." I started from Baltimore bearing the name of "Stanley." When I got to New York, I again changed my name to "Frederick Johnson," and thought that would be the last change. But when I got to New Bedford, I found it necessary again to change my name. The reason of this necessity was, that there were so many Johnsons in New Bedford, it was already quite difficult to distinguish between them. I gave Mr. Johnson the privilege of choosing me a name, but told him he must not take from me the name of "Frederick." I must hold on to that, to preserve a sense of my identity. Mr. Johnson had just been reading the "Lady of the Lake," and at once suggested that my name be "Douglass." From that time until now I have been called "Frederick Douglass;" and as I am more widely known by that name than by any of the others, I shall continue to use it as my own.

I was quite disappointed at the general appearance of things in New Bedford. The impression which I had received respecting the character and condition of the people of the north, I found to be singularly erroneous. I had very strangely supposed, while in slavery, that few of the comforts, and scarcely any of the luxuries, of life were enjoyed at the north, compared with what were enjoyed by the slaveholders of the south. I probably came to this conclusion from the fact that northern people owned no slaves. I supposed that they were about upon a level with the non-slaveholding population of the south. I knew *they* were exceedingly poor, and I had been accustomed to regard their poverty as the necessary consequence of their being non-slaveholders. I had somehow imbibed the opinion that, in the absence of slaves, there could be no wealth, and very little refinement. And upon coming to the north, I expected to meet with a rough, hard-handed, and uncultivated population, living in the most Spartan-like simplicity, knowing nothing of the ease, luxury, pomp, and grandeur of southern slaveholders. Such being my conjectures, any one acquainted with the appearance of New Bedford may very readily infer how palpably I must have seen my mistake.

In the afternoon of the day when I reached New Bedford, I visited the wharves, to take a view of the shipping. Here I found myself surrounded with the strongest proofs of wealth. Lying at the wharves, and riding in the stream, I saw many ships of the finest model, in the best order, and of the largest size. Upon the right and left, I was walled in by granite warehouses of the widest dimensions, stowed to their utmost capacity with the necessaries and comforts of life. Added to this, almost every body seemed to be at work, but noiselessly so, compared with what I had been accustomed to in Baltimore. There were no loud songs heard from those engaged in loading and unloading ships. I heard no deep oaths or horrid curses on the laborer. I saw no whipping of men; but all seemed to go smoothly on. Every man appeared to understand his work, and went at it with a sober, yet cheerful earnestness, which betokened the deep interest which he felt in what he was doing, as well as a sense of his own dignity as a man. To me this looked exceedingly strange. From the wharves I strolled around and over the town, gazing with wonder and admiration at the splendid churches, beautiful dwellings, and finely-cultivated gardens; evincing an amount of wealth, comfort, taste, and refinement, such as I had never seen in any part of slaveholding Maryland.

Every thing looked clean, new, and beautiful. I saw few or no dilapidated houses, with poverty-stricken inmates; no half-naked children and barefooted women, such as I had been accustomed to see in Hillsborough, Easton, St. Michael's, and Baltimore. The people looked more able, stronger, healthier, and happier, than those of Maryland. I was for once made glad by a view of extreme wealth, without being saddened by seeing extreme poverty. But the most astonishing as well as the most interesting thing to me was the condition of the colored people, a great many of whom, like myself, had escaped thither as a refuge from the hunters of men. I found many, who had not been seven years out of their chains, living in finer houses, and evidently enjoying more of the comforts of life, than the average of slaveholders in Maryland. I will venture to assert that my friend Mr. Nathan Johnson (of whom I can say with a grateful heart, "I was hungry, and he gave me meat; I was thirsty, and he gave me drink; I was a stranger, and he took me in") lived in a neater house; dined at a better table; took, paid for, and read, more newspapers; better understood the moral, religious, and political character of the nation,—than nine tenths of the slaveholders in Talbot county, Maryland. Yet Mr. Johnson was a working man. His hands were hardened by toil, and not his alone, but those also of Mrs. Johnson. I found the colored people much more spirited than I had supposed they would be. I found among them a determination to protect each other from the blood-thirsty kidnapper, at all hazards. Soon after my arrival, I was told of a circumstance which illustrated their spirit. A colored man and a fugitive slave were on unfriendly terms. The former was heard to threaten the latter with informing his master of his whereabouts. Straightway a meeting was called among the colored people, under the stereotyped notice, "Business of importance!" The betrayer was invited to attend. The people came at the appointed hour, and organized the meeting by appointing a very religious old gentleman as president, who, I believe, made a prayer, after which he addressed the meeting as follows: "*Friends, we have got him here, and I would recommend that you young men just take him outside the door, and kill him!*" With this, a number of them bolted at him; but they were intercepted by some more timid than themselves, and the betrayer escaped their vengeance, and has not been seen in New Bedford since. I believe there have been no more such threats, and should there be hereafter, I doubt not that death would be the consequence.

I found employment, the third day after my arrival, in stowing a sloop with a load of oil. It was new, dirty, and hard work for me; but I went at it with a glad heart and a willing hand. I was now my own master. It was a happy moment, the rapture of which can be understood only by those who have been slaves. It was the first work, the reward of which was to be entirely my own. There was no Master Hugh standing ready, the moment I earned the money, to rob me of it. I worked that day with a pleasure I had never before experienced. I was at work for myself and my newly-married wife. It was to me the starting-point of a new existence. When I got through with that job, I went in pursuit of a job of calking; but such was the strength of prejudice against color, among the white calkers, that they refused to work with me, and of course I could get no employment.* Finding my trade of no immediate benefit, I threw off my calking habiliments, and prepared

---

* I am told that colored persons can now get employment at calking in New Bedford—a result of anti-slavery effort.

myself to do any kind of work I could get to do. Mr. Johnson kindly let me have his wood-horse and saw, and I very soon found myself a plenty of work. There was no work too hard—none too dirty. I was ready to saw wood, shovel coal, carry the hod, sweep the chimney, or roll oil casks,—all of which I did for nearly three years in New Bedford, before I became known to the anti-slavery world.

In about four months after I went to New Bedford, there came a young man to me, and inquired if I did not wish to take the "Liberator." I told him I did; but, just having made my escape from slavery, I remarked that I was unable to pay for it then. I, however, finally became a subscriber to it. The paper came, and I read it from week to week with such feelings as it would be quite idle for me to attempt to describe. The paper became my meat and my drink. My soul was set all on fire. Its sympathy for my brethren in bonds—its scathing denunciations of slaveholders— its faithful exposures of slavery—and its powerful attacks upon the upholders of the institution—sent a thrill of joy through my soul, such as I had never felt before!

I had not long been a reader of the "Liberator," before I got a pretty correct idea of the principles, measures, and spirit of the anti-slavery reform. I took right hold of the cause. I could do but little; but what I could, I did with a joyful heart, and never felt happier than when in an anti-slavery meeting. I seldom had much to say at the meetings, because what I wanted to say was said so much better by others. But, while attending an anti-slavery convention at Nantucket, on the 11th of August, 1841, I felt strongly moved to speak, and was at the same time much urged to do so by Mr. William C. Coffin, a gentleman who had heard me speak in the colored people's meeting at New Bedford. It was a severe cross, and I took it up reluctantly. The truth was, I felt myself a slave, and the idea of speaking to white people weighed me down. I spoke but a few moments, when I felt a degree of freedom, and said what I desired with considerable ease. From that time until now, I have been engaged in pleading the cause of my brethren—with what success, and with what devotion, I leave those acquainted with my labors to decide.

APPENDIX.

I FIND, on reading over the foregoing Narrative that I have, in several instances, spoken in such a tone and manner, respecting religion, as may possibly lead those unacquainted with my religious views to suppose me an opponent of all religion. To remove the liability to such misapprehension, I deem it proper to append the following brief explanation. What I have said respecting and against religion, I mean strictly to apply to the *slaveholding religion* of this land, and with no reference whatever to Christianity proper; for, between the Christianity of this land, and the Christianity of Christ, I recognize the widest possible difference—so wide, that to receive the one as good, pure, and holy, is of necessity to reject the other as bad, corrupt, and wicked. To be the friend of the one, is of necessity to be the enemy of the other. I love the pure, peaceable, and impartial Christianity of Christ: I therefore hate the corrupt, slaveholding, women-whipping, cradle-plundering, partial and hypocritical Christianity of this land. Indeed, I can see no reason, but the most deceitful one, for calling the religion of this land Christianity. I look upon it as the climax of all misnomers, the boldest of all frauds, and the grossest of all libels. Never was there a clearer case of "stealing the livery of the court of heaven to serve the devil in." I am filled with unutterable loathing when I contemplate the religious pomp and show, together with the horrible inconsistencies, which every where surround me. We have men-stealers for ministers, women-whippers for missionaries, and cradle-plunderers for church members. The man who wields the blood-clotted cowskin during the week fills the pulpit on Sunday, and claims to be a minister of the meek and lowly Jesus. The man who robs me of my earnings at the end of each week meets me as a class-leader on Sunday morning, to show me the way of life, and the path of salvation. He who sells my sister, for purposes of prostitution, stands forth as the pious advocate of purity. He who proclaims it a religious duty to read the Bible denies me the right of learning to read the name of the God who made me. He who is the religious advocate of marriage robs whole millions of its sacred influence, and leaves them to the ravages of wholesale pollution. The warm defender of the sacredness of the family relation is the same that scatters whole families,—sundering husbands and wives, parents and children, sisters and brothers,—leaving the hut vacant, and the hearth desolate. We see the thief preaching against theft, and the adulterer against adultery. We have men sold to build churches, women sold to support the gospel, and babes sold to purchase Bibles for the *poor heathen! all for the glory of God and the good of souls!* The slave auctioneer's bell and the church-going bell chime in with each other, and the bitter cries of the heart-broken slave are drowned in the religious shouts of his pious master. Revivals of religion and revivals in the slave-trade go hand in hand together. The slave prison and the church stand near each other. The clanking of fetters and the rattling of chains in the prison, and the pious psalm and solemn prayer in the church, may be heard at the same time. The dealers in the bodies and souls of men erect their stand in the presence of the pulpit, and they mutually help each other. The dealer gives his blood-stained gold to support the pulpit, and the pulpit, in return, covers his infernal business with the garb of Christianity. Here we have religion and robbery the allies of each other; slavery and piety linked and interlinked; preachers of the gospel united with slaveholders! A horrible sight, to see devils dressed in angels' robes, and hell presenting the semblance of paradise.

> "Just God! and these are they,
>   Who minister at thine altar, God of right!
> Men who their hands, with prayer and blessing, lay
>   On Israel's ark of light.
>
> "What! preach, and kidnap men?
>   Give thanks, and rob thy own afflicted poor?
> Talk of thy glorious liberty, and then
>   Bolt hard the captive's door?
>
> "What! servants of thy own
>   Merciful Son, who came to seek and save
> The homeless and the outcast, fettering down
>   The tasked and plundered slave!
>
> "Pilate and Herod friends!
>   Chief priests and rulers, as of old, combine!
> Just God and holy! is that church which lends
>   Strength to the spoiler thine?"—*Whittier*.

The Christianity of America is a Christianity, of whose votaries it may be as truly said, as it was of the ancient scribes and Pharisees, "They bind heavy burdens, and grievous to be borne, and lay them on men's shoulders, but they themselves will not move them with one of their fingers. All their works they do for to be seen of men.—They love the uppermost rooms at feasts, and the chief seats in the synagogues, ... and to be called of men, Rabbi, Rabbi.—But woe unto you, scribes and Pharisees, hypocrites! for ye shut up the kingdom of heaven against men; for ye neither go in yourselves, neither suffer ye them that are entering to go in. Ye devour widows' houses, and for a pretence make long prayers; therefore ye shall receive the greater damnation. Ye compass sea and land to make one proselyte, and when he is made, ye make him twofold more the child of hell than your selves.—Woe unto you, scribes and Pharisees, hypocrites! for ye pay tithe of mint, and anise, and cumin, and have omitted the weightier matters of the law, judgment, mercy, and faith; these ought ye to have done, and not to leave the other undone. Ye blind guides! which strain at a gnat, and swallow a camel. Woe unto you, scribes and Pharisees, hypocrites! for ye make clean the outside of the cup and of the platter; but within, they are full of extortion and excess.—Woe unto you, scribes and Pharisees, hypocrites! for ye are like unto whited sepulchres, which indeed appear beautiful outward, but are within full of dead men's bones and of all uncleanness. Even so ye also outwardly appear righteous unto men, but within ye are full of hypocrisy and iniquity."

Dark and terrible as is this picture, I hold it to be strictly true of the overwhelming mass of professed Christians in America. They strain at a gnat, and swallow a camel. Could any thing be more true of our churches? They would be shocked at the proposition of fellowshipping a *sheep*-stealer; and at the same time they hug to their communion a *man*-stealer, and brand me with being an infidel, if I find fault with them for it. They attend with Pharisaical strictness to the outward forms of religion, and at the same time neglect the weightier matters of the law, judgment, mercy, and faith. They are always ready to sacrifice, but seldom to show mercy. These are they who are represented as professing to love God whom they have not seen, whilst they hate their brother whom they have seen. They love the heathen on the other side of the globe. They can pray for him, pay money to have the Bible put into his hand, and missionaries to instruct him; while they despise and totally neglect the heathen at their own doors.

Such is, very briefly, my view of the religion of this land; and to avoid any misunderstanding, growing out of the use of general terms, I mean, by the religion of this land, that which is revealed in the words, deeds, and actions, of those bodies, north and south, calling themselves Christian churches, and yet in union with slaveholders. It is against religion, as represented by these bodies, that I feel it my duty to testify.

I conclude these remarks by copying the following portrait of the religion of the south, (which is, by communion and fellowship, the religion of the north,) which I soberly affirm is "true to the life," and without caricature or the slightest exaggeration. It is said to have been drawn, several years before the present anti-slavery agitation began, by a northern Methodist preacher, who, while residing at the south, had an opportunity to see slaveholding morals, manners, and piety, with his own eyes. "Shall I not visit for these things? saith the Lord. Shall not my soul be avenged on such a nation as this?"

"A PARODY.

"Come, saints and sinners, hear me tell
How pious priests whip Jack and Nell,
And women buy and children sell,
And preach all sinners down to hell,
And sing of heavenly union.

"They'll bleat and baa, dona like goats,
Gorge down black sheep, and strain at motes,
Array their backs in fine black coats,
Then seize their negroes by their throats,
And choke, for heavenly union.

"They'll church you if you sip a dram,
And damn you if you steal a lamb;
Yet rob old Tony, Doll, and Sam,
Of human rights, and bread and ham;
Kidnapper's heavenly union.

"They'll loudly talk of Christ's reward,
And bind his image with a cord,
And scold, and swing the lash abhorred,
And sell their brother in the Lord
To handcuffed heavenly union.

"They'll read and sing a sacred song,
And make a prayer both loud and long,
And teach the right and do the wrong,
Hailing the brother, sister throng,
With words of heavenly union.

"We wonder how such saints can sing,
Or praise the Lord upon the wing,
Who roar, and scold, and whip, and sting,
And to their slaves and mammon cling,
In guilty conscience union.

"They'll raise tobacco, corn, and rye,
And drive, and thieve, and cheat, and lie,

And lay up treasures in the sky,
By making switch and cowskin fly,
In hope of heavenly union.

"They'll crack old Tony on the skull,
And preach and roar like Bashan bull,
Or braying ass, of mischief full,
Then seize old Jacob by the wool,
And pull for heavenly union.

"A roaring, ranting, sleek man-thief,
Who lived on mutton, veal, and beef,
Yet never would afford relief
To needy, sable sons of grief,
Was big with heavenly union.

"'Love not the world,' the preacher said,
And winked his eye, and shook his head;
He seized on Tom, and Dick, and Ned,
Cut short their meat, and clothes, and bread,
Yet still loved heavenly union.

"Another preacher whining spoke
Of One whose heart for sinners broke:
He tied old Nanny to an oak,
And drew the blood at every stroke,
And prayed for heavenly union.

"Two others oped their iron jaws,
And waved their children-stealing paws;
There sat their children in gewgaws;
By stinting negroes' backs and maws,
They kept up heavenly union.

"All good from Jack another takes,
And entertains their flirts and rakes,
Who dress as sleek as glossy snakes,
And cram their mouths with sweetened cakes;
And this goes down for union."

Sincerely and earnestly hoping that this little book may do something toward throwing light on the American slave system, and hastening the glad day of deliverance to the millions of my brethren in bonds—faithfully relying upon the power of truth, love, and justice, for success in my humble

efforts—and solemnly pledging my self anew to the sacred cause,—I
subscribe myself,

FREDERICK DOUGLASS.

LYNN, *Mass., April* 28, 1845.

THE END.

Historical Annotation

The two line counts supplied below for the annotation of passages in the text refer to first the Yale edition and then to the 1845 Boston edition. Line counts include chapter headings.

3.2/iii.2   I] The son of impoverished Nova Scotian immigrants to Massachusetts, William Lloyd Garrison (1805–79) learned the printer's trade as a youth and went on to become one of the nation's most influential reform journalists. In 1831, he brought out the first issue of the Boston *Liberator,* which endorsed immediate emancipation. Later Garrison became an advocate for temperance, women's rights, and many other causes. His uncompromising radical positions helped cause the schism in the abolitionist movement in 1840. Thereafter he served as president of the American Anti-Slavery Society and led the "Garrisonian" wing of abolitionism until the Civil War. John L. Thomas, *The Liberator: William Lloyd Garrison* (Boston, 1963); James Brewer Stewart, *William Lloyd Garrison and the Challenge of Emancipation* (Arlington Heights, Ill., 1992); *Dictionary of American Biography,* 20 vols. (New York, 1928–36), 7 : 168–72.

3.2–3/iii.2–3   an anti-slavery convention in Nantucket] On 10–12 August 1841, Douglass attended a special summer convention on the island of Nantucket called by the Massachusetts Anti-Slavery Society. Garrison also attended this gathering and strongly applauded Douglass's novice performance as an abolitionist orator. *Lib.,* 20 August 1841; McFeely, *Frederick Douglass,* 86–90.

3.10/iii.13   a resident of New Bedford] Douglass lived in New Bedford, Massachusetts, after his escape from slavery, staying in the city from 1838 until 1842. McFeely, *Frederick Douglass,* 74–92.

3.23–24/iv.1–2   "gave . . . MAN,"] *Hamlet,* act 3, sc. 4, line 62.

3.35–36/iv.18–19   "created. . . angels"] A close paraphrase of Ps. 8 : 5; Heb. 2 : 7.

4.8/iv.31   A beloved friend from New Bedford] In Chapter 11, Douglass identifies this individual as William C. Coffin. Coffin (1816–?) was a resident of New Bedford who in 1845 was an accountant for the local Mechanics Bank. An ardent abolitionist, Coffin was a good friend of William Lloyd Garrison and served as recording secretary of the Bristol County Anti-Slavery Society from the 1830s. Coffin, a Quaker, also advocated the doctrine of nonresistance and was jailed briefly in 1845 in New Bedford for refusing to swear an oath to the authority of a local judge. *Lib.,* 3 September 1841, 18 April, 23 May 1845; Henry H. Crapo, *New Bedford Directory [for 1845]* (New Bedford, 1845), 794; D. Hamilton Hurd, comp., *History of Bristol County, Massachusetts, with Biographical Sketches of*

Many of Its Pioneers and Prominent Men (Philadelphia, 1883), 105; Walter M. Merrill and Louis Ruchames, eds., *The Letters of William Lloyd Garrison,* 6 vols. (Cambridge, Mass., 1971–81), 2 : 712 (hereafter cited as *Garrison Letters*); *Narrative* (Boston, 1845), 117.20.

4.16/v.5–6   PATRICK HENRY] Patrick Henry (1736–99), a Virginia patriot, lawyer, and Revolutionary statesman, attended the First Continental Congress at Philadelphia and was governor of Virginia from 1776 to 1779. *DAB,* 7 : 554–59.

4.19–20/v.10–11   the peril which surrounded this self-emancipated young man] The vulnerability of fugitive slaves in Massachusetts had been highlighted by the capture of George Lattimer in Boston in October 1842. After abolitionists failed to find legal means to block his return to the South, Lattimer's freedom was purchased for four hundred dollars by northern sympathizers. Henry Wilson, *History of the Rise and Fall of the Slave Power in America,* 3 vols. (Boston, 1872–77), 1 : 477–87; Donald M. Jacobs, "A History of the Boston Negro from the Revolution to the Civil War" (Ph.D. diss., Boston University, 1968), 209–21.

4.25–26/v.19   the old Bay State] Massachusetts derived its nickname "Old Bay State" from its original name, the Massachusetts Bay Colony. Mitford M. Mathews, *A Dictionary of Americanisms on Historical Principles,* 2 vols. (New York, 1965), 2 : 1155.

4.26/v.19–20   "YES!" shouted the whole mass] Nantucket abolitionist Anna Gardner confirms that the convention members shouted their pledge to protect Douglass from reenslavement. McFeely, *Frederick Douglass,* 87–89, 394n.

4.27/v.21   Mason and Dixon's line] Disputes between Pennsylvania on the north and Maryland and Virginia on the south were resolved when English surveyors Charles Mason and Jeremiah Dixon determined and marked the precise borders between these colonies in 1763–67. Hubertis M. Cummins, *The Mason and Dixon Line: Story for a Bicentenary, 1763–1963* (n.p., 1962).

5.1/vi.1   Massachusetts Anti-Slavery Society] In late fall 1831, William Lloyd Garrison convened a series of meetings to advance support in the Boston area for the principles of immediate emancipation. Out of these meetings emerged the New England Anti-Slavery Society in early 1832. As abolitionist strength grew in the region, state-level societies were formed and the group renamed itself the Massachusetts Anti-Slavery Society in 1835. Dwight Lowell Dumond, *Antislavery: The Crusade for Freedom in America* (Ann Arbor, Mich., 1961), 172–73.

5.1/vi.2   JOHN A. COLLINS] Vermont native John Anderson Collins (1810–c. 1879) attended Middlebury College and Andover Theological Seminary before becoming a lecturer for the Massachusetts Anti-Slavery Society in the late 1830s. He broke his ties with the Garrisonian wing of the abolitionist movement in 1843 in order to devote himself to advancing the utopian philosophy of Robert Owen. Collins resided briefly on a communal farm near Skaneateles, New York, and ultimately settled in California. Carleton Mabee, *Black Freedom: The Nonviolent*

Abolitionists from 1830 Through the Civil War (London, 1970), 76, 80–82, 88, 112–25, 212, 264, 394n; *DAB,* 4 : 307–08.

5.8–9/vi.12   American . . . Anti-Slavery Society] Inspired by the success of the British emancipation movement, a group of sixty-two American abolitionists, representing Quakers, free blacks, New York evangelicals, and such New England radicals as William Lloyd Garrison, met in Philadelphia in December 1833 and founded the American Anti-Slavery Society. Garrison drafted most of the society's original Declaration of Sentiments, which endorsed a blend of immediatist principles and moral suasion tactics. By the time Douglass became a lecturer for the American Anti-Slavery Society in the early 1840s, the organization had suffered a serious schism when many abolitionists had quit in protest to Garrison's stands on women's rights, religious orthodoxy, and an independent antislavery political party. Merton L. Dillon, *The Abolitionists: The Growth of a Dissenting Minority* (DeKalb, Ill., 1974), 52–53, 113–26; James Brewer Stewart, *Holy Warriors: The Abolitionists and American Slavery* (New York, 1976), 50–51, 89–96.

5.18/vi.25–26   "grow . . . God,"] Garrison slightly adapts 2 Pet. 3 : 18.

5.25/vi.34–35   Charles Lenox Remond] Born to free black parents in Salem Massachusetts, Charles Lenox Remond (1810–73) was an early member of the New England Anti-Slavery Society. A talented abolitionist lecturer, Remond toured the British Isles in 1840–41. He and Douglass frequently traveled together as speaking agents of the Massachusetts Anti-Slavery Society. A loyal Garrisonian, Remond denounced Douglass's embrace of political abolitionism in the 1850s. Les Wallace, "Charles Lenox Remond: The Lost Prince of Abolitionism," *Negro History Bulletin,* 40 : 696–701 (May–June 1977); *DAB,* 15 : 499–500.

6.1–2/vii.19   Daniel O'Connell] Irish lawyer and parliamentarian, Daniel O'Connell (1775–1847) was a leader of the movements to repeal the Act of Union between England and Ireland and to remove civil disabilities on Roman Catholics. An abolitionist from the 1820s, O'Connell loyally supported William Lloyd Garrison and his followers' cause despite the backlash it caused for American support for the Irish repeal movement. Douglas C. Raich, "Daniel O'Connell and American Anti-Slavery," *Irish Historical Studies,* 20 : 3–25 (March 1976); Gilbert Osofsky, "Abolitionists, Irish Immigrants, and the Dilemmas of Romantic Nationalism," *American Historical Review,* 80 : 889–912 (October 1975); *DNB,* 14 : 816–34.

6.4–5/vii.22–23   speech . . . in the Conciliation Hall, Dublin] Garrison refers to a controversial speech that Daniel O'Connell delivered in Dublin's Conciliation Hall, the headquarters for the Loyal National Repeal Association. Founded in April 1840, that organization sought the repeal of the legislation of 1800 that abolished the separate Irish parliament and merged the governments of Ireland and Great Britain. O'Connell's speech denounced slavery, as Garrison reported, but it also pledged Irish support for British efforts to block American expansion. The speech produced dissension in Irish nationalist circles and hostile attacks from the

United States. Angus Macintyre, *The Liberator: Daniel O'Connell and the Irish Party, 1830–1847* (New York, 1965), 80, 162–63; Raich, "Daniel O'Connell," 19.

6.29/viii.20–21   arm . . . save] A paraphrase of Isa. 50 : 2: "Is my hand shortened at all, that it cannot redeem?"

6.30–31/viii.22–23   "in slaves and the souls of men."] Rev. 18 : 13.

6.34/viii.28   SLAVERY AS IT IS.] An allusion to Theodore Weld's *American Slavery As It Is: Testimony of a Thousand Witnesses* (New York, 1839).

7.18–22/ix.22–29   the description . . . spirit of freedom] Garrison alludes to a passage that appears in Chapter 10. *Narrative* (Boston, 1845), 64.4–65.26.

7.23–24/ix.30–31   a whole Alexandrian library of thought] Founded in the third century B.C. by Egyptian ruler Ptolemy I, the library at Alexandria was reputed to hold half a million literary works. Damaged in fighting when the Romans under Julius Caesar besieged Alexandria in 47 B.C., the library continued to function until the late third century A.D. Walter M. Ellis, *Ptolemy of Egypt* (London, 1994), 55–56.

8.24–25/xi.13–14   two instances of murderous cruelty] An allusion to Douglass's accounts of the murders of slave Bill Demby by overseer Austin Gore and of a second slave by Maryland farmer John Beale Bordley in Chapter 4. *Narrative* (Boston, 1845), 22.25–24.8, 25.19–26.4.

8.30–31/xi.22–23   The Baltimore American, of March 17, 1845] This news item from the Baltimore *American & Commercial Daily Advertiser* of 17 April, not March, 1845 appeared in Garrison's Boston *Liberator* of 9 May 1845, the same issue that contained a copy of the "Preface" he wrote for Douglass's *Narrative*.

8.33/xi.26   Charles county, Maryland] The site of the earliest European settlements in present-day Maryland, Charles County lies in the southern portion of the state along the Potomac River. Leon E. Seltzer, ed., *The Columbia Lippincott Gazetteer of the World,* rev. ed. (New York, 1962), 374.

8.34/xi.27   a young man, named Matthews] Probably William B. Matthews, a seventeen-year-old youth from Charles County, Maryland, at the time of the incident. 1850 U.S. Census, Maryland, Charles County, 578; Baltimore *Sun,* 18 April 1845.

8.35/xi.28–29   whose father . . . at Washington] William B. Matthews's father was John Matthews (c. 1783?), a wealthy slaveowner and landholder in Charles County, Maryland. The Matthews family owned property in the Middletown district of the county. 1850 U.S. Census, Maryland, Charles County, 578; Baltimore *Sun,* 18 April 1845.

9.5–6/xii.5   incompetent to testify against a white man] Garrison possibly relies on the compilation of slave codes by Theodore Weld that concluded that statutes, as well as public opinion, precluded testimony from slaves and free blacks when a white person was accused. [Weld,] *American Slavery,* 148–49.

9.14–15/xii.17   a cloud of witnesses] Heb. 12 : 1.

9.25–26/xii.31–32   " . . . NO UNION WITH SLAVEHOLDERS!"] In 1844, the

American Anti-Slavery Society adopted a resolution, penned by Garrison, branding the U.S. Constitution a proslavery document and calling for a dissolution of the Union. The motto Garrison quotes later appeared on the masthead of his Boston *Liberator*. Walter H. Merrill, *Against Wind and Tide: A Biography of William Lloyd Garrison* (Cambridge, Mass., 1963), 204–14, 255, 269–75; Thomas, *Liberator,* 328–59, 374.

10.2/xiii.2   WENDELL PHILLIPS] Boston-born and Harvard-educated Wendell Phillips (1811–84) ranked second only to Garrison in influence in the American Anti-Slavery Society in the 1840s and 1850s. A highly gifted orator, Phillips was in demand as a lecturer even in nonabolitionist circles. Besides abolition, Phillips championed woman suffrage, prohibition, penal reform, Indian rights, and legislative protection for workers. James Brewer Stewart, *Wendell Phillips: Liberty's Hero* (Baton Rouge, 1986); Irving H. Bartlett, *Wendell Phillips: Brahmin Radical* (Boston, 1961); *DAB,* 14 : 546–47.

10.5/xiii.5–6   "The Man and the Lion,"] Phillips loosely adapts a fable by Aesop, alternatively known as "The Lion and the Statue." Thomas Newbigging, *The Fables and Fabulists: Ancient and Modern* (1895; Freeport, N.Y., 1972), 9.

10.16/xiii.20   the West India experiment] The Abolition Act passed by Parliament on 28 August 1833 began the gradual emancipation of slavery in Great Britain's West Indian colonies. The following year, the legislation freed all slaves under six but held the remainder to work for the former masters as apprentices for a period ending 1 August 1838. The owners received twenty million pounds in compensation for the emancipated slaves. William A. Green, *British Slave Emancipation: The Sugar Colonies and the Great Experiment* (Oxford, 1976), 129–75.

10.26/xiv.5–6   the "white sails" of the Chesapeake] Phillips probably alludes to the same passage in Chapter 10 that Garrison earlier had.

10.36/xiv.19   Valley of the Shadow of Death] Ps. 23 : 4.

11.25–26/xv.19   the halter about their necks] Possibly an allusion to the statement that early U.S. historian Jared Sparks in 1840 claimed that Benjamin Franklin had made to John Hancock at the time of the signing of the Declaration of Independence: "Yes, we must indeed all hang together, or most assuredly we shall all hang separately." Carl Van Doren, *Benjamin Franklin* (Garden City, N.Y., 1941), 551–52.

12.8/xvi.12–13   "*hide* the outcast,"] A slight misquotation of Isa. 16 : 3.

13.5/1.2   in Tuckahoe, near Hillsborough] Talbot County, on Maryland's Eastern Shore, had been an important tobacco-growing region since colonial times. In 1788 the state legislature designated Easton, until then known as Talbot Town, as the administrative center for state operations for all nine Eastern Shore counties. Hillsborough (or Hillsboro) is situated northeast of Easton on Tuckahoe Creek, a tributary of the Choptank River that forms part of the eastern boundary of Talbot County. Dickson J. Preston, *Talbot County: A History* (Centreville, Md., 1983), 140, 191, 256; Paul Wilstach, *Tidewater Maryland* (Indianapolis, 1931), 104–05.

13.6–7/1.4   knowledge of my age] As nearly as can be determined, Douglass was born in February 1818. Ledger books kept by his master Aaron Anthony contain a table, "My Black People," with the notation "Frederick Augustus son of Harriott Feby 1818." Further evidence for the year 1818 is presented in Preston, *Young Frederick Douglass,* 31–34, 218–19nn1–5; Aaron Anthony Ledger B, 1812–26, folder 95, 165, Dodge Collection, MdAA.

13.16/2.3–4   my master] Aaron Anthony (1767–1826), Frederick Douglass's first owner and possibly his father, was born at Tuckahoe Neck in present-day Caroline County, Maryland. Anthony's father was a poor and illiterate farmer who died when Aaron was only two. Despite his impoverished origins, Anthony acquired a rudimentary education and a small amount of property. He became the captain in 1795 of the *Sally Lloyd,* the family schooner of Edward Lloyd IV, the wealthiest planter in Talbot County. In 1797 he increased his wealth through his marriage to Ann Catherine Skinner, the daughter of an old and prominent Eastern Shore family, who brought with her the slave family into which Douglass was later born. Soon thereafter, Anthony became chief overseer and general manager of the Lloyd family's thirteen farms, one of the largest estates in the United States. He remained in this position for the remainder of his life, all the while accumulating land and slaves of his own. By the time of his death in 1826, Anthony had become a moderately wealthy planter, accumulating three farms totaling 597 ½ acres, thirty slaves worth $3,065, and personal property. His estate was valued at $8,042. Anthony Family Bible, Oxford Museum, Oxford, Md.; Harriet L. Anthony, annotated copy of *My Bondage and My Freedom,* folder 93, 58, Dodge Collection, MdAA; Inventory of estate of Aaron Anthony, 13 January 1827, Talbot County Inventories, box 13, 5–9, MdTCH; Hulbert Footner, *Rivers of the Eastern Shore: Seventeen Maryland Rivers* (New York, 1944), 285, 299–304; Charles B. Clark, ed., *The Eastern Shore of Maryland and Virginia,* 3 vols. (New York, 1950), 1 : 491–92; Preston, *Young Frederick Douglass,* 22–30; idem, "Aaron Anthony" (unpublished paper, Easton, Md., 1977), MdTCH.

13.21/2.6   Harriet Bailey] Harriet Bailey (1792–1825) was the second child of a free black man, Isaac Bailey, and his enslaved wife, Betsey. She was owned by her mother's master, Aaron Anthony. From 1808 until her death, she was hired out by Anthony to local farmers as a field hand. In February 1818, while serving Perry Steward, a tenant farmer on Anthony's Holme Hill Farm in Tuckahoe Creek, she gave birth to Frederick Augustus Bailey, her fourth of six or seven children. In late 1825 or early 1826, she died on the Holme Hill Farm in Tuckahoe Creek after a long illness. Aaron Anthony, Ledger B, 1812–26, folder 95, 165, Dodge Collection, MdAA; Preston, *Young Frederick Douglass,* 8, 9, 17, 21, 34–35, 62–64, 205, 206, 219n9.

13.21/2.7   Isaac] Born some time before 1775, Isaac Bailey was a free black man and the husband of Betsey Bailey, a slave owned by Aaron Anthony. Isaac and Betsey lived together on Anthony's Tuckahoe Creek farm. A sawyer, Bailey was frequently employed by both Anthony and Edward Lloyd V to provide lumber for their plantations. On occasion, he hired one of Anthony's slaves to assist him in his work. He also sometimes earned wages as a plowman and harvest laborer on Anthony's farms. Bailey appears in the 1820 Talbot County census as a free black presiding over a large household with four adult women and nine children. The 1840 census lists him as living with one adult woman and a young boy. Bailey died during the 1840s. Ledger B, 1812–26, folder 95, Ledger C, 1809–27, folder 96, Anthony Family Papers, Dodge Collection, MdAA; 1820 U.S. Census, Maryland, Talbot County, 336; 1840 U.S. Census, Maryland, Talbot County, 9; Preston, *Young Frederick Douglass,* 17–20.

13.22/2.7   Betsy Bailey] Betsey Bailey (1774–1849), the maternal grand-mother of Frederick Douglass, grew up a slave on the Skinner plantation in Talbot County, Maryland. In 1797 she became the property of Aaron Anthony, who acquired her and several other slaves through his marriage to Ann Skinner. Anthony moved her to his farm on Tuckahoe Creek in Talbot County. She married Isaac Bailey, a free black who earned his living as a sawyer, and lived with him in her cabin. There she bore nine daughters and three sons. She was also a midwife, a service for which Anthony paid her. Upon Anthony's death in 1826, Bailey was inherited by Andrew Skinner Anthony, Aaron's son; when Andrew died in 1833, she became the slave of John Planner Anthony. Despite this succession of masters and the death of her husband, she remained in her cabin on the Tuckahoe Creek farm, living alone, nearly destitute, and going blind. In 1840, Thomas Auld, John Anthony's uncle, learned of Bailey's condition and sent for her, caring for her in his Talbot County home until her death. Aaron Anthony Slave Distribution, 22 October 1827, Talbot County Distributions, V.JP#D, 58–59, MdTCH; Inventory of Negroes owned by Aaron Anthony, 19 December 1826, folder 71, Aaron Anthony Slave Distribution, 27 September 1827, folder 77, "My Black People[s] Ages," Aaron Anthony Ledger A, folder 94, Aaron Anthony Ledger B, 1812–26, folder 77, 159, 165–68, Harriet Anthony's annotated copy of *Bondage and Freedom,* folder 93, 180, all in the Anthony Family Papers, Dodge Collection, MdAA; Douglass to Thomas Auld, 3 September 1848, 3 September 1849, in *NS,* 8 September 1848, 7 September 1849, reprinted in *Lib.,* 22 September 1848, 14 September 1849; Preston, *Young Frederick Douglass,* 8, 16–20, 167.

14.2/2.32   Mr. Stewart] From 1817 to 1821, Perry Ward Steward (?–1821), a tenant farmer, rented Holme Hill Farm from Aaron Anthony and hired the slave Harriet Bailey as a domestic servant. A Perry W. Stewart was listed in the 1820 Census as the head of a large household of eleven members. Aaron Anthony Ledger A, 1790–1818, file #94, 18, 19, 22, Dodge Collection, MdAA; 1820 U.S. Census, Maryland, Talbot County, 336; Preston, *Young Frederick Douglass,* 35, 219n7.

14.14/3.17   Lee's Mill] Levi Lee owned a mill near Holme Hill Farm and the Tuckahoe River in 1820. In that year, he headed a large household of eight family members and six slaves. 1820 U.S. Census, Maryland, Talbot County, 48; Preston, *Young Frederick Douglass,* 36.

15.14/5.8   God cursed Ham] Douglass refers to the account in the book of Genesis in which Noah curses Canaan, the son of Ham, for an offense that Ham had committed against his father, Noah. Through an obscure history the meaning of the curse "a servant of servants shall he be unto his brethren" had evolved in Christian Europe as a justification for the enslavement of Africans, the "sons of Ham." Proslavery advocates in the American South used this argument extensively in the renewed debates of the 1840s. Gen. 9 : 25; David Brion Davis, *The Problem of Slavery in the Age of Revolution, 1770–1823* (Ithaca, N.Y., 1975), 539–41, 555–56; Larry E. Tise, *Proslavery: A History of the Defense of Slavery in America, 1701–1840* (Athens, Ga., 1987), 106, 118, 189; George M. Fredrickson, *The Black Image in the White Mind: The Debate on Afro-American Character and Destiny, 1817–1914* (New York, 1971), 60–61.

15.25/5.24   Mr. Plummer] This individual is probably either James Plummer or Philemon Plummer. Both men were longtime residents of Talbot County and, at various times during Douglass's youth, worked for Aaron Anthony as overseers on his Tuckahoe farms. Philemon Plummer is listed in Anthony's accounting records for 1819. Aaron Anthony Day Books, folder 97, 30, Dodge Collection, MdAA; Preston, *Young Frederick Douglass,* 71, 222n7.

15.34–35/6.4–5   an own aunt of mine] Hester Bailey (1810–?) was one of twelve children born to Isaac and Betsey Bailey and owned by Aaron Anthony of Talbot County. The last trace of Hester and the lone child she bore was recorded in 1827, when she was awarded to Thomas Auld after the death of Aaron Anthony. Aaron Anthony Slave Distribution, 22 October 1827, Talbot County Distributions, V.JP#D, 58–59; Preston, *Young Frederick Douglass,* 18, 27, 206, 221n2.

16.15–16/7.1   Colonel Lloyd] Edward Lloyd V (1779–1834) of Wye House was the scion of Talbot County's first family. One of the state's largest landowners and slaveowners, he was also Maryland's most successful wheat grower and cattle raiser of his era. As a charter member of the Maryland Agricultural Society, a founder of at least two banks, and a speculator in coal lands, he became the wealthiest of a long line of Lloyds that reached back to colonial Maryland. In terms of slaves alone, his huge holdings increased from 420 in 1810 to 545 in 1830. An eager student of politics as an adolescent and a frequent auditor of political debate at the Annapolis State House, Edward V became a Republican delegate to the state legislature as soon as he reached the age of majority in 1800. The following year, he was active in securing passage of a bill removing all restrictions to white male suffrage. From 1806 to 1808 he was a U.S. congressman, voting in 1807 against a bill to end the African slave trade. For the next two years he was governor of Maryland, and from 1811 to 1816 he returned to the state legislature. In 1819 he was elected to the U.S. Senate, from which he resigned in 1826 to return to the Maryland senate, where he was president until 1831. Edward V married Sally Scott

Murray on 30 November 1797 and had six children with her. 1810 U.S. Census, Maryland, Talbot County, 342; Oswald Tilghman, *History of Talbot County, Maryland, 1661–1861,* 2 vols. (Baltimore, 1915), 1 : 184–210; Footner, *Rivers of the Eastern Shore,* 283–90; Preston, *Young Frederick Douglass,* 26, 30, 48–54, 57–58, 74, 82; *Biographical Directory of the American Congress, 1774–1989: Bicentennial Edition* (Washington, D.C., 1989), 1381.

16.16/7.2   Ned Roberts] Ned Roberts (1810–?) was a slave owned by Edward Lloyd V. It was 1825 when Aaron Anthony discovered that his slave Hester Bailey was continuing to see Ned Roberts. Return Book, 1 January 1824, Land Papers—Maintenance of Property, Land Volume 39, reel 10, Lloyd Family Papers, MdHi.

17.8/8.11   two sons, Andrew] Andrew Skinner Anthony (1797–1833) was the eldest son of Aaron and Ann Catherine Skinner Anthony and the nephew of Edward Lloyd V. His father apprenticed him as a young man to James Neall, a cabinetmaker, in Easton, Maryland. After completing his apprenticeship, Anthony migrated to Indiana, where he married Ann Wingate of Martin County in 1823. He and his bride returned to Talbot County shortly thereafter. In 1826 Andrew's father died and he inherited a third of his estate, including eight slaves. Although he increased his estate and owned twenty slaves, Andrew suffered from alcoholism and operated a whiskey shop in his final years. John Manross to Douglass, 14 January 1856, General Correspondence File, reel 1, frames 654–56, FD Papers, DLC; Harriet Anthony's annotated copy of *Bondage and Freedom,* folder 93, 176 Dodge Collection, MdAA; 1830 U.S. Census, Maryland, Talbot County, 51; Preston, *Young Frederick Douglass,* 26, 29, 218n17, 224n10.

17.8/8.12   Richard] Richard Lee Anthony (1800–28), the second eldest of three children born to Aaron and Ann Anthony, was trained as a blacksmith for five years before inheriting land, money, and slaves after his father's death in November 1826. Douglass incorrectly asserted that Richard died before his father. Harriet L. Anthony's annotated copy of *Bondage and Freedom,* folder 93, 173–74, Dodge Collection, MdAA; Aaron Anthony Slave Distribution, 22 October 1827, Talbot County Distributions, V.JP#D, 58–59, MdTCH; Preston, *Young Frederick Douglass,* 27, 28, 29, 52, 91, 218n17.

17.8–9/8.12   one daughter, Lucretia] Lucretia Planner Anthony Auld (1804–27) was the third child and only daughter of Aaron and Ann Anthony. In 1823 she married Thomas Auld, a boarder in her father's household and an employee of Edward Lloyd. Lucretia subsequently moved to Hillsborough, Maryland, where she and her husband opened a store. Following the deaths of her father and brother Richard Lee, Lucretia and her older brother Andrew inherited their father's estate. Her portion included the young slave Frederick Douglass. She died in 1827 and was survived by one child, Arianna Amanda Auld. Auld Family Bible (courtesy of Carl G. Auld); McFeely, *Frederick Douglass,* 27; Preston, *Young Frederick Douglass,* 28, 30, 62, 87–88, 223n6; Preston, *Talbot County,* 191; Emerson B. Roberts, "A Visitation of Western Talbot," *MdHM,* 41 : 244–45 (September 1946).

17.9/8.13   Captain Thomas Auld] Born in St. Michaels, Maryland, Thomas
Auld (1795–1880) was the eldest son of Hugh and Zipporah Auld. Trained as a
shipbuilder, Auld supervised the construction of the Lloyd sloop, the *Sally Lloyd,*
and subsequently became its captain. In 1823, he met and married Lucretia Anthony while a boarder in the Anthony home. Shortly thereafter, in 1827, Auld
became a storekeeper in Hillsborough, Maryland, and inherited Douglass along
with ten other slaves from the estate of Aaron Anthony. He later kept store in St.
Michaels where he also served as postmaster, before retiring to a nearby farm. The
1850 census listed him as a "farmer" with $8,500 worth of real estate. References
to Thomas Auld in Douglass's *Narrative* and public speeches are generally uncom-
plimentary although Douglass disclaimed any personal hostility toward his former
owner. A reconciliation occurred in the post-Reconstruction period when Douglass visited the dying Auld in St. Michaels. *NASS,* 25 November 1845; *NS,* 8
September 1848, 7 September 1849; Baltimore *Sun,* 19 June 1877; Aaron Anthony
Slave Distribution, 22 October 1827, Talbot County Distributions, V.JP#D, 58–
59, MdTCH; 1850 U.S. Census, Maryland, Talbot County, 1169 (schedule of free
inhabitants); Benjamin Quarles, *Frederick Douglass* (Washington, D.C., 1948),
342–43; Tilghman, *Talbot County,* 1 : 395; Preston, "Aaron Anthony," 5; Roberts,
"Visitation of Western Talbot," 235–45.

17.10/8.14   the home plantation of Colonel Edward Lloyd] Settled by Edward
Lloyd I in 1658, Wye House, the home plantation of the Lloyds, was situated on a
peninsula formed by the Wye River on the north and the Miles River on the south.
By 1790, Edward Lloyd IV, father of Edward Lloyd V, owned 11,884 acres in the
region. The mansion house to which Douglass refers was built in 1784 and over-
looks Lloyd's Cove on the Wye River. Aaron Anthony and his family lived in the
"Captain's House," a brick outbuilding near the mansion. Douglass lived at Anthony's home at Wye House from August 1824 to March 1826. Footner, *Rivers of
the Eastern Shore,* 269–93; H[enry] Chandlee Forman, *Old Buildings, Gardens,
and Furniture in Tidewater Maryland* (Cambridge, Md., 1967), 51–80; Preston,
Young Frederick Douglass, 37–40, 199.

17.21–22/9.4–5   This sloop was named Sally Lloyd] In 1819 Edward Lloyd V
ordered the construction of a new sloop to replace the aging schooner *Elizabeth &
Ann,* which carried his crops to markets in Baltimore and Annapolis and brought
back supplies to his scattered Talbot County farms. Thomas Auld had supervised
the construction, in Joseph Kemp's St. Michaels shipyard, of the replacement
vessel, named the *Sally Lloyd* in honor of the colonel's eldest daughter, Sally Scott
Lloyd. Auld remained in Lloyd's employment as the master of the *Sally Lloyd,*
which was manned by a slave crew. The latter gained celebrity status among the
Lloyd slaves because of their contact with the world outside the rural plantations
and their ability to purchase small items in the cities for resale to other slaves.
Various account books and cash books, Land Papers—Maintenance of Property,
Land Volume 39, reel 10, Lloyd Family Papers, MdHi.

17.22/9.5   one of the colonel's daughters] Sally Scott Lloyd Lowndes, the second daughter of Edward Lloyd V, was the namesake of her mother Sally Scott Murray Lloyd. She married Charles Lowndes, a U.S. Navy officer, on 24 May 1824. Colonel Lloyd purchased an estate called the Anchorage on the Miles River as a gift for the couple. Their son Lloyd Lowndes served as governor of Maryland from 1896 to 1900. Rossiter Johnson, ed., *The Twentieth Century Biographical Dictionary of Notable Americans,* 10 vols. (Boston, 1904), 7:n.p.; Tilghman, *Talbot County,* 1 : 207; Preston, *Young Frederick Douglass,* 47, 222n4.

17.24–25/9.8–9   Peter, Isaac, Rich, and Jake] Two of the slaves who served as the crew of the *Sally Lloyd* appear in the business records of Edward Lloyd V: Peter (1799–?) and Rich (1817–?). Various account books and cash books, Land Papers—Maintenance of Property, Land Volume 39, reel 10, Lloyd Family Papers, MdHi.

17.28/9.13–14   three to four hundred slaves] Douglass exaggerates the number of slaves owned by Edward Lloyd V. In 1824, the year Douglass arrived on the Lloyd's main plantation, there were 181 slaves at Wye House, including the fifteen owned by Aaron Anthony who also lived there. The Lloyds owned slaves on adjoining farms as well, though their number is not available. Edward Lloyd IV owned 305 slaves in 1790, and his grandson, Edward Lloyd VI, owned an estimated 700 slaves, including those on his Mississippi Valley plantations. Return Book, 1 January 1824, Land Papers—Maintenance of Property, Land Volume 39, reel 10, Lloyd Family Papers, MdHi; Footner, *Rivers of the Eastern Shore,* 280–81; Tilghman, *Talbot County,* 1 : 225; Preston, *Young Frederick Douglass,* 48, 220n13.

17.31/9.17   Wye Town] Wye Town is located at the confluence of the Miles River and the Wye River in Talbot County, next to the main Lloyd plantation Wye House. At the urging of the Lloyds, the Maryland General Assembly had established the site of a town here in 1683 which was later abandoned. Wye Town Farm, part of the land owned here by the Lloyds, encompassed 260 acres. Henry Chandlee Forman, *Tidewater Maryland Architecture and Gardens* (New York, 1956), 49–54.

17.31/9.17   New Design] New Design Farm was one of several smaller plantations owned by Edward Lloyd V in Talbot County. At least through the 1820s, Lloyd used it primarily for growing wheat. Various account books and cash books, Land Papers—Maintenance of Property, Land Volume 39, reel 10, Lloyd Family Papers, MdHi.

17.32/9.19   Noah Willis] In 1819 Aaron Anthony's records indicate that he employed a Noah Willes. A Noah Willis is listed in the 1820 census as an overseer in Talbot County. He was between 26 and 45 years old. Willis is listed again in the 1830 census but without any job designation. He was married by then, having eight children under 15 in his household, and owned four slaves. Willis held over 400 acres of land by the late 1820s. Aaron Anthony Papers, Ledger A, 1790–1818, file

94, 19; 1820 U.S. Census, Maryland, Talbot County, 7; 1830 U.S. Census, Mary-land, Talbot County, 14; Whitman H. Ridgway, *Community Leadership in Mary-land, 1790–1840: A Comparative Analysis of Power in Society* (Chapel Hill, 1979), 339.

17.33/9.20   Mr. Townsend] Between 1809 and 1812, George Townsend worked for Aaron Anthony, probably as an overseer. In 1820, he was between twenty-six and forty years of age, and managed a farm which had 23 slaves. 1820 U.S. Census, Maryland, Talbot County, 6; Aaron Anthony Ledger C, 1809–27, folder 96, 3, 35, 69, 114, 119, 128, 171, 177, 286, 315, Dodge Collection, MdAA.

18.3/9.30   Austin Woolfolk] Austin Woolfolk of Augusta, Georgia, became a slave trader serving the Southwest, which rapidly expanded following the Battle of New Orleans in 1815. He settled in Baltimore in 1819 to avail himself both of the large surplus slave population in the state and the excellent shipping facilities which the port afforded. During the 1820s he lived on Pratt Street to the west of the city's commercial center. Woolfolk's business prospered as he sent agents through-out Maryland ready to pay high prices in cash for young black males. He annually transported from 230 to 460 slaves to markets in New Orleans, many of them having been purchased from planters on the Eastern Shore. In the 1830s, however, Woolfolk's business declined due to increased competition from larger firms, a decrease in the number of slaves for sale owing to manumissions and owner emigrations, and the heightened opposition of Marylanders to the interstate slave trade. Preston, *Young Frederick Douglass,* 50, 58, 76–80, 96, 102; William Cal-derhead, "The Role of the Professional Slave Trader in a Slave Economy: Austin Woolfolk, A Case Study," *Civil War History,* 23 : 195–211 (September 1977).

18.10–11/10.8   negro cloth] Coarse, durable, inexpensive cloth manufactured for sale to slaveowners for their servants.

18.34/11.8–9   Mr. Severe] During the years 1809–12 and possibly thereafter, William Sevier worked for Aaron Anthony, probably as an overseer on his farms. In 1820, he was between twenty-six and forty years old. At that time Sevier occupied a small red frame house on the east side of Wye House's Long Green, and was Edward Lloyd V's overseer for the more than 150 slaves at the main planta-tion. Aaron Anthony Ledger A, 1790–1818, folder 94, 19, Ledger C, 1809–27, folder 96, 1, 3, 13, 87, 119, 124, 177, 286, 291; 1820 U.S. Census, Maryland, Talbot County, 7; Preston, *Young Frederick Douglass,* 70–71, 222n5 and n6.

19.14/12.3   Mr. Hopkins] James Hopkins briefly took the place of William Sevier as overseer of the Wye House plantation. Preston, *Young Frederick Doug-lass,* 73.

19.25–26/12.20   the *Great House Farm*] A reference to the principal planta-tion of Edward Lloyd V, the Wye House plantation. Douglass visited there in June 1881 and several younger members of the Lloyd family escorted him around the grounds. Preston, *Young Frederick Douglass,* 192–96.

21.2/14.29–30   "there . . . heart."] Douglass quotes line 8 from *The Time*

Piece by William Cowper. J.C. Bailey, ed., *The Poems of William Cowper* (London, 1905), 267.

21.17–18/15.19–20   the chief gardener, (Mr. M'Durmond.)] In 1824 Aaron Anthony hired William McDermott to work for Edward Lloyd V. McDermott lived and ate at Anthony's house at least through spring 1825. Aaron Anthony Ledger A, 1790–1818, folder 94, 42, 43, Dodge Collection, MdAA.

22.3–4/16.24   Old Barney and Young Barney] Old Barney was Barnett Sampson (c. 1768–?). He was owned by Edward Lloyd V and was the father of Young Barney, Barnett Bentley (c. 1810–?). He was listed as fifty-five years old in January 1824. Return Book, 1 January 1824, Land Papers—Maintenance of Property, Land Volume 39, reel 10, Lloyd Family Papers, MdHi.

22.31/17.31   Edward] Born in the Annapolis home of his maternal grandparents, Edward Lloyd VI (1798–1861) was the oldest child and principal heir of his father's great wealth. Educated at the Wye House plantation by tutors, the younger Lloyd received charge of a nearby plantation where his father built him the beautiful Wye Heights mansion upon his marriage in 1824 to Alicia McBlair, daughter of a Baltimore merchant. She died prematurely in 1838 after bearing five children. After inheriting the bulk of his father's landholdings, Lloyd successfully shifted from tobacco to grain farming and weathered the agricultural depression that struck most of the Eastern Shore in the 1840s and 1850s. Lloyd also purchased cotton growing land in Mississippi in 1837 and later added more in Arkansas and Louisiana. He transferred some of his swelling slave population to those new plantations. Although reputedly a stern disciplinarian, he did try to avoid separating families during these relocations and when sales occurred. A life-long Democrat, Lloyd served as a delegate to the Maryland constitutional convention of 1850 and as a state senator (1851–52). 1850 U.S. Census, Maryland, Talbot County, 6–10 (slave schedule); Tilghman, *Talbot County,* 1 : 210–21; Preston, *Young Frederick Douglass,* 42–43, 44–45, 70, 192; J. Donnell Tilghman, "Wye House," *MdHM,* 48 : 89–108 (June 1953).

22.31/17.31   Murray] James Murray Lloyd (1803–47) was the middle son of Edward Lloyd V and Sally Murray Scott. When he married, his father built a mansion for him called Presqu'ile which quickly became a Talbot County showplace. In 1840, he was one of the region's richest farmers, owning 113 slaves. 1840 U.S. Census, Maryland, Talbot County, 60; Stella Pickett Hardy, *Colonial Families of the Southern States of America* (New York, 1911), 387; Preston, *Young Frederick Douglass,* 47, 49–50, 69, 70; Tilghman, *Talbot County,* 1 : 207, 222.

22.31/17.31   Daniel] Daniel Lloyd (1811–75) was the sixth-born child and youngest son of Edward Lloyd V. Daniel became a farmer and his wealth increased steadily, expanding the number of slaves he owned from 18 to 36 between 1840 and 1850. By the latter year, he possessed real estate valued at $25,000. After the death of his father, Lloyd resided at the nearby Wye Heights Plantation, earlier built for Edward Lloyd VI and his wife. Daniel's son, Henry, was Maryland's governor in the 1880s. 1840 U.S. Census, Maryland, Talbot County, 59; 1850 U.S. Census, Maryland, Talbot County, 11a (free schedule), 14 (slave schedule); Preston, *Young Frederick Douglass,* 54–55, 61, 81, 221n21; Tilghman, *Talbot County,* 1 : 207, 212.

22.32/17.32   Mr. Winder] Edward Stoughton Winder, son of Levin Winder, the sixteenth governor of Maryland, and Mary Sloss, married Elizabeth Tayloe Lloyd, the eldest daughter of Edward Lloyd V, in 1820. Their son, Charles Sidney Winder, became a Confederate brigadier general. Edward most likely died before 1850 as that year's census lists Elizabeth, rather than him, as the family head. 1850 U.S. Census, Maryland, Talbot County, 52; Tilghman, *Talbot County,* 1 : 207; Preston, *Young Frederick Douglass,* 221–22; Hardy, *Colonial Families,* 387; *National Cyclopaedia of American Biography* (New York, 1898), 5 : 514.

22.32/17.32   Mr. Nicholson] Joseph Nicholson was the son of Rebecca Lloyd, Edward V's sister, and her husband, Joseph Hopper Nicholson (1770–1817), a Democratic-Republican congressman from Baltimore from 1799 through 1806 and thereafter a prominent Maryland jurist. The younger Nicholson was the nephew of Edward Lloyd V, not the son-in-law, as Douglass identifies him. Preston, *Young Frederick Douglass,* 70, 222n4; Hardy, *Colonial Families,* 500–11; *DAB,* 13 : 505–06; *BDAC,* 1570.

22.32/17.32–18.1   Mr. Lowndes] Born in Kent County, Maryland, Charles Lowndes (1798–1885) entered the navy as a midshipman in 1815. He married Sally Scott Lloyd in the mid-1820s and by 1840 was a prosperous Talbot County farmer with thirty-five slaves. By the start of the Civil War, he had risen to the rank of captain in the U.S. Navy. Suspected of Confederate sympathies, he was placed on the retired list in 1862 and later promoted to commodore and placed on a war prize commission. 1840 U.S. Census, Maryland, Talbot County, 70; Preston, *Young Frederick Douglass,* 47, 222; Johnson, *Twentieth Century Biographical Dictionary,* 7 : n.p.; Christopher Johnston, "Lowndes Family," *MdHM,* 2 : 279 (September 1907); *Appleton's Cyclopaedia of American Biography,* 6 vols. (New York, 1888–89), 4 : 44.

22.34/18.3–4   William Wilkes] William Wilks (c. 1791–?) was a slave of Edward Lloyd V. Sometime in the first half of the 1830s he purchased his freedom and moved to Baltimore. In that city, Wilks worked as a general laborer and resided on Lexington Street, east of Park Street. Return Book, 1 January 1824, Land Papers—Maintenance of Property, Land Volume 39, reel 10, Lloyd Family Papers, MdHi; *Matchett's Baltimore Director[y] . . . 1835–6* (Baltimore, 1835), 275; *Matchett's Baltimore Director[y] . . . 1837–8* (Baltimore, 1837), 472.

22.39/18.9   the riches of Job] Douglass refers to the biblical story of Job, where his wealth is enumerated and he is described as "the greatest of all in the east." Job 1 : 1–3.

23.26–27/19.13–14   a still tongue makes a wise head] This saying probably had its roots in an old English epigram, "Hauyng a styll toung he had a besy head." *The Proverbs and Epigrams of John Heywood* (1562; New York, 1967), 214.

24.5/20.6–7   Jacob Jepson] Jacob Gibson (1759–1818), a slaveowner locally feared for his volatile temper, resided at Marengo, a plantation bordering the Lloyd property. Douglass mistakenly refers to him as "Jacob Jepson." Appointed an associate judge for Talbot County in 1802, Gibson won election to the legislature in 1806. Residents remembered him because of his numerous vitriolic broadsides and newspaper essays as well as his physical assaults on his enemies. The 1810 U.S. census listed him as the owner of thirty-four slaves, whom Gibson reputedly ruled over as a stern taskmaster. Gibson's plantation belonged to his son Fayette at the time to which Douglass refers. 1810 U.S. Census, Maryland, Talbot County, 342; Tilghman, *Talbot County,* 1 : 231–56; Preston, *Young Frederick Douglass,* 60, 221n28.

24.18–19/20.25   Mr. Austin Gore] Austin Gore (1794–1871), also referred to as Orson Gore in the Lloyd family account and cash books, was the overseer of Edward Lloyd V's Davis's Farm plantation where in 1822 a young slave named Bill Demby died. A friend of Gore's later challenged Douglass's assertion that Gore coolly murdered Demby, insisting that he was "a respectable citizen living near St. Michaels, and . . . a worthy member of the Methodist Episcopal Church; . . . all who know him, think him anything but a murderer." Lloyd apparently tolerated Gore's brutal actions because he later promoted him to be overseer of the much larger Wye House plantation. The 1830 U.S. census listed Gore as the head of a household which contained three boys and two girls under 10, his wife, and an elderly woman. Only a child at the time of Demby's death, Douglass must have constructed his narrative of the incident from plantation legends. A. C. C. Thompson, "To the Public—Falsehood Refuted," reprinted in the *NASS,* 25 November 1845 and in *Lib.,* 12 December 1845; Various account books and cash books, Land Papers—Maintenance of Property, Land Volume 39, reel 10, Lloyd Family Papers, MdHi; 1830 U.S. Census, Maryland, Talbot County, 14.

25.27/22.29   by the name of Demby] Bill Demby (c. 1802–22) lived with twenty-two other slaves, including his family, on Davis's Farm, one of several Talbot County plantations owned by Edward Lloyd V. Plantation records indicate that Demby, a prime field hand, died sometime during the year 1822. Return Book, 1 January 1822, 1 January 1823, Land Papers—Maintenance of Property, Land Volume 39, reel 10, Lloyd Family Papers, MdHi; Preston, *Young Frederick Douglass,* 72–73, 213n10.

26.22/24.12   Mr. Thomas Lanman] Thomas H. W. Lambdin (c. 1807–?) had labored at a number of trades by 1850: ship carpenter, schoolteacher, town bailiff for St. Michaels (1848), and miller (1850). In 1850 he was married and had five young children. He owned real estate valued at $1,000.00 in that year. In a rebuttal to Douglass's negative characterization, a Maryland friend described Lambdin as "too good-natured and harmless to injure any person but himself." A. C. C.

Thompson, "To the Public—Falsehood Refuted," reprinted in *NASS,* 25 November 1845 and in *Lib.,* 12 December 1845; Tilghman, *Talbot County,* 2 : 395.

26.28/24.21   Mr. Giles Hicks] A Giles Hicks resided in Caroline County, Maryland in 1820. 1820 U.S. Census, Maryland, Talbot County, 92.

26.29/24.22   my wife's] Anna Murray Douglass (c. 1813–82), Frederick Douglass's first wife, was born free in Denton, Caroline County, Maryland. She was the eighth child of Bambarra Murray and his wife Mary, slaves who had been manumitted shortly before Anna's birth. At seventeen she moved to Baltimore, where she worked as a domestic. She met Douglass at meetings of the East Baltimore Mental Improvement Society, helped finance his escape, and, according to plan, joined him in New York City, where they were married on 15 September 1838. During Douglass's tour of the British Isles in 1845–47 she remained in Lynn, Massachusetts, where she supported herself by binding shoes. There she gained a reputation for frugality and skillful household management—qualities that would contribute greatly to her family's financial prosperity over the years. A member of the Lynn Ladies' Anti-Slavery Society and a regular participant in the annual antislavery bazaars in Boston, she continued her antislavery activities after moving to Rochester in 1847. Unlettered, reserved, and, according to her husband, never completely at ease in white company, she seldom appeared at public functions with Douglass. She was nevertheless affectionately remembered by her husband's associates as a "warm" and "hospitable" hostess at their home. On 9 July 1882, Anna Douglass suffered an attack of paralysis in Washington, D.C. She died there on 4 August. In January 1884 Douglass married Helen Pitts, a white woman. *Lib.,* 18 November, 2 December 1853; Philadelphia *Christian Recorder,* 20 July 1882; Washington *Post,* 5 August 1882; Rosetta Douglass Sprague, *Anna Murray Douglass: My Mother as I Recall Her* (1900; Washington, D.C., 1923); Jane Marsh Parker, "Reminiscences of Frederick Douglass," *Outlook* 51 : 552–53 (6 April 1895); Preston, *Young Frederick Douglass,* 149, 151, 154, 159; Quarles, *Frederick Douglass,* 9–10, 100–01, 106, 109–10, 297–98.

27.15/25.25   Mr. Beal Bondly] John Beale Bordley (1800–82) was the son of Matthias Bordley (1757–1828) and the grandson of John Beale Bordley (1727–1804), a noted agriculturalist and Revolutionary War era patriot from Maryland. Often called simply Beale Bordley, John Beale Bordley was born on his father's Wye Island estate, across the river from the Lloyd plantation, and remained there until his mid-twenties when he moved to Philadelphia to study law with Pennsylvania Chief Justice John Bannister Gibson. Quickly tiring of the law, Bordley came to develop a very successful career as a portrait painter of prominent figures in Baltimore, Philadelphia, and elsewhere. A number of his paintings are held by the Maryland Historical Society. Francis Sims McGrath, "A Letter to Eileen," *MdHM,* 24 : 306 (December 1929); Eugenia Calvert Holland and Louisa MacGill Gray, comps., "Miniatures in the Collection of the Maryland Historical Society," *MdHM,* 51 : 342, 346, 353 (December 1956); Anna Wells Rutledge, "Portraits

Painted Before 1900 in the Collection of the Maryland Historical Society . . . ,"
MdHM, 41 : 35, 36, 43 (March 1946); Baltimore *American and Commercial
Advertiser,* 14 March 1882; Francis Sims McGrath, *Pillars of Maryland* (Richmond, 1950), 393.

28.3/26.26   tow linen] Rough, unbleached cloth manufactured from tow, the
shortest fibers taken from flax or hemp.

28.19/27.24   Mr. Hugh Auld] Born in Talbot County, Maryland, Hugh Auld
(1799–1861) moved as a young man to Baltimore. There he worked as a ship's
carpenter, master shipbuilder, shipyard foreman, and occasionally served as a
magistrate. Prior to moving to Baltimore, Hugh married Sophia Keithley. Between
1826 and 1833 and again between 1836 and 1838, the young Frederick Douglass
lived and worked in their household, lent to them by his owner, Hugh's brother
Thomas. In 1845, Hugh, incensed by Douglass's depiction of his family in the
Narrative, bought Douglass, then on a lecture tour of Britain, from his brother
Thomas. According to the *Pennsylvania Freeman,* Auld was determined to reenslave Douglass and "place him in the cotton fields of the South" if the fugitive ever
returned to the United States. In 1846, two British abolitionists, Anna and Ellen
Richardson, offered to buy Douglass from Auld; in exchange for $711.66 (£150
sterling) raised among British reformers, Auld signed the manumission papers that
made Douglass a free man. *PaF,* 26 February 1846; *Lib.,* 6 March 1846; Walter
Lourie to Ellis Gray Loring, 15 December 1846, reel 1, frame 644, Benjamin F.
Auld to Douglass, 11, 27 September 1891, reel 6, frames 240–41, 257–58, Douglass to Benjamin F. Auld, 16 September 1891, reel 6, frames 246–47, J. C. Schaffer
to Helen Pitts Douglass, 21 October 1896, reel 8, frames 92–93, General Correspondence File, FD Papers, DLC; Talbot County Records, V.60, 35–36, MdTCH,
Easton, Md. (a copy is found on reel 1, frames 637–39, FD Papers, DLC); Hugh
Auld Family Genealogical Chart, prepared by Carl G. Auld, Ellicott City, Md., 5
June 1976; Preston, *Young Frederick Douglass,* 81, 84–85, 92, 143, 173–75.

28.23/27.29   scurf] Scales of epidermis continually being detached from the
skin.

28.38–39/28.19–20   I had two sisters] Sarah Bailey (1814–?) was Frederick
Douglass's oldest sister and the second of seven children born to Harriet Bailey.
Aaron Anthony owned Sarah but after his death in 1826, she became the chattel of
his son, Andrew Skinner Anthony. In 1832, Andrew sold Bailey, her son Henry,
and four other slaves to Perry Cohee of Lawrence County in south Mississippi.
Douglass and Sarah remained separated until 1883, when she, then living in
Louisville, Kentucky, and calling herself Mrs. Sarah Pettit, wrote to Douglass and
reestablished their relationship. Sarah O. Pettit to Douglass, 26 September 1883,
General Correspondence File, reel 3, frame 778–80, FD Papers, DLC; Aaron
Anthony Slave Distribution, 22 October 1827, Talbot County Distributions,
V.JP#D, 58–59, MdTCH; Sale of Slaves, Andrew S. Anthony to Perry Cohee, 14
July 1832, Talbot County Records, V. 50, 192–93, MdTCH.

28.38–39/28.19–20   I had two sisters] The third oldest of six children born to
Harriet Bailey and the sister of Frederick Douglass, Eliza Bailey (1816–c. 1876)
was a slave owned by Aaron Anthony. When Anthony died in 1826, Eliza became
the property of Thomas Auld, Anthony's son-in-law. Eliza married Peter Mitchell,
a free black who worked as a field hand in Talbot County, with whom she had nine
children. In 1836, Mitchell bought Eliza and their then two children from Thomas
Auld for one hundred dollars. After settling on an acre of land which they rented
from Samuel and John Hambleton of Talbot County, they raised their own vegetables and meat and hired themselves out as a domestic and a field hand, respec-
tively. Eliza and her brother Frederick were separated after the latter's escape from
slavery in 1838. On 6 June 1844, Mitchell freed Eliza and the other children
because state laws no longer required removal from Maryland upon manumission.
Eliza and Frederick were reunited in 1865 when Douglass stopped in Baltimore
while on a speaking tour. New York *Independent,* 2 March 1865; Lewis Douglass
to Douglass, 9 June 1865, FD Papers, Moorland-Spingarn Library, DHU; Aaron
Anthony Slave Distribution, 22 October 1827, Talbot County Distributions,
V.JP#D, 58–59, Sale of Slaves, Thomas Auld to Peter Mitchell, 25 January 1836,
Talbot County Records, V.52, 258, Manumission of Eliza Mitchell, 1 July 1844,
Talbot County Records, V.58, 234–35, all in MdTCH; Preston, *Young Frederick
Douglass,* 164–65, 184, 206–07, 229n7.

28.39/28.20   and one brother] Perry Bailey (1813–?), the oldest of seven
children born to Harriet Bailey and Frederick Douglass's brother, was the slave of
Aaron Anthony. When Anthony died in 1826, Perry was inherited by Anthony's
son, Andrew J. Anthony. Andrew died in 1832, leaving Perry, now married to a
slave named Maria, to John P. Anthony, who sold Maria to a slaveowner in Brazos
County, Texas. Perry followed his wife to Texas, where a post-emancipation labor
shortage allowed him to earn "fifteen dollars gold wages a month." In 1867, Perry,
Maria, and their four children traveled to Rochester to reunite with Frederick.
Elated by this reunion, Douglass built a cottage for them on his Rochester estate,
where the family stayed for two years. In 1869, Perry and Maria returned to
Maryland's Eastern Shore where Perry died some time after 1878. Perry Downs to
Douglass, 21 February 1867, Douglass Papers, Moorland-Spingarn Library, DHU;
Douglass to J. J. Spelman, 11 July 1867, reprinted in New York *Independent,* 25
July 1867; Douglass to Theodore Tilton, 2 September 1867, FD Papers, NHi; Anna
Downs to Douglass, 5 October 1869, General Correspondence File, reel 2, frames
497–99, FD Papers, DLC; Aaron Anthony Slave Distribution, 22 October 1827,
Talbot County Distributions, V.JP#D, 58–59, MdTCH; Preston, *Young Frederick
Douglass,* 175–77, 206.

29.11/29.5   Cousin Tom] Tom Bailey (1814–?), the fourth of Milly Bailey's
seven children and Douglass's cousin, was a slave belonging to Aaron Anthony.
When Anthony died in 1826, Bailey became the property of Thomas Auld. Auld
granted Bailey his freedom in 1845. The last record of Bailey's existence is a letter

to Douglass from his son Lewis, who visited Talbot County in 1865. During his visit, Lewis wrote, he met with Bailey, who was still living in St. Michaels. Lewis Douglass to Douglass, 9 June 1865, FD Papers, Moorland-Spingarn Library, DHU; Aaron Anthony Slave Distribution, 22 October 1827, Talbot County Distributions, V.JP#D, 58–59, MdTCH; Preston, *Young Frederick Douglass,* 91, 174, 206, 221n29, 230n25.

29.21/29.18   Miles River] Originally known as the St. Michaels River, the twelve-mile-long Miles River lies entirely within Talbot County. The right-angled river flows southwest for its first eight miles and then flows northwest to meet the Chesapeake Bay at the town of St. Michaels. Footner, *Rivers of the Eastern Shore,* 236, 239–40, 255.

29.21/29.18–19   on a Saturday morning] Douglass departed St. Michaels for Baltimore on a Saturday in March 1826, probably the 18th. Preston, *Young Frederick Douglass,* 82.

29.34–35/30.5   at Smith's Wharf, not far from Bowley's Wharf] Smith's Wharf and Bowley's Wharf were two sturdily-built wharves below Pratt Street in Baltimore's inner harbor, the Basin, west of Fells Point. The city directory at times spelled the latter as "Bowly's Wharf." *Matchett's Baltimore Directory for 1827* (Baltimore, 1827), 18–19 (street register); Sherry H. Olson, *Baltimore: The Building of an American City* (Baltimore, 1980), 60.

29.36–39/30.7–8   the slaughterhouse of Mr. Curtis] The Baltimore city directory of 1824 lists two "victuallers": Thomas Curtain on Eden Street and James Curtain on Bond Street. Three years later the city directory lists Thomas Curtis as a "victualler." *Matchett's Baltimore Directory for 1824,* 74; *Matchett's Baltimore Directory for 1827,* 70.

29.38/30.10   my new home in Alliciana Street] Neither the 1824 nor 1827 Baltimore directories, the only extant directories in this period, list Hugh Auld's residence. The Baltimore City Commission on Historical and Architectural Preservation established that Hugh Auld's house was on the southeast corner of Aliceanna and Durham (formerly Happy Alley) streets in Fells Point. Contemporary sources spelled the street "Alisanna" (1824) or "Alice Anna" (1827). *Matchett's Baltimore Directory, for 1824* (Baltimore, 1824), 343; *Matchett's Baltimore Directory for 1827,* 1 (street register); Fielding Lucas, Jr., *Plan of the City of Baltimore* (Baltimore, 1836); Preston, *Young Frederick Douglass,* 223n1.

29.39/30.11   near Mr. Gardner's ship-yard] William Gardner, a ship carpenter or shipbuilder, resided on Fleet Street, Fells Point, between 1827 and 1836. The shipyard of George and William Gardner was at the "lower end of Fountain Street," on the eastern edge of the Fells Point wharf area. *Matchett's Baltimore Director[y] . . . 1831* (Baltimore, 1831), 141, 5 (street register).

29.39/30.11   on Fells Point] Fells Point, first settled by William Fell in 1726, was a separate enclave east of Baltimore center not annexed to Baltimore until 1773. This hooked piece of land jutting into the outer harbor had been a shipbuilding site since the mid-eighteenth century. After the War of 1812 it was the construction site for the famous Baltimore clipper ships. By the time of Douglass's arrival, Fells Point was a heavily-populated neighborhood whose residents worked in shipbuilding and other maritime pursuits. Shipyards and wharves for unloading cargo lined its waterfront. To reduce the frequency of yellow fever epidemics, a marshy area between Fells Point and the central city was dredged in the 1820s to form the City Dock, also called the City Block, which added to the Fells Point wharf area. A drawbridge at the entrance to the City Dock connected Block Street in Fells Point to the Basin area wharves. J. Thomas Scharf, *History of Baltimore City and County from the Earliest Period to the Present Day* (Philadelphia, 1881), 54, 59–60, 292–94; Olson, *Baltimore,* 52–53, 85.

30.1–2/30.13   their little son Thomas] Thomas Auld (1824–48), the son of Hugh and Sophia Auld and the nephew of Thomas Auld, Aaron Anthony's son-in-law, was the charge of the young slave Douglass. He died in an unsuccessful attempt by the brig *Tweed* to rescue a sinking British vessel. Benjamin F. Auld to Douglass, 11 September 1891, General Correspondence File, reel 6, frame 240, FD Papers, DLC; Preston, *Young Frederick Douglass,* 148, 228n10.

30.4/30.17   Sophia Auld] Sophia Keithley Auld (1797–1880) was born in Talbot County, Maryland, to Richard and Hester Keithley. Her parents were poor, devout Methodists who held to the antislavery teachings of their church. Before marrying Hugh Auld, she worked as a weaver. Soon after their marriage, the couple moved to Baltimore, where Hugh worked as a ship's carpenter, master shipbuilder, and shipyard fireman. Between 1826 and 1833, and again in 1836–38, the young slave Frederick Douglass lived and worked in their household. Both Douglass and Sophia Auld retained enormous affection for one another long after Douglass had established himself in the North. Douglass tried to visit Auld in Baltimore during the Civil War. Years after her death, Auld's son Benjamin told Douglass that "mother would always speak in the kindest terms of you, whenever your name was mentioned." Baltimore *Sun,* 5 July 1880; Benjamin F. Auld to Douglass, 11 September 1891, General Correspondence File, reel 6, frame 240, FD Papers, DLC; Preston, *Young Frederick Douglass,* 87, 165–66, 168.

31.28/33.12–13   If you give nigger an inch, he will take an ell. A paraphrase of the old English proverb, "For whan I gaue you an ynche, ye tooke an ell." An ell is an antiquated English unit of length equal to forty-five inches. Heywood, *Proverbs and Epigrams,* 78.

32.35/35.13   Philpot Street] Philpot Street ran east to west, parallel to the waterfront on Fells Point. The Aulds moved to Philpot Street in 1827 or 1828 soon after Hugh Auld began working at Durgin and Bailey's shipyard. Benjamin F. Auld to Douglass, 27 September 1891, General Correspondence File, reel 6, frames 257–58, FD Papers, DLC; Lucas, *Plan of the City of Baltimore.*

32.35/35.13   Mr. Thomas Hamilton] Thomas Hamilton, a ship carpenter, lived at 22 Philpot Street in Baltimore from at least 1831 through 1838. In 1833 his address was probably incorrectly listed as 18 Philpot Street. *Matchett's Baltimore Director[y]. . . 1831,* 163; *Matchett's Baltimore Director[y]. . . 1833* (Baltimore, 1833), 83; *Matchett's Baltimore Director[y] . . . 1835–6,* 110; *Matchett's Baltimore Director[y] for 1837–8,* 154.

33.9/35.31   *gip*] Gypsy.

34.2/37.13–14   for every mourner that came within her reach] Possibly a loose paraphrase of Prov. 25 : 20–23.

34.38/38.31–32   Durgin and Bailey's ship-yard] John Durgin and Thomas Bailey operated a shipwright business on Philpot Street in Fell's Point in the late 1820s and the 1830s. Douglass later recalled that as a boy he carried Auld's dinner to him while Auld was employed as a carpenter at this shipyard near the Auld home. Bailey continued as a ship carpenter in the same area into the 1830s. Douglass to Benjamin F. Auld, 24 March 1894, SC-163, Mrs. Howard V. Hall Collection of Auld Family Papers, MdAA; *Matchett's Baltimore Director[y] . . . 1829* (Baltimore, 1829), 94; *Matchett's Baltimore Director[y] . . . 1831,* 21; *Matchett's Baltimore Director[y] . . . 1835–36,* 12.

35.8/39.12   "The Columbian Orator"] Boston schoolteacher and book-seller Caleb Bingham (1757–1817) authored the *Columbian Orator* (1797; Boston, 1827), one of the first textbooks on English grammar and rhetoric published in the United States. It contained short extracts from speeches by such famous orators as William Pitt, George Washington, Charles James Fox, and Cicero, as well as plays and poems on the themes of patriotism, education, and freedom. The *Columbian Orator* remained one of the most popular textbooks of its kind in America through the 1820s. Bingham himself contributed an essay on oratorical skills, "General Directions for Speaking," whose rules Douglass followed in his early years as a public speaker. *NCAB,* 8 : 19; *DAB,* 2 : 273–74.

35.9–10/39.14–15   a dialogue between a master and his slave] The anonymous "Dialogue between a Master and Slave" is a conversation between a master and slave in which the slave is caught trying to run away for the second time. Bingham, *Columbian Orator,* 1827 ed., 240–42.

35.19–20/39.27–28   Sheridan's mighty speeches on and in behalf of Catholic Emancipation] Although Richard Sheridan (1751–1816), the Irish orator, playwright, and politician who entered Parliament in 1780, championed Irish and other reform causes, the only speech extracted in the *Columbian Orator* is "Mr. Sheridan's Speech Against Mr. Taylor," which is not on Catholic "emancipation." Douglass is probably referring to another selection in the anthology entitled "Part of Mr. O'Connor's Speech in the Irish House of Commons, in Favor of the Bill for Emancipating the Roman Catholics, 1795." Arthur O'Connor (1763–1852), a liberal Protestant member of the Irish parliament, was a strong supporter of Catholic rights, including "Catholic emancipation" or the right of Catholics to hold office and sit in Parliament. O'Connor resigned his seat after delivering this speech.

Bingham, *Columbian Orator,* 1827 ed., 130–31, 243–48; *Dictionary of National Biography,* 21 vols. (London, 1921–22), 18 : 78–85, 21 : 394–95.

36.29–30/42.1–2   petitions from the north] The sending of petitions to Congress, calling for an end to the slave trade and to slavery in the District of Columbia, dated back to the early years of the federal government. In 1828, a national petition drive had helped force the House of Representatives to vote on abolishing slavery in the District of Columbia. The newly organized movement for immediate emancipation adopted the petition strategy in the 1830s and deluged Congress with antislavery memorials bearing thousands of signatures. Louis Filler, *The Crusade Against Slavery, 1830–1860* (New York, 1960), 3, 99; Russel B. Nye, *Fettered Freedom: Civil Liberties and the Slavery Controversy, 1830–1860* (1949; Ann Arbor, Mich., 1963), 41–51.

36.34–35/42.9   on the wharf of Mr. Waters] George P. Waters was a ship chandler and grocer who operated both of his businesses very near the wharf he owned at the south end of Fell Street in Fell's Point. *Matchett's Baltimore Director[y] . . . 1833,* 189, 15 (street register); *Matchett's Baltimore Director[y] . . . for 1835–6,* 267; Lucas, *Plan of the City of Baltimore.*

37.18/43.9   larboard side] The left side of a ship when looking toward the bow.

37.34/44.1   Webster's Spelling Book] The first version of the spelling book, *A Grammatical Institute of the English Language* (Hartford, Conn., 1783), by Noah Webster (1758–1843), a Connecticut teacher, editor, and Federalist politician, rapidly became the standard spelling and pronunciation guide in the new nation. In 1788 the title became *The American Spelling Book* and in 1829 *The Elementary Spelling Book.* Harry R. Warfel, *Noah Webster: Schoolmaster to America* (New York, 1936); Richard J. Moss, *Noah Webster* (Boston, 1984); *DAB,* 19 : 594–97.

37.39/44.7–8   the Wilk Street meeting-house] The Fifth Methodist Episcopal Church, on the corner of Wilke (Wilks) Street and Apple Alley, was about seven blocks from Auld's house on Philpot Street. *Matchett's Baltimore Director[y] . . . 1831,* 16 (street register); *Matchett's Baltimore Director[y] . . . 1837–8,* 18; Lucas, *Plan of the City of Baltimore.*

38.8/44.18   youngest son, Richard, died] Douglass is mistaken in believing that Richard died before his father. According to the Anthony Family Bible, Richard did not die until 18 May 1828, and had shared in the division of his father's estate. Harriet Anthony's annotated copy of *Bondage and Freedom,* folder 93, 173–74, Aaron Anthony Slave Distribution, 27 September 1827, folder 77, both in Dodge Collection, MdAA; Preston, "Aaron Anthony," 5.

38.9/44.20   Captain Anthony, died] Aaron Anthony died on 14 November 1826, at age 59. According to his great-granddaughter Harriet Lucretia Anthony, he was buried in an unmarked grave in the family graveyard on Holme Hill Farm. Harriet Anthony's annotated copy of *Bondage and Freedom,* folder 93, 173–74, Harriet Anthony mss. notes, 1919, folder 89, 9–11, both in Dodge Collection, MdAA; Preston, *Young Frederick Douglass,* 29–30.

38.19/45.7   Captain Rowe] Captain Joseph H. Rowe lived in Baltimore on Market Street south of Bank Street from at least 1831 through 1836. *Matchett's Baltimore Director[y] . . . 1831,* 320; *Matchett's Baltimore Director[y] . . . 1833,* 159; *Matchett's Baltimore Director[y] . . . 1835–6,* 222.

38.19/45.7–8   the schooner Wild Cat] The schooner *Wild Cat* was a slow, shallow-draft merchant ship designed to carry cargo up and down the tidal creeks of the Chesapeake Bay. Preston, *Young Frederick Douglass,* 88.

38.33/45.27   then came the division] Aaron Anthony's heirs, Richard Anthony, Andrew Anthony, and Thomas Auld, agreed to the division of his slaves on 27 September 1827. Twenty-eight slaves, including Frederick Douglass, comprised the division and were valued at $2,805. Frederick was among the slaves awarded to Thomas Auld, widower of Lucretia Anthony Auld. Aaron Anthony Slave Distribution, 27 September 1827, folder 77, Dodge Collection, MdAA; Aaron Anthony Slave Distribution, 22 October 1827, Talbot County Distributions, V.JP#D, 58–59, MdTCH.

39.26/47.5–6   was sent immediately back to Baltimore] After court-appointed appraisers oversaw the actual assignment of Aaron Anthony's slaves to each of his heirs, Douglass probably returned to Baltimore by November 1827 at the latest. Preston, *Young Frederick Douglass,* 90.

39.31/47.12–13   my mistress, Lucretia, died] Lucretia Anthony Auld died 6 July 1827. Douglass is mistaken in his recollection that he was awarded to Lucretia, as she had died after her father Aaron Anthony but before his estate was settled. County records indicate that Frederick was awarded to her husband Thomas Auld as her heir. Anthony Family Bible, Oxford Museum, Oxford, Md.; Aaron Anthony Slave Distribution, 22 October 1827, Talbot County Distributions, V.JP#D, 58–59, MdTCH; Preston, "Aaron Anthony," 5.

39.32/47.13–14   one child, Amanda] Born in Hillsborough, Maryland, Arianna Amanda Auld Sears (1826–78) was the only child of Thomas and Lucretia Anthony Auld. With her mother's death in 1826 and her father's subsequent remarriage, she fell under the charge of her stepmother Rowena Hambleton Auld. In 1843 she married John L. Sears, a Philadelphia coal merchant, with whom she bore four children. The Sears moved to Philadelphia, but returned to Maryland in the early 1860s, settling in Baltimore. Amanda Auld's childhood acquaintance with Frederick Douglass was reestablished in 1859 when he called upon her while on a speaking engagement in Philadelphia. Douglass and Auld maintained a warm friendship over the years that followed; after her death in 1878, Auld's husband John wrote to Douglass, "God bless you for your kindness to her." Auld Family Bible (courtesy of Carl G. Auld); New York *Herald,* 6 September 1866; Philadelphia *Evening Bulletin,* 6 September 1866; John L. Sears to Douglass, 10 January 1878, Thomas E. Sears to Douglass, 1 February 1878, General Correspondence File, reel 3, frames 215–16, reel 3, frame 225, FD Papers, DLC; Preston, *Young Frederick Douglass,* 30, 106–

07, 168–70; McFeely, *Frederick Douglass,* 297, 306; Roberts, "Visitation of Western Talbot," 245.

39.32–33/47.14–15   after her death, Master Andrew died] Andrew Anthony died in June 1833 but not before he had sold several of Douglass's Bailey relatives to a Mississippi slaveholder. Andrew Anthony Slave Distribution, 28 August 1835, Talbot County Distributions, V.JB#D, 1825–45, 185–86, MdTCH; Preston, *Young Frederick Douglass,* 110, 225.

40.20–21/48.20–21   the slave's poet, Whittier] Born in Haverhill, Massachusetts, Quaker poet and abolitionist John Greenleaf Whittier (1807–72) was a journalist and editor for such journals as *Free Press, American Manufacturer,* Washington (D.C.) *National Era,* and the *Atlantic Monthly.* Among Whittier's volumes of poetry are *Voices of Freedom* (1846), *The Panorama and Other Poems* (1856), and *At Sundown* (1890). Douglass often quoted Whittier's poems in his speeches. Edward Wagenknecht, *John Greenleaf Whittier: A Portrait in Paradox* (New York, 1967); *DAB,* 20 : 174.

40.33/48.33   Woe is me, my stolen daughters] Douglass quotes the first twelve lines from the 1838 poem, "The Farewell of a Virginia Slave Mother to Her Daughter Sold into Southern Bondage," by John G. Whittier. *The Poetical Works of John Greenleaf Whittier,* 4 vols. (Boston, 1892), 3 : 56.

41.13/49.25   Rowena Hamilton] Rowena Hambleton Auld (1812–42) was the eldest daughter of William Hambleton, a wealthy slaveowner in Martingham, Maryland. She became the second wife of Thomas Auld on 21 May 1829. Auld Family Bible (Courtesy of Carl G. Auld); Preston, *Young Frederick Douglass,* 106–07; Roberts, "Visitation of Western Talbot," 245.

41.14/49.26   Mr. William Hamilton] William Hambleton (c. 1783–?), not Hamilton, descended from an old Eastern Shore family and lived at Martingham, a Talbot County plantation. He was the father of Rowena Hambleton Auld and the brother of "Purser" Samuel Hambleton who had won national fame as a hero at the Battle of Lake Erie. In 1850 Hambleton possessed real estate valued at $10,000 and owned ten slaves. 1850 U.S. Census, Maryland, Talbot County, 1016 (schedule of free inhabitants), 32 (slave schedule); Preston, *Young Frederick Douglass,* 108, 109, 130.

41.17/49.30   to live with himself at St. Michael's] Hugh Auld returned Douglass to Thomas Auld in St. Michaels in March 1833 not 1832 as Douglass erroneously believed at the time of writing the *Narrative.* Preston, *Young Frederick Douglass,* 104–05.

41.35/50.21   Captain Edward Dodson] Edward Dodson was captain of a packet ship that conveyed passengers and freight between St. Michaels, Talbot County, and Baltimore during the early nineteenth century. In 1830 he was in his twenties and lived in Talbot County. The members of his household included three children, two white women both in their twenties, and a slightly older free black woman. 1830 U.S. Census, Maryland, Talbot County, 37; Tilghman, *Talbot County,* 2 : 396.

41.37/50.24   on reaching North Point] North Point, on Chesapeake Bay east of Baltimore, is located at the mouth of the Patapsco River at the tip of Patapsco River Neck. To reach northern ports from Baltimore, ships traveled around North Point and headed north on the bay to the Chesapeake and Delaware Canal, which opened to navigation in 1830. Scharf, *Baltimore City and County,* map preceding p. 13; George Rogers Taylor, *The Transportation Revolution, 1815–1860* (New York, 1951), 41–42.

42.5–6/51.4   at St. Michael's, in March, 1832] Actually March 1833.

42.25/52.4   my aunt Priscilla] Priscilla Bailey (1816–?), the eleventh of twelve children born to Isaac and Betsey Bailey, was a slave belonging to Aaron Anthony. When Anthony died in 1826, his son Richard Lee Anthony inherited her. Aaron Anthony Slave Distribution, 22 October 1827, Talbot County Distributions, V.JP#D, 58–59, MdTCH; Preston, *Young Frederick Douglass,* 18, 206.

42.26/52.4   Henny] Henny Bailey (1816–?), a cousin of Frederick Douglass, was one of seven children born to Milly Bailey, a slave on one of Aaron Anthony's farms. Henny was apparently ill-fitted for work: Anthony estimated her value at fifty dollars in 1826, less than half the value he placed on her younger cousin Frederick. When Anthony died in 1826, his son-in-law Thomas Auld inherited Bailey and four other slaves. Some time before 1840, Auld granted Bailey her freedom. The last record of Henny's existence is an entry in the 1840 U.S. Census, which identifies her as a free black, between the age of thirty-six and fifty-five, living in St. Michaels District. Inventory of Negroes owned by Aaron Anthony, 19 December 1826, folder 71, Aaron Anthony, Ledger B, 1812–1826, folder 95, 159, both in Dodge Collection, MdAA; Aaron Anthony Slave Distribution, 22 October 1827, Talbot County Distributions, V.JP#D, 58–59, MdTCH; 1840 U.S. Census, Maryland, Talbot County, 42; Preston, *Young Frederick Douglass,* 91, 174, 225n14.

43.29–30/53.30–31   my master attended a Methodist camp-meeting] Douglass accompanied his master, Thomas Auld, to some of the services at a Methodist camp meeting held at Haddaway's Woods on what is presently known as the Tilghman Peninsula along the Chesapeake. The meeting lasted from 16 to 21 August 1833 and attracted people from as far as Baltimore. Preston, *Young Frederick Douglass,* 111–13.

44.9/54.24–25   Mr. Storks] The Reverend Levi Storks was the circuit preacher of the Talbot Circuit of the Methodist Episcopal Church in 1832 and 1833. When the British invaded the Eastern Shore in 1814, Storks served as a private in a local regiment. In 1820 he was probably an overseer in Talbot County and in 1834, he married Anne G. Nicholson. 1820 U.S. Census, Maryland, Talbot County, 6; William M. Marine, *The British Invasion of Maryland, 1812–1815* (Baltimore, 1913), 451; Edith G. Bevan, "Maryland Bookplates," *MdHM,* 39 : 93–94 (March 1944); Thomas H. Sewell, "St. Michaels Methodism" (unpublished paper, 1894), 717, 723, MdAA.

44.9/54.25   Mr. Ewery] In 1832, William Uriey (c. 1810–80) was a circuit preacher for the Methodist Episcopal Church's Talbot Circuit, which included St. Michaels Parish. Sewell, "St. Michaels Methodism," 717.

44.9/54.25   Mr. Humphry] Joshua Humphries (c. 1801–79) entered the Methodist Episcopal ministry in 1829 and soon became a prominent member of that faith in Talbot County. In 1834 he was the presiding elder and circuit preacher for the Talbot Circuit. Humphries continued in charge in the Talbot Circuit in 1835 when he issued an important report on the state of Sunday schools. James M. McCarter and Benjamin F. Jackson, eds., *Historical and Biographical Encyclopedia of Delaware* (Wilmington, Del., 1882), 410; Sewell, "St. Michaels Methodism," 675, 730.

44.9/54.25   Mr. Hickey] William—or possibly Thomas—Hickey was a Methodist preacher who in the 1830s rode a circuit which included St. Michaels Parish. Sewell, "St. Michaels Methodism," 723; Preston, *Young Frederick Douglass,* 114, 226n16.

44.10/54.26   Mr. George Cookman] Born into a wealthy family in Hull, England, George Cookman (1800–41) began working in his father's merchant firm at the age of twenty. Between 1821 and 1823, he visited the United States on business and during this sojourn became convinced of his duty to preach the gospel. Despite his father's protestations, he resolved to settle permanently in America and become a Methodist minister. Soon after migrating in 1825, Cookman became a popular figure in the Methodists' Philadelphia Conference, preaching throughout parts of Pennsylvania, New Jersey, Maryland, and the District of Columbia. His powerful sermons won him the position of chaplain to the U.S. Congress. As revivals were sweeping the Eastern Shore, Cookman became the minister of the St. Michaels Methodist Episcopal church in the summer of 1829 and labored to hold it in the denomination. He remained in that position at least through the early 1830s. By 1830 Cookman was married and had two young sons. He had some antislavery leanings and apparently persuaded Samuel Harrison, one of Talbot County's largest slaveholders, to emancipate all of his adult male slaves in his will. In March 1841, the steamship *President* on which Cookman was sailing for England was lost at sea. 1830 U.S. Census, Maryland, Talbot County, 6; Matthew Simpson, ed., *Cyclopaedia of Methodism,* 5th rev. ed. (Philadelphia, 1882), 255–56; Preston, *Young Frederick Douglass,* 114–15, 226n17; Sewell, "St Michaels Methodism," 665–67, 675–76, 677–78, 680, 707; *ACAB,* 1 : 722.

44.12/54.29   Mr. Samuel Harrison] Samuel Harrison (?–1837) was one of the wealthiest slaveholders in Talbot County: in 1802 he inherited a lucrative import and export business from his father Thomas Harrison. He increased his fortune in the 1810s by lending money and supplies to those engaged in the then booming shipbuilding industry of Talbot County and by 1830 he owned 84 slaves. At the request of his friend and confidante, the Reverend George Cookman, Harrison stipulated in his will that all adult male slaves be manumitted upon his death. 1830

U.S. Census, Maryland, Talbot County, 42; Tilghman, *Talbot County,* 2 : 379, 383, 389–90, 397; Preston, *Young Frederick Douglass,* 115, 226n17.

44.21/55.8   Mr. Wilson] Nathan Wilson (c. 1797–c. 1861), an unmarried Quaker about fifty years old, taught at a local school for whites in the early 1840s near Denton in Caroline County, only a few miles from Talbot County. While Quakerism no longer was the influential religious force on the Eastern Shore that it had been in the eighteenth century, numerous Quakers remained in the region and some continued to argue against slavery and for teaching the slaves to read the Scriptures. This particular teacher could plausibly have been interested in opening a Sabbath school for blacks, as could have any of the other various Quaker Wilsons who populated Talbot and other Eastern Shore counties. Among other local whites interested in black education was Louisa Hambleton from the Eastern Shore's famous first family, who unsuccessfully attempted to open a Sabbath school for St. Michaels' slaves in 1843. Robert Todd, *Methodism of the Peninsula* (Philadelphia, 1886), 249–53; Kenneth Carroll, *Quakerism on the Eastern Shore* (Baltimore, 1970), 219, 245; Sewell, "St. Michaels Methodism," 687.

44.23/55.11   Mr. West] Garretson West (1800–53) was famous among Methodists in St. Michaels, Maryland, for his religious enthusiasm and moral zeal. Although he worked first as an oysterman and later as a teamster, West primarily devoted himself to spurring public prayer, exhorting the faithful at the Methodist classes he led, and—despite his illiteracy—conversing at length with others over the meaning of various biblical passages. In 1829, West was elected to the board of trustees of the Methodist church in St. Michaels and held that position until 1836. He also was appointed that church's sexton in 1830 and again in 1836. At the time of his death, West was married, had at least one child, and had accumulated little wealth. 1850 U.S. Census, Maryland, Talbot County, 80; Tilghman, *Talbot County,* 2 : 400–01; Todd, *Methodism of the Peninsula,* 113–23; Preston, *Young Frederick Douglass,* 116; Sewell, "St. Michaels Methodism," 672–74, 680–81, 701, 707, 727.

44.23/55.12   Mr. Fairbanks] Wrightson Fairbank or Fairbanks (c. 1806–?) was a resident of Talbot County who in 1850 worked as a merchant and headed a household that included his wife, four children, and two female relatives. He owned neither land nor slaves. Fairbanks was an active member of the Methodist Episcopal Church in St. Michaels and ran unsuccessfully for the board of trustees of the parish in September 1835. 1850 U.S. Census, Maryland, Talbot County, 80; Sewell, "St. Michaels Methodism," 725.

44.32–33/55.25   beaten with many stripes] A paraphrase of Luke 12 : 47.

45.25/57.5–6   Edward Covey] Edward Covey (1806?–75), who started out as a poor farm-renter from Talbot County, Maryland, managed to accumulate $23,000 in real estate by 1850. Covey's reputation as a slave breaker enabled him to rent or even to receive the free use of field hands from local slaveowners anxious to have their slaves taught proper discipline. Harriet Lucretia Anthony, the great granddaughter of Aaron Anthony, remembered that "Mr. Covey was really noted for his cruelty and meanness." Inventory of the Estate of Edward Covey, 15 May 1875, Talbot County Inventories, TNC#3, 578, MdTCH; Harriet Anthony's annotated copy of *My Bondage and My Freedom*, folder 93, 203, Dodge Collection, MdAA; 1850 U.S. Census, Maryland, Talbot County, 240 (schedule of free inhabitants); Preston, *Young Frederick Douglass*, 117–31.

46.13/58.15   in-hand . . . off-hand] In a team of harnessed animals, the in-hand one is directly under control of the driver.

50.5/65.4   ague] A fit of shaking or shivering, often accompanying a violent fever.

50.27/66.2   Bill Smith] Bill Smith (1804–?) was a slave owned by Samuel Harrison of Rich Neck Manor and hired out as a servant to Edward Covey in 1834. Smith probably received his freedom in 1837, as Samuel Harrison's will stipulated that all adult male slaves should be freed upon his death. Simpson, *Cyclopaedia of Methodism*, 225; Preston, *Young Frederick Douglass*, 119, 122, 123, 128, 226n17.

50.28/66.4   fanning wheat] Exposing cut grain to the wind to have the chaff blown away.

51.1–2/66.21   treading-yard] Place where plants are beaten down into a smaller size for storage by means of treading.

52.29/69.19   Mrs. Kemp's fields] Elizabeth Doyle Kemp (c. 1787–?) probably owned a farm adjacent to the farm Edward Covey rented from her son, John. Married to the shipbuilder Thomas Kemp in Baltimore in November 1809, Elizabeth moved with him in 1816 to a 236-acre farm, Wades Point, west of the town of St. Michaels in Talbot County. After his death in March 1824, most of his property was divided between his two eldest sons, Thomas and John, but provisions were also made for Elizabeth. In 1830 she was the head of a household which comprised five white males, two white females, six male slaves, and three female slaves. 1830 U.S. Census, Maryland, Talbot County, 38; M. Florence Bourne, "Thomas Kemp, Shipbuilder, and His Home, Wades Point," *MdHM*, 49 : 271–89 (December 1954); Preston, *Young Frederick Douglass*, 118.

52.38/69.32   Sandy Jenkins] Sandy Jenkins was a slave owned by William Groomes of Easton, Maryland, who often hired him out to farmers in Talbot County. Preston, *Young Frederick Douglass*, 125–26, 131, 134–36, 138–39, 227n3.

57.5–6/77.4   Mr. William Freeland] William Freeland, the son of William and Elizabeth Freeland of Talbot County, Maryland, was a farmer and slaveowner near St. Michaels. The 1820 U.S. Census lists William as a young adult between sixteen and twenty-five years of age. Between 1820 and 1830, and perhaps later, he lived in a household headed by his mother. They shared their home with two white boys and six slaves. By 1830 the Freeland's household had diminished: Elizabeth and William now lived with only one young white man and four slaves. 1820 U.S. Census, Maryland, Talbot County, 10; 1830 U.S. Census, Maryland, Talbot County, 35.

57.32/78.9   the Rev. Daniel Weeden] Daniel Weeden (c. 1794–?) was a farmer and Methodist minister in Talbot County. Although an overseer without any of his own slaves in 1820, Weeden appears by 1830 to have become an independent farmer with two slaves and a growing family. By 1850 he owned six slaves. In 1839 Weeden forced a free black man back into slavery by revealing that he had served time in a Maryland jail. He then purchased the man at a greatly reduced price. By the early 1840s Weeden was well established as a local minister, having presided over a number of Talbot County weddings in 1843 and 1844. 1820 U.S. Census, Maryland, Talbot County, 7; 1830 U.S. Census, Maryland, Talbot County, 32; 1840 U.S. Census, Maryland, Talbot County, 36a; 1850 U.S. Census, Maryland, Talbot County, 37 (slave schedule); Preston, *Young Frederick Douglass,* 130, 227n8; Charles Montgomery Haddaway III, "Marriages Recorded in Talbot County Newspapers: 1819–1823, 1841–1843, & 1870," *MdHM,* 81 : 254, 260, 262, 267, 268, 270 (Fall 1986).

57.32–33/78.10   the Rev. Rigby Hopkins] Rigby Hopkins was a Methodist minister who had long lived and farmed in Talbot County. In 1830 he was between 50 and 60 years old and had within his household two white males, six white females, and one black female. While in 1820 he owned seventeen slaves, in 1830 he had none, possibly indicating a preference for renting black labor by then. 1820 U.S. Census, Maryland, Talbot County, 19; 1830 U.S. Census, Maryland, Talbot County, 31; Preston, *Young Frederick Douglass,* 130.

57.33–34/78.11–12   the Reformed Methodist Church] An agitation for greater lay authority inside the Methodist Episcopal Church resulted in the expulsion of a small number of members and some congregations from the Methodist Episcopal Church in the mid-1820s. Additional sympathizers of this reform movement withdrew and formed the Associate Methodist Church in 1828, soon after renamed the Methodist Protestant Church. This controversy inspired a large majority of the members of the Sardis Chapel in St. Michaels to affiliate with the new denomination. The minority led by the Reverend George Cookman and Garretson West successfully retained the original church building and eventually rebuilt their congregation's numbers. In the late 1850s, the Methodist Protestant Church underwent a sectional schism over the slavery issue as had its parent Methodist Episcopal Church in the mid-1840s and the Maryland conference sided with the South. Sewell, "St. Michaels Methodism," 674–99; Ancel H. Bassett, *A Concise History of the Methodist Protestant Church from Its Origin* (Pittsburgh, 1887), 167–221; Simpson, *Cyclopaedia of Methodism,* 602–07.

62.11/85.29   " . . . that we knew not of"] *Hamlet,* act 3, sc. 1, lines 81–82.

62.13/85.31–86.1   resolved upon liberty or death] Douglass paraphrases Patrick Henry's speech in a Virginia revolutionary convention, on 23 March 1775. William Wirt, *Sketches of the Life and Character of Patrick Henry,* 7th ed. (New York, 1835), 141.

62.17/86.6   Henry Bailey] Henry Bailey (1820–?) was the youngest of twelve children born to Douglass's maternal grandparents, Isaac and Betsey Bailey. Henry was owned by Aaron Anthony of Talbot County; when Anthony died in 1826, Henry became the property of Richard Lee Anthony. When Richard died in 1828, Thomas Auld, Richard's brother-in-law, became Henry's master. Aaron Anthony Slave Distribution, 22 October 1827, Talbot County Distributions, V.JP#D, pp. 58–59, MdTCH; Preston, *Young Frederick Douglass,* 18, 109, 206.

62.22/87.1   Easter holidays] Easter Sunday in 1836 fell on 3 April.

64.21–22/89.24   Tom Graham, the constable] Thomas Graham was the constable for St. Michaels Parish in 1833 and the next-door neighbor of Thomas Auld. In 1830 he was between the age of forty and fifty, married, the father of one son, and the owner of one female slave. He appears to have died between 1846 and 1850 as he was not listed in the census for the latter year. After the publication of the *Narrative,* Graham publicly disputed Douglass's characterization of his treatment by Auld. *Lib.,* 20 February 1846; 1830 U.S. Census, Maryland, Talbot County, 39; 1840 U.S. Census, Maryland, Talbot County, 48a; Preston, *Young Frederick Douglass,* 116, 136–37.

65.28–29/91.23–24   the sheriff, Mr. Joseph Graham] Joseph Graham (c. 1797–?) was the sheriff of Talbot County in 1836. By 1830 he was married and the father of two young daughters. Graham was still alive in 1878 when Douglass returned to visit Talbot County. 1830 U.S. Census, Maryland, Talbot County, 36; Preston, *Young Frederick Douglass,* 139, 190.

66.36/93.24–25   to my old home at Baltimore] Douglass returned to Baltimore in mid-April 1836. While Douglass makes no mention of the Aulds having moved, Benjamin Auld thought that his family had moved from Philpot Street to "Fell Street" around 1834. The Baltimore city directories list Hugh Auld as residing on Philpot Street until 1837, when he is listed as a shipwright on "Falls Street south of Thames." Benjamin F. Auld to Douglass, 27 September 1891, General Correspondence File, reel 6, frames 257–58, FD Papers, DLC; *Matchett's Baltimore Director[y] . . . 1837–8,* 50.

67.14/94.17   cant] To tilt or turn over an object.

67.18/94.22   fall] The loose end of a hoisting tackle.

67.22/94.28   *bowse*] To haul an object by means of a tackle.

67.37–38/95.19–20   at once to put a stop to it] Most free blacks in Baltimore held jobs as laborers, draymen, and servants, though they also held such craft positions as carpenter, blacksmith, barber, and caulker. They dominated the latter two trades through the 1850s. In the mid-1830s Baltimore witnessed increasing mob violence, brought on by worsening economic conditions and the failure of the Bank of Maryland in 1834. Claiming that free blacks were depriving them of jobs, white Baltimore workers unsuccessfully petitioned the Maryland legislature in the 1830s and 1840s to restrict free blacks from working in certain trades. Economic competition between the races continued, and in 1845 Dr. R. S. Steuart of Baltimore claimed that white labor had driven blacks out of many unskilled jobs in the Fells

Point area. "The Condition of the Coloured Population of the City of Baltimore," *Baltimore Literary and Religious Magazine* 4 : 174–75 (April 1838); Ira Berlin, *Slaves Without Masters: The Free Negro in the Antebellum South* (New York, 1974), 217–49; Jeffrey R. Brackett, *The Negro in Maryland: A Study of the Institution of Slavery* (Baltimore, 1889), 210; James M. Wright, *The Free Negro in Maryland, 1634–1860* (New York, 1921), 154–55, 172; Olson, *Baltimore,* 98–101; M. Ray Della, Jr., "The Problems of Negro Labor in the 1850s," *MdHM,* 66 : 25 (Spring 1971).

68.27/96.28   death by Lynch law] The actual individual for whom the term "lynch law" derived its name has been disputed but the expression was in common use by the early nineteenth century as a description for the punishment of individuals without due process of law. David C. Roller and Robert W. Twyman, eds., *The Encyclopedia of Southern History* (Baton Rogue, 1979), 762–64.

69.4–5/97.19   to Esquire Watson's, on Bond Street] William H. Watson (?–1846) was a justice of the peace and prominent attorney, who lived at 76 Bond Street in Baltimore's Fells Point district in the late 1830s. He joined a Baltimore volunteer battalion as a captain during the war with Mexico. Watson quickly rose to the rank of lieutenant colonel but died in the Battle of Monterey in October 1846. *Matchett's Baltimore Director[y] . . . 1837–8,* 321; J. Thomas Scharf, *The Chronicles of Baltimore; Being a Complete History of "Baltimore Town" and Baltimore City from the Earliest Period to the Present Time* (Baltimore, 1874), 516, 517; Morris Radoff, ed., *The Old Line State: A History of Maryland* (Baltimore, 1971), 258.

69.28/98.21   Mr. Walter Price] Walter Price, whose family had long been engaged in shipbuilding, operated a shipyard on Fell Street south of Thames Street along the waterfront in the 1830s. By the latter part of the decade, a number of Baltimore shipbuilders had begun construction of fleet clippers which found their way into the international slave trade. Brazilian and Cuban slave traders prized these ships for their ability to evade the British blockade of Africa's Slave Coast. Benjamin Auld thought that Hugh Auld began working for Walter Price about 1834, after serving a short period as a master builder in partnership with Edward Harrison. Both Auld and Douglass worked for Price during the construction of at least three ships, which he covertly sold in Cuba or Brazil. *Matchett's Baltimore Director[y] . . . 1837–8,* 258; Benjamin F. Auld to Douglass, 27 September 1891, General Correspondence File, reel 6, frames 257–58, FD Papers, DLC; Howard I. Chapelle, *The Search for Speed Under Sail, 1700–1855* (New York, 1967), 297–312; Preston, *Young Frederick Douglass,* 145–47, 228n8.

69.31/98.25–26   to the most experienced calkers] Blacks, both free and slave, dominated the semi-skilled caulking occupation in Baltimore in the 1830s. The largest Baltimore slaveholders in the 1810s and 1820s included master shipbuilders who used slave caulkers in their own shipyards or hired them out to other shipbuilders. Though information on caulkers' wages in the 1830s is elusive, free black caulkers earned $1.50 per day in 1812 and during the height of wartime building had raised their daily wages to $1.67 1/4. Slave caulkers in the same year earned $1.25 to $1.31 1/4 per day. By 1838 free blacks had formed their own organization, the Caulker's Beneficial Association. Controlling the trade through the 1850s, by the end of that decade members of the Association were receiving $1.75 a day, while their apprentices were paid $1.50. The black caulkers owed their power to an alliance with the white shipwrights' association to control wages and conditions in shipbuilding. Blacks' hold on the trade was shaken when clashes erupted in 1858 between black Association members and white caulkers who were willing to accept lower wages. Blacks faced increasing discrimination in the 1860s, prompting black carpenters and caulkers to organize their own shipyard in 1866. In 1871 Douglass visited the Fells Point shipbuilding area and commented on the success of the black shipyard, noting that the "leading shipbuilders [of] forty years ago, are all gone, and have not even left their firms behind to perpetuate their names." Ironically, in 1836–38 some of the Fells Point shipyards where Douglass worked as a caulker built ships destined for the illegal African slave trade. [Washington, D.C.] *New National Era,* 6 July 1871; "Condition of the Coloured Population," 174; Charles G. Steffen, *The Mechanics of Baltimore: Workers and Politics in the Age of the Revolution, 1763–1812* (Urbana, Ill., 1984), 38–42; Barbara Jeanne Fields, *Slavery and Freedom on the Middle Ground: Maryland During the Nineteenth Century* (New Haven, 1985), 37–38, 40–62; Wright, *Free Negro in Maryland,* 154–55; Preston, *Young Frederick Douglass,* 145–47, 228; Bettye C. Thomas, "A Nineteenth Century Black Operated Shipyard, 1866–1884: Reflections upon its Inception and Ownership," *JNH,* 59 : 1–3 (January 1974); Della, "Problems of Negro Labor," 14–32.

71.6/101.6   the *underground railroad*] Northern blacks along with some sympathetic white supporters maintained a loose, clandestine system to clothe, feed, and shelter fugitive slaves from the South. In addition, "vigilance committees" operated in many northern communities to expose the presence of slave hunters and, on occasion, to rescue fugitives in the process of rendition to their masters. Larry Gara, *The Liberty Line: The Legend of the Underground Railroad* (Lexington, Ky., 1961), *passim.*

72.8/102.31–32   came to Baltimore to purchase his spring goods] This visit apparently occurred in March 1838. McFeely, *Frederick Douglass,* 64.

73.5/103.1   allow me to hire my time] In the urban South masters commonly hired their slaves out to other employers for specified periods of time. The less common practice of allowing their slaves to seek their own employment and pay their masters a specified sum grew over time, causing public fears that it would undermine the slave system itself. The Maryland legislature periodically passed legislation to control or abolish this practice, with little result. Richard C. Wade, *Slavery in the Cities: The South, 1820–1860* (New York, 1964), 38–54; Robert S. Starobin, *Industrial Slavery in the Old South* (New York, 1970), 128–37; Brackett, *Negro in Maryland,* 104–08, 174.

73.7–8/104.22–23   my attending a camp meeting] Douglass attended a camp meeting on the weekend of 4–5 August 1838. Revivals abounded in the South in the hot month of August, two more occurring near Baltimore the following weekend. Baltimore *Sun,* 8 August 1838; Preston, *Young Frederick Douglass,* 152–53.

73.38/106.2–3   Mr. Butler, at his ship-yard] Samuel Butler, a Baltimore ship carpenter, established a shipyard in 1819 in partnership with Robert Lambdin. Apparently Lambdin moved to St. Michaels, Talbot County, in 1830 while maintaining his financial interest in the yard. Butler remained to manage the operation throughout the 1830s during which time it launched the noted ship *Catherine.* Entries for Samuel Butler, a ship carpenter on Exeter Street, and Robert Lamden, a ship carpenter on City Block, appear in the 1840 city directory. *Matchett's Baltimore Director[y], for 1840–41* (Baltimore, n.p.), 86, 221; Chapelle, *Search for Speed Under Sail,* 302; John Philips Cranwell, ed., "Ship-Building on the Chesapeake: Recollections of Robert Dawson Lambdin," *MdHM,* 36 : 172 (June 1941); Lewis Addison Beck, "The *Seaman* and the *Seaman's Bride,* Baltimore Clipper Ships," *MdHM,* 51 : 305 (December 1956).

74.31/107.16–17   succeeded in reaching New York] Not until 1881 did Douglass publicly reveal the details of his escape from slavery. On 3 September 1838, he boarded a train bound from Baltimore to New York City. Douglass had borrowed the uniform and seaman's protection papers of a free black friend in Baltimore. Fortunately for Douglass the conductor did not check the description in the papers carefully and several white acquaintances on the train failed to recognize him. Douglass, "My Escape from Slavery," *Century Magazine,* 23 : 125–31 (November 1881), reprinted in idem, *Life and Times of Frederick Douglass* (1894; New York, 1941), 218–23.

75.36/109.16   Mr. DAVID RUGGLES] David Ruggles (1810–49), a free black man, was born and educated in Norwich, Connecticut. In 1827 he moved to New York, where he worked as a grocer. In 1834 he opened a printing and book shop that specialized in abolitionist literature. Ruggles became active in the New York antislavery movement, serving as a writer, lecturer, and traveling agent for the reform publication, *Emancipator and Journal of Public Morals.* He also was a conductor on the Underground Railroad, editor of the *Genius of Freedom* and the *Mirror of Liberty,* and secretary to the New York Vigilance Committee. His career in the antislavery movement ended abruptly in 1842 when temporary blindness, an illness that would plague him for the remainder of his life, forced him to curtail his activities and seek medical attention. At the Northampton Association of Education and Industry in Florence, Massachusetts, he underwent hydrotherapy, which temporarily relieved his blindness. Soon thereafter he began a new career as a hydrotherapist in Northampton, Massachusetts, treating such celebrated individuals as Sojourner Truth and William Lloyd Garrison. His reputation as a hydrotherapist gave him a prominence that rivaled his stature as an abolitionist. *NASS,* 20 December 1849; *Lib.,* 21 December 1849; New York *Evangelist,* 27 December

1849; *ASB,* 29 December 1849; *NS,* 1 February 1850; I. Garland Penn, *Afro-American Press and Its Editors* (Springfield, Mass., 1891), 118; Rayford W. Logan and Michael R. Winston, eds., *Dictionary of American Negro Biography* (New York, 1982), 536–38.

76.5/109.26–27   the memorable *Darg* case] The Darg case became a celebrated example of the persecution of abolitionists by established local authorities and proslavery newspapers. In August 1838, Thomas Hughes, a slave, escaped from his owner, John P. Darg of Arkansas, while the two were in New York City. Hughes also stole approximately $8,000 from Darg. He soon sought assistance from Isaac T. Hopper, a leading Quaker abolitionist. Suspicious of Hughes, Hopper housed him for only one night and soon thereafter learned of the stolen money. While Hopper did not want to harbor a felon, he also did not want to return a man to slavery. Seeking counsel from David Ruggles and other abolitionists, Hopper learned that Darg would free Hughes and not charge him if all of his money was returned. The abolitionists immediately commenced recovering the money but local police officials working with Darg were intent upon convicting Hopper, Ruggles, Barney Corse, and others as accomplices to the theft. Only after sixteen months of legal hearings and the brief imprisonment of both Ruggles and Corse did the prosecution abandon its case as hopeless. The outcome for Hughes is not known. New York *Colored American,* 15 September 1838, 26 January 1839; Isaac T. Hopper, *Exposition of the Proceedings of John P. Darg, Henry W. Merritt, and Others, in Relation to the Robbery of Darg, . . .* (New York, 1840); Dorothy B. Porter, "David M. Ruggles, An Apostle of Human Rights," *JNH,* 28 : 23–50 (January 1943).

76.18/110.13   the Rev. J. W. C. Pennington] Born into slavery as Jim Pembroke, James William Charles Pennington (1809–71) was owned by Frisbie Tilghman of Maryland's Eastern Shore until the age of twenty-one, when he fled north to the home of a Pennsylvania Quaker who taught him to read and write. Later Pennington found work in Long Island, attended night school and private tutorials, and taught black children in Newtown, New York, and New Haven, Connecticut. In 1840, after studying theology in New Haven, Pennington entered the Congregational ministry in Hartford, Connecticut, where he ministered to a black congregation. In 1847 he left to serve another black church in New York City. Committed to a variety of reform causes such as temperance, missionary work, and world peace, Pennington's greatest exertions were devoted to the antislavery movement. In 1843 he traveled to England as a delegate-at-large to the World's Anti-Slavery Convention in London and lectured throughout Europe. Fearing recapture after the passage of the Fugitive Slave Law, Pennington again traveled abroad in 1850, remaining there until a Hartford friend, John Hooker, was able to purchase his freedom. In addition to many sermons, addresses, and regular contributions to the *Anglo-African Magazine,* Pennington wrote *A Text Book of the Origins and History, &c., &c. of the Colored People* (1841), and an autobiography.

J. W. C. Pennington, *The Fugitive Blacksmith*, 3d ed. (London, 1850); *DANB*, 488–90; *DAB*, 14 : 441–42.

76.18–19/110.14   Mrs. Michaels] In the late 1830s, Mrs. D. Michaels owned and operated a boardinghouse in New York City at 33–36 Lespanard Street. She was married to Joseph Michaels who made floor mats and dealt in scrap metal, glass, and rags. [New York] *Weekly Advocate*, 14 January 1837; [New York] *Colored American*, 20 October 1838.

76.30/111.1–2   Mr. Shaw in Newport] George C. Shaw lived in Newport, Rhode Island. In 1840, he was the corresponding secretary for the Newport Anti-Slavery Society, a group supporting William Lloyd Garrison's New England Anti-Slavery Society. *Lib.*, 21 February 1840.

77.1/111.11   Joseph Ricketson] Joseph Ricketson (1771–1841) was the owner of a candle factory and oil refinery in New Bedford, Massachusetts. He also helped form the New Bedford Fire Society in 1807, served as a cashier and a director of the New Bedford Commercial Bank and as a trustee of the New Bedford Lyceum and Antheneum. Ricketson was a Quaker and committed to various reform and antislavery endeavors. Although a scrupulously honest and hard-working businessman, Ricketson's last years were spent close to poverty because of several serious business reversals. Henry H. Crapo, *The New Bedford Directory [for 1836]* (New Bedford, 1836), 18; idem, *The New Bedford Directory [for 1841]* (New Bedford, 1841), 30; *Vital Records of New Bedford, Massachusetts, to the Year 1850*, 3 vols. (Boston, 1932), 1 : 386, 3 : 138; Leonard Bolles Ellis, *History of New Bedford and Its Vicinity, 1602–1892* (Syracuse, 1892), 252, 509, 516, 517, 629; *Our County and Its People: Descriptive and Biographical Record of Bristol County, Massachusetts* (Boston, 1899), 351n1, 353, 406; Daniel Ricketson, *The History of New Bedford, Bristol County, Massachusetts* (New Bedford, 1858), 232–34; Hurd, *Bristol County*, 92, 105, 111.

77.2/111.11–12   William C. Taber] A descendant of one of the earliest settlers of New Bedford, Massachusetts, William C. Taber (1797–?) operated a profitable store which sold books, stationery, charts, and engravings. In the 1850s Taber led local businessmen in converting from whale oil for illumination to gas, coal oil, and kerosene and was the first president of the New Bedford Gas-Light Company. He was long active in the city's financial institutions, having served at different times as a director of both the Marine Bank and the New Bedford Institution For Savings. Taber also represented New Bedford at one point in the Massachusetts legislature. An ardent Quaker, Taber held the post of first clerk at the New Bedford Monthly Meeting for nineteen years. He married Hannah Shearman of the same town. Crapo, *New Bedford Directory [for 1836]*, 84; idem, *New Bedford Directory [for 1841]*, 19; idem, *New Bedford Directory [for 1845]*, 14; idem, *The New Bedford Directory [for 1856]* (New Bedford, 1856), 164; Hurd, *Bristol County*, 91–92, 105, 148; Ellis, *New Bedford*, 422, 469, 475, 517, 566, 638, 721; *Our County*, 353–54, 372–73, 416–17, and "Personal References," 343.

77.7/111.19   Mr. and Mrs. Johnson] Owners of a confectionery shop and a thriving catering business, Nathan Johnson (?–1880) and Mary Page Johnson (?–c. 1870) were two of the most prominent blacks in New Bedford, Massachusetts. They had helped and housed black fugitives on many occasions and Nathan had long been an active abolitionist, serving as a manager of the American Anti-Slavery Society at one point. In 1832, Nathan represented New Bedford at the National Negro Convention in Philadelphia and in 1837 he was one of three local African Americans chosen to question all county political candidates as to their view on slavery and the slave trade. Johnson left New Bedford for California in 1849 and did not return until 1871 after his wife, who had remained behind, died. [New York] *Colored American,* 18 November 1837; Henry H. Crapo, *The New Bedford Directory [for 1838]* (New Bedford, 1838), 77; *Vital Records of New Bedford,* 2 : 309, 396; Barbara Clayton and Kathleen Whitley, *Guide to New Bedford* (Chester, Conn., 1979), 134–35; Merrill and Ruchames, *Garrison Letters,* 2 : 712; McFeely, *Frederick Douglass,* 76, 77, 78, 84.

77.26–27/112.15   the "Lady of the Lake,"] Sir Walter Scott (1771–1832) published *The Lady of the Lake* in Edinburgh in 1810. Ellen Douglas and her father, Lord James of Douglas, are the principal characters. *The Poetic Works of Sir Walter Scott,* 12 vols. (Edinburgh, 1880,) 8 : 8, 63, 75–76; Paul Harvey, ed., *The Oxford Companion to English Literature,* 4th ed. (New York, 1967), 458, 735–36.

79.1–2/114.28   " . . . and he took me in"] Douglass paraphrases Matt. 25 : 35.

80.8/116.25   the "Liberator."] Pioneer abolitionist William Lloyd Garrison published the weekly Boston newspaper, the *Liberator,* from 1831 to 1865. The paper advocated women's rights, temperance, pacifism, and a variety of other reforms in addition to immediate emancipation. Thomas, *The Liberator,* 127–28, 436; *DAB,* 7 : 168–72.

80.23–24/117.17   an anti-slavery convention at Nantucket] A reference to the same abolitionist convention at Atheneum Hall in Nantucket, Massachusetts, on 10–12 August 1841, which Garrison described in his Preface to the *Narrative.* Douglass spoke in favor of a resolution condemning northern white racial prejudice on 11 August. Douglass had earlier addressed antislavery meetings in New Bedford, Massachusetts. *Lib.,* 29 March, 9 July, 20 August 1841.

81.16/118.26–119.1   "stealing . . . in."] Robert Pollok, *The Course of Time, A Poem* (Boston, 1843), Book 8, lines 616–18: "He was a man / Who stole the livery of the court of heaven, / To serve the Devil in."

82.26/120.13–28   Strength to the spoiler thine?] With minor punctuation changes, Douglass quotes the first four stanzas of John Greenleaf Whittier's 1835 poem, "Clerical Oppressors." *Poetical Works of John Greenleaf Whittier,* 3 : 38–39.

82.28–83.12/121.1–30   "They bind . . . of hypocrisy and iniquity."] An adaptation of Jesus' denunciation of the scribes and Pharisees in Matt. 23 : 4–28.

84.1–84.3/123.4–6   "Shall I . . . a nation as this?"] Jer. 5 : 9, 29.

85.5/124.15   Bashan bull] A paraphrase of Ps. 22 : 12.

Reader Responses, 1845–49

Douglass reproduced many of the newspaper and periodical reviews of the *Narrative* in an appendix to later editions of the book, entitled "Critical Notices." What follows are other contemporary reviews located by the editors. Because many of these reviews contain lengthy excerpts from the *Narrative* text, they have been abridged when a quoted passage exceeds one hundred words. Deleted passages are indicated by means of ellipses and a notation of the page and line location of the omitted text in the 1845 Boston edition. Lengthy portions of these reviews assessing or describing books other than the *Narrative* have been deleted by means of ellipses.

FREDERICK DOUGLASS. [Anon.]. Lynn *Pioneer,* n.d., reprinted in *Lib.,* 30 May 1845.

My readers will be delighted to learn that Frederick Douglass—the fugitive slave—has at last concluded his narrative. All who know the wonderful gifts of friend Douglass know that his narrative must, in the nature of things, be written with great power. It is so indeed. It is the most thrilling work which the American press ever issued—*and the most important.* If it does not open the eyes of this people, they must be petrified into eternal sleep.

The picture it presents of slavery is too horrible to look upon, and yet it is but a faint *picture* of what to millions is a vivid *life.* It is evidently drawn with a nice eye, and the coloring is chaste and subdued, rather than extravagant or overwrought. Thrilling as it is, and full of the most burning eloquence, it is yet simple and unimpassioned. Its eloquence is the eloquence of truth, and so is as simple and touching as the impulses of childhood. There are passages in it which would brighten the reputation of any living author,—while the book, as a whole, judged as a mere work of art would widen the fame of Bunyan or De Foe. A spirit of the loftiest integrity, and a vein of the purest religious sentiment, runs through its pages, and it must leave on every mind a deep conviction of the author's strength of mind and purity of heart. I predict for it a sale of at least twenty thousand in this country, and equally great in Europe. It will leave a mark upon this age which the busy finger of time will deepen at every touch. It will generate a public sentiment in this nation, in the presence of which our pro-slavery laws and constitutions shall be like chaff in the presence of fire. It contains the spark which will kindle up the smoldering embers of freedom in a million souls, and light up our whole continent with the flames of liberty. Great efforts will be made in the name of the Constitution and the Bible, of James Polk and the Apostle Paul, to suppress it: but it will run through this nation from house to house, and from heart to heart, as the wild fire, *finding wings in every wind which blows,* flies across the tall and boundless prairies. Its stirring incidents will fasten themselves on the eager minds of the youth of this country with hooks of steel. The politics of the land will stand abashed before it, while her more corrupt religion will wish to sink back into the hot womb which gave it birth. It will fall in among the churches and state-houses of the land like a bomb-shell, and those who madly undertake to pick it to pieces will share the fate of that poor New-Yorker who attempted something of the kind on a bomb-shell picked up on the shores of Jersey, i.e., they will be blowed to atoms at the first blow.—*Lynn Pioneer.*

NARRATIVE OF DOUGLASS. A. M. *Lib.,* 6 June 1845.

DEAR GARRISON: I received, yesterday, through the kindness of some friend in Boston, the Narrative of Frederick Douglass—his *multum in parto.* His account is brief, though admirable for its comprehensiveness. Whole volumes are therein contained, it being replete with the strong features of that most odious monster Slavery. The scenes through which he passed are exhibited with a clearness, and stamped upon the mind with a strength, which ever accompanies a strong, commanding evidence of truth.

My language is inadequate; therefore I shall not attempt to describe my feelings, as I went with the Narrator through his twenty years' experience in slavery.

I have wept over the pages of Dickens' 'Oliver Twist'—I have moistened with my tears whole chapters of Eugene Sue's Mysteries of Paris—but Douglass's history of the wrongs of the American Slave, brought, not tears—no, tears refused me their comfort—its home truths crowded in such quick succession, and entered so deep into the chambers of my soul, as to entirely close the relief valve. For I am an American woman, and for American women I bleed. I groaned in the agony of my spirit, and said, 'Oh, Lord! how long shall these things be? How long shall the spoiler mark his prey?' I have many times heard the author vividly portray the evils of slavery. I have often heard him recount with deep feeling the endless wrongs they are made to endure—but, oh! never before have I been brought so completely in sympathy with the slave—never before have I felt myself so completely bound with them—never before have I so fully realized the doctrine of our blessed Savior, 'whatsoever ye do unto the least one of these, ye do it unto me.'

May his Narrative incite us to renewed diligence in our labors for the slave! May the author become a mighty instrument to the pulling down of the strong holds of iniquity, and to the establishing of righteousness in our land!

Affectionately thine for the slave,

A. M.

P.S.—I know of no way in which I can better serve the cause of the oppressed, than to enclose $5 to the author of the book, for the extension of its publicity.

Albany, May 24, 1845.

☞ Our correspondent chooses to affix to her letter only the initials of her name; but we know her to be a most faithful friend of the oppressed. Copies of the Narrative, to the extent of her donation, shall be distributed with judgment and care.

In this connexion, we make other extracts from this remarkable work. The following sketch of the effects of the holidays which are granted to the slaves, is highly instructive, as revealing the arts of the slaveholders to make their victims disgusted with the idea of perpetual liberty:

The days between Christmas . . . [74.2–77.2] . . . a very common one.

How startling, yet how true is the description of the religion of the United States, given in the following extract:—

What I have said . . . [118.8–120.12] . . . the semblance of paradise.

Dark and terrible as . . . [121.31–122.26] . . . my duty to testify.

NARRATIVE OF THE LIFE OF FREDERICK DOUGLASS, AN AMERICAN SLAVE. Margaret Fuller. New York *Daily Tribune,* 10 June 1845.

NARRATIVE OF THE LIFE OF FREDERICK DOUGLASS, AN AMERICAN SLAVE. Written by himself. Boston: Published at the Anti-Slavery Office. No. 25 Cornhill. 1845.

Frederick Douglass has been for some time a prominent member of the Abolition party. He is said to be an excellent speaker—can speak from a thorough personal experience—and has upon the audience, beside, the influence of a strong character and uncommon talents. In the book before us he has put into the story of his life the thoughts, the feelings and the adventures that have been so affecting through the living voice; nor are they less so from the printed page. He has had the courage to name the persons, times and places, thus exposing himself to obvious danger, and setting the seal on his deep convictions as to the religious need of speaking the whole truth. Considered merely as a narrative, we have never read one more simple, true, coherent, and warm with genuine feeling. It is an excellent piece of writing, and on that score to be prized as a specimen of the powers of the Black Race, which Prejudice persists in disputing. We prize highly all evidence of this kind, and it is becoming more abundant. The Cross of the Legion of Honor has just been conferred in France on Dumas and Soulie, both celebrated in the paths of light literature. Dumas, whose father was a General in the French Army, is a Mulatto: Soulie, a Quadroon. He went from New Orleans, where, though to the eye a white man, yet, as known to have African blood in his veins, he could never have enjoyed the privileges due to a human being. Leaving the Land of Freedom, he found himself free to develope the powers that God had given.

Two wise and candid thinkers,—the Scotchman, Kinment, prematurely lost to this country, of which he was so faithful and generous a student, and the late Dr. Channing,—both thought that the African Race had in them a peculiar element, which, if it could be assimilated with those imported among us from Europe, would give to genius a development, and to the energies of character a balance and harmony beyond what has been seen heretofore in the history of the world. Such an element is indicated in their lowest estate by a talent for melody, a ready skill at imitation and adaptation, an almost indestructible elasticity of nature. It is to be remarked in the writings both of Soulie and Dumas, full of faults but glowing with plastic life and fertile in invention. The same torrid energy and saccharine fulness may be felt in the writings of this Douglass, though his life being one of action or resistance, was less favorable to *such* powers than one of a more joyous flow might have been.

The book is prefaced by two communications,—one from Garrison, and one from Wendell Phillips. That from the former is in his usual over emphatic style. His motives and his course have been noble and generous. We look upon him with high respect, but he has indulged in violent invective and denunciation till he has spoiled the temper of his mind. Like a man who has been in the habit of screaming himself hoarse to make the deaf hear, he can no longer pitch his voice on a key agreeable to common ears. Mr. Phillips's remarks are equally decided, without this exaggeration in the tone Douglass himself seems very just and temperate. We feel that his view, even of those who have injured him most, may be relied upon. He knows how to allow for motives and influences. Upon the subject of Religion, he speaks with great force, and not more than our own sympathies can respond to. The inconsistencies of Slaveholding professors of religion cry to Heaven. We are not disposed to detest, or refuse communion with them. Then blindness is but one form of that prevalent fallacy which substitutes a creed for a faith, a ritual for a life. We have seen too much of this system of atonement not to know that those who adopt it often began with good intentions, and are at any rate, in their mistakes worthy of the deepest pity. But that is no reason why the truth should not be uttered trumpet tongued, about the thing. "Bring no more vain oblations": sermons must daily be preached anew on that text. Kings, five hundred years ago built Churches with the spoils of War; Clergymen to-day command Slaves to obey a Gospel which they will not allow them to read, and call themselves Christians amid the curses of their fellow men.—The world ought to get on a little faster than that, if there be really any principle of improvement in it. The Kingdom of Heaven may not at the beginning have dropped seed larger than a mustard-seed, but even from that we had a right to expect a fuller growth than can be believed to exist, when we read such a book as this of Douglass. Unspeakably affecting is the fact that he never saw his mother at all by day-light.

"I do not recollect of ever seeing my mother by the light of day. She was with me in the night. She would lie down with me; and get me to sleep, but long before I waked she was gone."

The following extract presents a suitable answer to the hacknied argument drawn by the defender of Slavery from the songs of the Slave, and is also a good specimen of the powers of observation and manly heart of the writer. We wish that every one may read his book and see what a mind might have been stifled in bondage,—what a man may be subjected to the insults of spendthrift dandies, or the blows of mercenary brutes, in whom there is no whiteness except of the skin, no humanity except in the outward form, and of whom the Avenger will not fail yet to demand—"Where is thy brother?"

"The home plantation of . . . [12.10–15.15] . . . by the same emotion."

☞Copies of the work may be had of W. H. Graham, Tribune Buildings. Price, 50 cents.

NARRATIVE OF THE LIFE OF FREDERICK DOUGLASS. [Maria Weston] C[hapman]. *NASS,* 12 June 1845.

Narrative of the life of Frederick Douglass, written by himself. Boston. Anti-Slavery Office, 23 Cornhill, pp. 125.

This book ought be read by all before whose mental blindness visions of happy slaves continually dance. It is the story of the life of a man of great intellectual power, in the very circumstances so often alluded to by the advocates for the longer continuance of Slavery;—in the Northernmost of the slave States, and under kind masters. No wonder that those States patronize the Colonization Society for the removal of characters so dangerous to the perpetuity of Slavery. Once, the kind master made a merit of giving *such* a slave his freedom on condition of consenting to go to Liberia. *Nous avons changé tout cela;* the anti-slavery enterprise has drawn to itself the most effectual advocates from the victims of the system it opposes. It has, while shaking that system to its foundation, been unavoidably and incidentally the means of freeing and educating in their own native country, more of these single victims, than the Colonization Society, while doing its best to uphold Slavery, has been able to doom to African exile.

All pro-slavery men, all Abolitionists, and all those who are merely indifferent should buy this book. It will convince the first class, confirm the second, and by the mere interest of its delineation, amply satisfy the third. It is illustrated by a remarkably good engraving of the author. The condition of the infant and of the aged slave, the sorrowful songs of bondage so often quoted by Northern men as an excuse for standing aloof from the Anti-Slavery enterprise, and the swell of heart with which the thought of freedom fills the bosom of the fugitive, are all dwelt upon with that deep impressment which artistical skill strives in vain with melancholy experience, to equal. "I never saw my mother in the day-time. She used to travel in the evening twelve miles to see me, and return before morning." Shall not the simple pathos of this fact, one of a class of facts necessary in Slavery, raise the soul of every mother that reads it?

We have no space for extracts this week, nor do we wish to lessen the value of the narrative to purchasers by forestalling its deeply interesting contents. It is accompanied by a letter from Wendell Phillips, which so truly expresses our own feelings, that we subjoin it.—c.

FREDERICK DOUGLASS—HORRORS OF SLAVERY. [Anon.]. *Religious Spectator,* n.d., reprinted in *NASS,* 7 August 1845.

We had a book put into our hands the other day, purporting to be the autobiography of a slave, who had escaped from bondage, by the name of Frederick Douglass, and we frankly acknowledge, that had it not been for our confidence in the good judgment of the friend from whom the book came, who we knew had little sympathy with the class of technical Abolitionists, we might possibly have laid it aside, without reading it, from perceiving that it was published under the patronage of several individuals, whose course on the subject of Slavery we have never regarded as either politic or right.

On looking into the book, however, we have found it to contain one of the most remarkable and thrilling narratives that have ever fallen under our eye; and though there are some things in it which we regret, particularly the strong expressions against professing Christians at the South, yet we see nothing to cast even a shade of doubt over the authenticity of the narrative, even in respect to its minutest details. We should indeed, have made a single exception to this remark—that is, we should have doubted the practicability of such a book being produced by a poor runaway slave, had it not been that we are assured that his efforts as a public speaker are quite equal to what he has here shown himself to be as a writer; and we have it upon good authority, that his lectures are characterized by as able reasoning, as genuine wit, and as bold and stirring appeals, as we almost ever find in connection with the highest intellectual culture.

Unless we greatly mistake, this small work to which we are referring is destined to exert a mighty influence in favor of the great cause of Emancipation. We acknowledge for ourselves, that we might have heard the system of Slavery reasoned against abstractly, no matter how ably, and no matter how long, and yet we could not have been so deep impressed with it as an outrage against humanity, as we have been by reading this simple story. It is especially fitted to correct a too prevalent error that Slavery *in itself* is not deserving of any severe reprobation—that it is only the abuses of the system with which we have a right to find fault.

And we acknowledge ourselves to be among those who look for its removal at no distant day. It seems to us as clear as the shining of the sun, that there are signs of the times which betoken a speedy and mighty revolution on this subject. The march of public opinion is evidently in favor of emancipation; and opposition can no more arrest it than it can arrest the motion of the planets. There is a spirit awake throughout all the North, that cries out for universal Freedom, and all the agitation and opposition that we witness at the South is but the heaving of the same spirit under different circumstances. It tells of a terrible conflict between selfishness and conscience, which will certainly terminate at last in favor of the better principle.

What particular mode of abolishing Slavery from our land, Providence may ordain—whether it shall be by bringing the South to bow to the high dictates of conscience and of duty, or by suffering the slaves themselves to become minisers of vengeance toward their oppressors, or by some other means, of which we know nothing—we pretend not to say; but the event of ultimate emancipation, in some way, we consider as absolutely certain; and while we would have all labor to bring it about, we would have all take counsel of the spirit of prudence, as well as philanthropy, in respect to the channel in which their labors shall be directed.

GLEAMS OF LIGHT. A Citizen of Maryland. *Lib.,* 26 September 1845.

A Baltimore correspondent of the Albany Patriot writes to the editor of that paper a letter, which contains the following interesting and encouraging statements:

We can buy anti-slavery documents now in this city at Shurtz & Wilde's Periodical Bookstore. The following are for sale: Review of West India Emancipation, by a Virginian; Bascom's and Peck's Pamphlets; Wayland and Fuller's Letters; and 'Slavery in Maryland,' by John L. Carey of this city, Editor of the Baltimore American. Frederick Douglass's Narrative is now circulating and being read in this city, and five hundred copies are still wanted here. They would be read with avidity, and do much good. And thus Garrison, who is proscribed here in person, would be heard in Baltimore, in the burning language of his Preface to the Narrative.

One word in regard to the truth of the narrative. I have made some inquiry, and have reason to believe his statements are true. Col. Edward Lloyd's relatives are my relatives! Let this suffice for the present. There is one particular slave mentioned in the book that I have often heard spoken of; that is, poor 'Jake,' who was bought by my brother-in-law, a nephew of Col. L. The northern people fight slavery at a distance: I have to fight it every day, and every where, in all the highways and byways of life. I board with a slaveholder, and am waited on by a slave, and see all the laziness and inefficiency on the part of the whites, and the *puttering,* do-nothing, sulky habits of the poor blacks. Every thing about slavery is mean, dirty, lazy, hateful, and *undignified.* There is nothing about it to promote self-respect, or any other noble or virtuous feeling.

Dr. Stewart, a noble-minded philanthropist, the owner of 150 slaves and a plantation, is now writing a pamphlet on slavery and emancipation, and in favor of the freedom of the slaves. Dr. S. is a brother of Gen. Stewart of this city, of whom your correspondent some months since stated, that he sold a colored woman by whom he had children with her offspring, his own flesh and blood, to Hope H. Slatter. No wonder Dr. Stewart is disgusted with slavery, when his own brother is such a monster of iniquity.

We are full of hope in this State. The 'Saturday Visiter' is our leader. Pray for us, till hope is lost in victory.

A CITIZEN OF MARYLAND.

NARRATIVE OF THE LIFE OF FREDERICK DOUGLASS—AN AMERI-CAN SLAVE:—Dublin: WEBB & CHAPMAN, pp. 128. 1845. [Anon.]. *British Friend,* 3:174 (November 1845), reprinted in *Lib.,* 26 December 1845.

WE would especially call the attention of our readers to this deeply interesting little volume. It is impossible to read it and not have every sympathy awakened in behalf of our fellow beings, held as "chattels," in that land of professed Republicans and Christians—the United States of America. The reader is impressed with a feeling that the *slave-holding* portions of that country are yet in ignorance of the first principles of liberty, of justice, and Christianity. Truth seems stamped on every page of this narrative. If it be true, as no reader can doubt that it is, how fearful the responsibility of the General Assembly of the Free Church of Scotland, of the American Board of Commissioners for Foreign Missions, and of all professedly religious bodies that stand sponsor for the Christianity of American Slave-holders! We earnestly entreat all our readers, and every abolitionist, and friend of justice, and humanity, in this kingdom, to obtain and read this little work. It will do more to give them correct views of American Republicanism, and American Religion, as these are developed in the Slave-States, and do more to give them just views of duty in reference to the Slave-holding churches, and minsters of America—than a thousand lecturers could do.

This is a plain, but eloquent narrative of the experience of a man who was born and trained to regard himself, and to be regarded by all around him, as a "chattel." In reading it, one sees before him the fearful tossings and heavings of an immortal soul, herded with beasts, and compelled to grope about, feeling after God among reptiles. The reader feels himself in communion with immortality—sunk to a thing—with the image of God turned into a brute. One feels that the distinction between Christianity and the Slave-holding Religion of America, is justly and forcibly drawn. It is impossible for the American Slaves not to be infidels to the religion of their masters. Every reader of this narrative must feel, that a religion which can receive a Slave-holder to its loving and honoured embrace, cannot be true Christianity—cannot be of God. This book clearly indicates that the only way peacefully to abolish American Slavery is, to exclude all Slave-holders from all respectable and Christian society.

FREDERICK DOUGLASS, THE FUGITIVE SLAVE. [Anon.]. Bristol *Mercury,* 6 January 1846, reprinted in *NASS,* 5 March 1846.

But little is yet known in England respecting this remarkable man. A few years ago he was suffering under the horrors of hopeless slavery, in Maryland, United States. Happily for him, and probably for his suffering fellow-slaves, he escaped from his cruel bondage to the free States of America, where he remained in obscurity for a year or two, working at any employment he could procure, exposed only to the contempt and indignity with which *independent* and republican America, even its *free* States, treats that portion of its population, however well educated and refined they may be, whose misfortune it is to have any color in their skin. After a time, on a casual attendance upon an anti-slavery meeting, Douglass ventured to make himself known to some members of an abolition society. The Abolitionists found him to be a young man of unusual ability, of sound judgment, serious, of excellent character, and with a degree of cultivation of mind quite extraordinary for the opportunities he had while in the slave States, where teaching slaves to read, and even giving them Bibles, subject the offenders to severe penalties! The American Anti-Slavery Society having ascertained that, in addition to the dependence that could be placed upon all of Frederick Douglass's statements, he had a peculiar facility of expressing himself with fluency and correctness, employed him as a lecturer upon Slavery, the evils of which he was able to expose from personal experience. His lectures occasioned much excitement in the free States, and much indignation, when his statements had gone southward, in the slave States from whence he had escaped. Doubts having been circulated as to the truth of the appalling revelations he made, he resolved to publish a narrative of his life, giving the names of the masters under whom he had lived, and dates and events which would at once prove the correctness of his account, and suppressing only some names and circumstances connected with his escape, which, if known, would have involved some of his benefactors in difficulties, and have diminished the facility of escape of other slaves by similar means. Wendell Phillips, Esq. an eminent barrister of Massachusetts, and an active Abolitionist, to whom Douglass showed his narrative in MS., advised him not to publish it, as it would probably lead to successful efforts for his being re-taken, and returned to Slavery, a fugitive slave not being safe even in the free States, their laws compelling them to give up such runaways if claimed by their owners. Douglass, however, with that courage which has distinguished him throughout his career, printed the narrative, and most rapid was its sale in America. Prudence, however, as well as other powerful motives, decided him upon taking the occasion of the excitement produced by the wide dissemination of his narrative, to leave America for awhile, and visit Great Britain. In accordance with this intention he sailed in the *Cambria,* Government steamer, from Boston, last August, in company with Mr. Buffum, a highly respectable man, an Abolitionist, and with the Hutchinsons, a remarkable family of singers, consisting of four brothers and one sister, who have been performing in Liverpool, and occasioning much interest by the originality of their music and their anti-slavery songs. The party arrived in Liverpool, August 28th, and Douglass immediately repaired to Dublin, where, as well as in Cork and at Belfast, (where he at present is,) he has been lecturing to thronged assemblies.

The papers contained an account of a fracas on board the *Cambria* when Douglass came to England. The passengers having ascertained what an interesting man they had with them, expressed a desire to hear him give some history of himself and of Slavery, and the captain saw no reason for objecting to their wishes. Notice having been given of what was to take place, that the passengers might attend or absent themselves as they wished, Douglass began to speak, but he had not proceeded far, before he was interrupted by two American gentlemen accusing him of falsehood. Douglass, to prove his statements, began to read the laws of the slave States; the Americans, however, would not allow him to proceed, and threatened to throw him overboard. An Irish gentleman assured them that any attempt at violence would be a dangerous expedient for their own safety. The disturbance rose so high, that Captain Judkins was at length compelled to declare he would put in irons any one who ventured upon an act of aggression. The Abolitionists in Massachusetts have been voting resolutions of thanks to Captain Judkins for his manliness on the occasion, and the papers in the interest of the slaveholders abuse him, and threaten him with no more American passengers for allowing their nation to be insulted.

Douglass's lectures are said to be very eloquent. He is now finishing some at Belfast, where the chapels of the Wesleyan Methodists, Independents, and Presbyterians have been thrown open to him. His next visit will be to Glasgow, and he will probably come to Bristol (an invitation from which place he has accepted) in the spring.

A more deeply interesting "Narrative" than Douglass's can hardly ben conceived. An edition of it has been reprinted by a warm friend of his in Dublin, and is being sold chiefly among private friends, without any advertisements or commission charges, for Douglass's benefit. A few copies have come to Bristol. Douglass, whose feelings are very independent, hopes to support himself while in England solely by the sale of the "Narrative."

He states in his preface to the Irish edition that his inducements to come to Great Britain were—First, to be absent from America during the sale of his book, on account of his personal safety, "lest his *owner* should adopt measures to restore him to his '*patriarchal care*.'" Second, that he might improve his stock of knowledge by visiting this kingdom. Third, chiefly to extend in England an enlightened knowledge of the contaminating and degrading influences of American Slavery upon both slaveholders and slaves, and thus excite such an intelligent interest in behalf of his suffering countrymen as may react upon America, and aid in the eventual extinction of this sinful institution.

Mr. Douglass speaks with much feeling of the gratification it has been to him, during his limited experience of travelling in this country, to move about from place to place in public conveyances without being despised and insulted in consequence of his color, and of his meeting everywhere with that respect which is due from man to man; and he has drawn a strong contrast on this point, between the freedom of monarchical England, and the thraldom of republican America.

NARRATIVE OF FREDERICK DOUGLASS. [Anon.]. Albany *Patriot,* reprinted in *Lib.,* 20 February 1846.

In the Patriot of Dec. 31, we published an article from the Delaware Republican, signed 'A. C. C. Thompson,' in which the truthfulness of Douglass's narrative is denied—to which we subjoined a remark or two of our own, and also some extracts of letters recently received in this country from Ireland, showing the opinion formed there in relation to the character of Douglass, and his abilities as a man—the latter having been impugned and denied by Mr. Thompson, no less than his veracity.

We have received from Mr. Thompson the following letter, enclosing a slip cut from some newspaper, containing the four certificates which we insert at his request. The certificates are evidently cut out of the body of some article, the whole of which he seems unwilling we should see. Why did he not send us the paper?

WILMINGTON, (Del.) Jan. 12, 1846.

To the Proprietor of the Albany Patriot:

DEAR SIR:—In your paper of Dec. 31, I notice that you have copied my communication to the Delaware Republican, upon which you make some very worthy comments. You say:

'Mr. Thompson will have to produce some better testimony than his own opinion of the general religious character of slaveholders, before he can disturb the stern facts recorded by Frederick Douglass.'

Herein you grossly misrepresent me, as you do every thing connected with slavery. It would not answer your purposes to publish plain truth upon all occasions, as it would not coincide with your perverted opinions.

What I intended by my communication in the Delaware Republican, was only to prove the assertions in the narrative of Frederick Douglass to be false, which I knew to be so. But as you do not consider the evidence of one respectable white man as creditable as the assertions of a ranting negro, I will produce other testimony than my own, from gentlemen of respectable standing, to show you that the assertions of this negro Douglass are nothing more than gross misrepresentations. Now for the testimony.

Extracts from the letter of Mr. Auld, the master of Frederick Douglass.

'He states that I used to flog and starve him; but I can put my hand upon my Bible, and with a clear conscience swear that I never struck him in my life, nor caused any person else to do it. I never allowanced one of my slaves: but the tale would not have answered their (the Abolitionists,) purposes, unless the slave had been starved, or nearly whipped to death.

Can it be believed that Mr. Gore should deliberately shoot one of Col. Lloyd's slaves, and still be retained in his employ? Col. Lloyd was not the man to suffer such an imposition, and I know the whole story to be false.

I placed him in Baltimore to learn a trade, and told him that if he would behave himself and learn his trade well, when he was 25 years old I would emancipate him; and he promised me faithfully that he would do it. He does not say one word about this in his Narrative, as it would not have answered to have mentioned so much truth.'

Extract from the letter of Dr. A. C. Thompson.

CAMBRIDGE, Dorchester Co., Md.

'I always knew Thomas Auld to be a worthy and pious man, but he was never a class leader nor an exhorter.'

Letter from Dr. James Dawson.

ST. MICHAELS, Talbot Co., Md.

DEAR SIR:—I have seen and read a Narrative of the life of negro Frederick Douglass, purporting to have been written by himself; (doubtful) in which the character of Mr. Thomas Auld is most foully aspersed. I lived in the family of Mr. Auld at the time when this cruel and inhuman conduct is said to have taken place; and so far as my knowledge of himself and an acquaintance with his domestic affairs goes, (which was thorough) I can unhesitatingly pronounce it a base and villanous fabrication. I could say much more in confirmation of the falsity of the charges, but deem it unnecessary.

Yours, &c.

JAMES DAWSON.

A. C. C. THOMPSON, Wilmington.

Letter from Mr. Thomas Graham.

ST. MICHAELS, Talbot Co., Md.

Mr. A. C. C. THOMPSON:

DEAR SIR:—During Mr. Auld's entire residence in St. Michaels, he was my immediate neighbor, and the intercourse between our families gave me an opportunity of knowing the situation and condition of his servants. The statements of Frederick Douglass respecting Mr. Auld's treatment to them, is, in every word, most basely false. They were well fed and well clothed; never allowanced in food, but had as much as they could eat.

Mr. Auld's indulgence to his servants is well known throughout this neighborhood; and I have no hesitancy in saying that I know beyond the possibility of a doubt that the whole statement relating to this gentleman is most ungrateful and false. And from my acquaintance with other individuals accused, and from their unimpeachable Christian character, I believe the entire narrative of accusations to be a manufactured compound of falsehoods.

I lived within 30 feet of Mr. Auld's residence for several years, and during that time his conduct to his servants was more like an indulgent father than a master. He has invariably emancipated his slaves when they arrived at the age of 25 years, and their services to him were almost voluntary.

THOMAS GRAHAM.

Letter from L. Dodson.

St. MICHAELS, Talbot Co., Md.

Mr. THOMPSON:

DEAR SIR:—If it will be of any service to you, in your attempt to expose the base falsehoods contained in the 'Narrative of Frederick Douglass,' I will say, that so far as his narrations refer to Mr. Auld's treatment toward his servants, they are most palpably untrue. For nine years I was connected with Mr. Auld's family; the greater part of the time boarding with him; and I speak from personal knowledge, when I say that Fred. and all his servants were treated well. Indeed, I never knew him to strike, much less abuse them.

I knew Fred. well; we were boys together, in the same family, and his narrations are little less than gross misrepresentations.

The cruelties which are charged upon Mr. Covy, Gore, and others, are equally false; for every man acquainted with these gentlemen will say that they are incapable of such offences against humanity.

You may confidently hold up this 'Narrative' as the latest and perhaps the most unpardonable effort of Abolitionism. If 'truth is mighty and must prevail,' I have no doubt that this attempt like many others will prove ineffectual.

Yours truly,

L. DODSON.

If you are not carried away by prejudice, I think the evidence I have adduced from these gentlemen's letters should be sufficient to convince you that 'the stern facts recorded by Mr. Douglass' are very stern falsehoods. I care not how great a man you make of him—if he is 'one of God's best gifts to the world'—yet with all his greatness, he is a liar. And surely you will never again attempt to palm his narrative upon the public for truth.

I do not wish to be understood as advocating slavery, for I am convinced that it is a great evil—but not sinful under ordinary circumstances. Neither do I attempt to vindicate the religious character of the slaveholders of the South; for it is evident that there are bad men among them, as well as in every other community. But tell me, is the Southerner to be deprecated because he owns a slave, more than the Northern Abolitionist, who, in defiance of all law and honor, steals a slave from his lawful owner, and will then manufacture an incredible story without the least shadow of truth, to defame the character of slaveholders? If such is your opinion, you have studied some code of morality that I have never seen.

If you wish to persuade the Southerners to abolish slavery, you must talk to them in a more sensible manner; you must not fabricate such horrid tales of murder, man-stealing, &c., as you have done heretofore. And perhaps when you shall be cured of this evil spirit, then the slaveholders will have some confidence in your abilities to advise. But be assured that all the venom that you can disgorge will never add one laurel to your brow, but on the contrary, will engender jealousy and hatred, and make the condition of the slave much worse.

Yours, very respectfully,

A. C. C. THOMPSON.

We publish with the utmost willingness the above letter and certificates, not only because it is fair play to let the slaveholders, as well as other evil doers, be heard in their own defence, but also because we want no better confirmation of the general credibility and truth of Douglass's narrative than such certificates afford.

If any of our readers have never read the Narrative, we wish they would do so. It purports to be a plain statement of facts and circumstances which occurred to the writer, or within his immediate knowledge—giving names and incidents, and a part of the time, dates, with minute particularity. Scenes of common and ordinary interest exemplifying many of the peculiar characteristics of the slave system as it prevails in Maryland, are detailed, and others of great cruelty, and inhumanity are narrated. Of a great part of this cruelty, Douglass was the victim, and of many other instances he was the witness. There is a peculiarity of detail, and other internal evidence of veracity, which, we repeat, will require something more than Mr. Thompson's opinion that the story is false, or the certificates of the good character of Mr. Auld which he has published, to overthrow. In all the above certificates, formidable as they may seem, there is but one distinct fact stated by Douglass contradicted. Douglass says, page 57:

'I had lived with him (Auld) nine months, during which time he had given me a number of severe whippings, all to no good purpose.

This Mr. Auld in his certificate denies. He says he never struck him in his life, 'nor caused any person else to do it.' It must be borne in mind, that Mr. Auld is the accused person, and is testifying in his own behalf—so it is a question of credibility. Douglass says he was whipped and ill-fed by Auld. Auld denies it—pleads not guilty, as accused people generally do. All the other certificates, and the things stated in them, amount to this, and this only—that the certifiers have too good an opinion of Mr. Auld, Mr. Gore, and Mr. Covy, to believe they would do the inhuman and abominable things Douglass says they did.

Mr. Thompson must be very green, or else he must suppose others very green, if he thinks that such wordy opinions of accomplices in wickedness will satisfy the candid public mind of this nation, which has commenced a searching scrutiny into the secret and hidden, as well as manifest abominations of the infernal system of slavery, that Mr. Douglass's statements are 'stern falsehoods.'

We hope Mr. Thompson will not rest here, but will proceed with his investigations into the truth or falsity of Douglass's statements, and give the public the *evidences* of lying which he shall discover—not the opinions of one man as to what another would do, who should be as deep in the mud as the witness himself might be in the mire, but good legal testimony, such as courts would receive in a *civilized* country—as to *facts,* some of the specific occurrences with which the narrative abounds. Come, Mr. Thompson, an honest, manly effort to overthrow by disproving the *events* which he states took place, would do you good. And when you have done that, we will give you another batch of facts to work at. We will furnish you with a book entitled 'American Slavery as it is, or the Testimony of 1000 Witnesses,' published in 1839. Perhaps our friends C. D. Cleveland or Thomas Earle, of Philadelphia, can furnish you with the book now, if you choose. Come, go at that book, and not spend your time upon such small game as poor Frederick Douglass, the 'recreant slave.' These 1000 witnesses are not abolitionists generally, but Southern men and women, statesmen, governors, congressmen, bad men and good men, from high places and low places and sacred places, ministers, deacons, and bishops—and their testimony challenges scrutiny. The vouchers are mostly on file. The work has been extensively circulated for the last six years, as well at the South as the North, and no man has yet undertaken to invalidate the horrid charges it prefers against the system. If Mr. Thompson will once peruse that work with candor and attention, he will find a larger business than defending the religion of the South against the slanders of a 'ranting negro.' He will find also that we have some reasons to know, that high professions of religion, and exalted piety towards God, are, in the ethics of the slave code, deemed consistent with monstrous inhumanity to man.

Index

Abolition Act, 91

Abolitionists: bazaars of, 102; blacks as, 5, 76, 77, 89, 102, 119, 122, 127; churches and, 83; edit fugitive slave narratives, xvii–xx, xxi, 134, 135; District of Columbia and, 36; Douglass and, xxii, xxix, xxxiv, 3–4, 124, 125, 131; in Great Britain, xxxv, 89, 103; in Ireland, xxix–xxx, xxxi, xxxiv, 6, 35, 89, 132; in Massachusetts, 3–13, 87–88, 90–91, 102, 110, 121–22, 131; meetings of, 3, 80, 87, 88, 122, 131; *Narrative* circulated by, xxx–xxxiii, 125; in New York, 88, 120, 125; newspapers of, xv–xvi, xviii, xxv–xxvii, 80, 122, 127–28, 131–33; opposition to, 127, 136; petition Congress, 108; in Pennsylvania, 89, 103; purchase slaves' freedom, 88, 103, 120; Quakers as, xviii, 87, 89, 113, 120, 121; in Rhode Island, 121; schism of, 87; suppressed in South, 69; temperance and, 91; women in, 125; women's rights and, 91. *See also* American Anti-Slavery Society; Garrisonians; Underground Railroad; *Liberator* (Boston); *National Anti-Slavery Standard* (New York)

Act of Union (Great Britain), 89

Aesop's Fables, 10, 91

Africa: black slavery in 35; whites enslaved in, x, xxi, 6

African slave trade, 35, 94, 118

Alabama, xix, 6, 66

Albany, N.Y., xxxi, 125, 129

Albany *Patriot,* 129, 133–37

Alexandrian Library (Egypt), 7, 90

Alice Anna Street. *See* Aliceanna Street

Aliceanna Street (Baltimore), 29, 105

Alisanna Street. *See* Aliceanna Street

Alliciana Street. *See* Aliceanna Street

Amanda (ship), 41

American and Foreign Anti-Slavery Reporter (New York), xv–xvi

American Anti-Slavery Society: disunionism and, 90–91; employs Douglass, xxx, 5, 131; free blacks and, 122; Garrison leads, 87, 91; *Narrative* and, xxix, xl, 125; publishes fugitive slave narratives, xvii; schism of, 89

American Board of Commissioners for Foreign Missions, 130

American Colonization Society, 127

American Manufacturer (Pittsburgh), 110

American Slavery As It Is: Testimony of a Thousand Witnesses (Weld), xx, 6, 90; influence on Douglass, xvi

American Spelling Book, The (Webster), 37, 108

Amistad (ship), xvi

Anchorage (estate), 97

Andover Theological Seminary, 88

Anglo-African Magazine (New York), 120

Annapolis, Md., 21; Douglass visits, 29; Lloyd family and, 94, 99; as market center, 96; state house, 94

Antheneum Hall (Nantucket, Mass.), 122

Anthony, Aaron: Thomas Auld and, 17, 94–96, 104, 109, 111; death of, 38, 93–96, 103–04, 108–09, 111, 116; as Douglass's master, 13, 15–17, 28, 92; family of, 17, 38, 92, 95, 98, 106, 109, 114; farms of, 92–95, 108, 111; Austin Gore and, 26; Lloyd family and, 17, 92, 96, 99; overseers of, 26, 15, 93–94, 98; portrayal in *Narrative,* xxxiii; as possible father of Douglass, 13; as ship captain, 15, 17, 92; slaves of, 38–39, 92–97, 103–04, 109, 111, 116; A. C. C. Thompson defends, xxxiii

Anthony, Andrew J., 104

Anthony, Andrew Skinner, 17; character of, 39; death of, 35, 110; slaves of, 38, 93, 95, 103, 109

Anthony, Ann Catherine Skinner, 92–93, 95

Anthony, Harriet Lucretia, 108, 113

Anthony, John Planner, 93, 104

Anthony, Lucretia. *See* Auld, Lucretia Planner Anthony

Anthony, Richard Lee, 17; death of, 38, 95, 108; slaves of, xii, 109, 111, 116

Anti-Slavery Almanac (Boston and New York), xv

Apple Alley (Baltimore), 108

Arabic, 6

Arkansas, 99, 120

Armistead, Wilson, xxxi

Associate Methodist Church. *See* Methodist Protestant Church

At Sundown (Whittier), 110

Atlantic Monthly (Boston), 110

Augusta, Ga., 98

Auld, Amanda. *See* Sears, Amanda Auld

Auld, Arianna Amanda, 95
Auld, Benjamin F., 106, 116–17
Auld, Hugh, Jr.: attacks *Narrative*, 103; character of, 39, 103; Douglass resides with, 28, 30–38, 42, 66–74, 103, 106, 110; hires Douglass out, 68, 69–70, 71–73, 79; home of, 29–30, 105, 106, 116; manumits Douglass, 103; opposes Douglass's education, 31–32, 35; purchases Douglass, xxxv, 103; quarrels with Thomas Auld, 41; as ship carpenter, 107, 116–17
Auld, Hugh, Sr., 96
Auld, Lucretia Planner Anthony, 38; death of, 39, 41, 95, 109; Douglass and, 17, 27–28, 39, 95; marries Thomas Auld, 95–96
Auld, Rowena Hambleton, 41, 43, 68, 69, 109–10
Auld, Sophia Keithley: character of, 30–31, 33–35, 37, 39; teaches Douglass, 31–33, 103, 106
Auld, Thomas: Aaron Anthony and, 17, 94–96, 104, 109, 111; Betsey Bailey and, 93; character of, 42–44, 68, 134–35; children of, 30, 37, 106, 109; Edward Covey and, 52; defenders of, xxxiii–xxxv, 133–37; Douglass criticizes in *Narrative*, xxxv, 96, 133–37; Douglass resides with, 42–46, 110, 134–35; Douglass sold by, xxxv, 66, 103; Douglass writes to, xxiii, xxxv–xxxvi; *Narrative* criticized by, xxxiii–xxxvi, xl; owns Douglass, 8, 28, 66, 72, 96; promises to manumit Douglass, 71, 134; quarrels with Hugh Auld, 41; religion and, 43–45, 111, 134–35; in St. Michaels, 41, 134–35; sells Douglass to brother, xxxv, 103; as ship captain, 17, 43, 96; slaves of, 94, 111, 116, 134–35; A.C.C. Thompson and, xxxiii–xxxv, 134
Auld, Tommy, 38; Douglass and, 30, 37, 106
Auld, Zipporah, 96
Autobiography: black authors of, xx, xxi, xxiv, xxv, xxxvi, xl; credibility of, xiii–xiv, xxii, xxxvi, xl; didactic purpose of, xii–xiii, xx–xxi; Indian captivity narratives and, x, xx; literary theorists and, xi–xv, xx, xxxvi; salvational, xl–xli. *See also* fugitive slave narratives

Bacon, Jarvis C., xxxii–xxxiii
Bailey, Betsey, 28; Isaac Bailey and, 13, 92, 93; children of, 13, 94, 116; Douglass lives with, 17; mistreatment of, 39–41; physical description of, 13
Bailey, Eliza, 42, 104
Bailey, Frederick Augustus Washington. *See* Douglass, Frederick
Bailey, Harriet: Thomas Auld and, 93; children of, 103–04, 111; death of, 28, 92; Douglass and, 14, 126–27; master of, 13, 92; physical description of, 13

Bailey, Henny, 42, 44–45, 111
Bailey, Henry, 103, 115–116; escape plot and, 62, 65–66
Bailey, Hester, 94; Ned Roberts and, 15, 95; whipping of, 15–16
Bailey, Isaac, 93; Betsey Bailey and, 13, 93; children of, 94, 111, 116; physical description of, 13, 92
Bailey, Maria, 104
Bailey, Milly, 104, 111
Bailey, Perry, 104
Bailey, Priscilla, 42, 111
Bailey, Sarah, 103
Bailey, Thomas, 107
Bailey, Tom (cousin), 29, 104–05
Ball, Charles, xxiv
Baltimore, Md., 21, 129; churches of, 108, 119; compared to North, 78; Douglass resides in, 28–42, 65–74, 77, 103–06, 109, 110, 116–18, 134; free blacks in, 67, 100, 102, 110, 116–19; government of, 100, 103; as market center, 17, 96, 98–99, 111; *Narrative* circulated in, xxxii; ship-yards of, 29, 34, 37, 67–70, 73, 103, 106–07, 114, 117, 119; slave-trade in, 18, 98; slaves in, 28–42, 62–63, 65–74, 77, 104–06, 109–10, 116–18, 134; wharfs of, 29, 36, 105, 108. *See also* Fells Point (Baltimore)
Baltimore *American & Commercial Daily Advertiser*, 8, 90, 129
Baltimore clipper ships, 106, 117
Bank of Maryland, 116
Bank Street (Baltimore), 109
Barney (Old). *See* Sampson, Barnett
Barney (Young). *See* Bentley, Barnett
Bascom's Pamphlets, 129
Basin area (Baltimore), 106
Bay-side, Md., 43
Belfast, Ire., 132
Bentley, Barnett (slave), 22, 99
Bible: allusions to in literature, x, 81, 84–85, 126; books of, 94, 113, 122; denied to slaves, 131; as proslavery argument, 123–24; quoted, 3, 5, 6, 9, 10, 11, 12, 15, 21, 22, 34, 44, 79, 81, 82, 87, 89, 90, 91, 94, 100, 107, 113, 122, 124, 127
Bingham, Caleb, xv, 107
Birney, James, xix
Blacks: as abolitionists, 5, 76–77, 89, 102, 119, 122, 127; as autobiographers, xiv, xx, xxi, xxv, xxxvi, xl; intellectual capacities of, xxvi
Block Street (Baltimore), 106
Bond Street (Baltimore), 69, 105, 117
Bondly, Beal. *See* Bordley, John Beal
Bordley, John Beal, 27, 90, 102

Bordley, Matthias, 102
Boston, abolitionists in, 3–9, 10–13, 91, 102, 122, 124, 131; fugitive slaves in, 88
Boston *Courier,* xxvii
Boston *Transcript,* xxvii
Bowley's Wharf (Baltimore), 29, 105
Brazos County, Tex., 104
British Friend (Glasgow), xxviii, xxx, 130
Bristol, Eng., 132
Bristol County Anti-Slavery Society, 87
Bristol *Mercury,* xxviii, 131–33
Brown, William Wells, xxxvi
Buffum, James N., 131
Bunyan, John, 123
Butler, Samuel, 73, 119

Caesar, Julius, 90
Caldwell, Handy (slave), 59
California, 88, 122
Cambria (ship), 131
Cambridge, Md., 134
Camp-meetings, 73
Canaan, 94
Canada, xvii, 61, 76
Carey, John L., 129
Caroline (slave), 48–49
Caroline County, Md., 92, 102, 113
Catherine (ship), 119
Caulker's Beneficial Association (Baltimore), 118
Chamber's Edinburgh Journal, xxvii
Channing, William E., 126
Chapman, Maria Weston, 127–28
Charles County, Md., 8, 90
Chesapeake Bay, 105; Aaron Anthony and, 15; commerce on, 41, 50, 109, 111; Douglass describes, xxxii, 7, 10, 49–50, 91; as slave escape route, 62–63
Child, Lydia Maria, xviii
Choptank River (Md.), 91
Christian Examiner (Boston), xxxvi
Church Street (New York City), 76
Cicero, 107
City Block. *See* City Dock (Baltimore)
City Dock (Baltimore), 73, 106, 119
Civil War, 87, 100, 106
Clarke, Lewis, xvi, xxxvi, xxxviii–xxxix
Clarke, Milton, xxxvi, xxxviii–xxxix
"Clerical Oppressors" (Whittier), 122
Coffin, William C., 80, 87
Cohee, Perry, 103
Collins, John Anderson, 5, 88
Columbian Orator, The (Bingham), 107; influence upon Douglass, xv, 35
Conciliation Hall (Dublin), 6, 89

Confederate States of America, 100
Congregational Church, 120
Connecticut, 108, 119, 120
Cookman, George, 44, 112, 115
Cork, Ire., xxv, 132
Cork *Examiner,* xxvii
Corn, 17
Corse, Barney, 120
Cotton, 103
The Course of Time, A Poem (Pollok), 122
Covey, Edward, 68; Thomas Auld and, 52; Douglass fights, 51–54, 68; Douglass resides with, 46–55, 57; as slave-breaker, 45, 55, 57, 113–14; portrayal in *Narrative,* xxxiii, 47–49, 57–59; A. C. C. Thompson defends, 135–36; whips Douglass, 46–47, 50–54
Cowper, William, quoted, 98–99
Cross of the Legion of Honor, 125
Cuba, 117
Curry, James, xvi
Curtain, James, 105
Curtain, Thomas, 105
Curtis, Thomas, 29, 105

Darg case, 76, 120
Darg, John P., 120
Datsun, L., xxxiv
Davis's Farm, 101
Dawson, James, xxxiii, 134
Declaration of Independence, 11, 91
DeFoe, Daniel, 123
Delaware, 50
Delaware Canal, 111
Delaware Republican (Wilmington, Del.), xxxiii, 133–37
Demby. *See* Denby, Bill
Democratic party, 99, 100
Denby, Bill, 25–26, 90, 101
Denton, Md., 102, 113
"Dialogue between a Master and a Slave" (anon.), 107
Dickens, Charles, xxxi, 124
Disunionism, 12, 90–91
Dixon, Jeremiah, 88
Dodson, Edward, 41, 110
Dodson, L., 135
Domestic Slavery Considered as a Scriptural Institution (Wayland and Fuller), 129
Dorchester County, Md., 134
Douglas, Ellen, 122
Douglas, Lord James, 122
Douglass, Anna Murray: marries Douglass, 76, 102; in New Bedford, 3, 76–77, 79–80, 87
Douglass, Frederick: as abolitionist, xxii, xxiv, xxv, xxx, 3, 5, 80, 87–89, 122, 125, 131–33;

Hugh Auld and, xxxv, 28, 30–38, 42, 66–74, 103, 106–07, 109, 110; Lucretia Auld and, 17, 27–28, 95; Thomas Auld and, xxiii, xxxv, 42–46, 66, 71, 96, 103, 110, 133–37; as autobiographer, ix, xv, xvii, xxii–xxiv; in Baltimore, 28–42, 65–74, 77, 103–06, 109–10, 116–18, 134; birth date of, 8, 13, 92; birthplace of, 8, 11, 13; as caulker, 67–70, 76, 79–80; childhood of, 13–29, 135; children of, 105; Edward Covey and, 46–55, 57; credibility of, 11, 70, 133–37; criticizes slaveholders' religion, 9, 80–86, 111, 123, 126, 128, 130; daguerreotype of, xxii; discontented as slave, 24–36, 41–42, 60–61, 70–72; edits *North Star,* xxxv; encounters discrimination in North, 79–80, 130; family of, 103–05, 111; father of, 13; Benjamin Franklin's influence upon, xv; William Freeland and, 57–58, 60, 64; as fugitive slave, ix, 4–5, 87, 103, 123–24, 131; William Lloyd Garrison and, 3, 90; Garrisonians and, xvii, xxxiv, 3; in Great Britain, xxii, xxiv–xxv, xxix, xxxiii, xxxv, 103, 131–32; hires himself out, 68–70, 71–72, 79; intellectual development of, ix, xv–iv, xxii, xxiii, xxxi, xxxix, 10, 30–33, 36–38, 41, 54, 128–29, 131; in Ireland, xxiv–xxv, xxix, 132; jailed for running away, 64–66; letters to, 12; in Lynn, Mass., xxxiv, 86, 102; malnourishment of, 28, 42, 45; manumission of, 103; marries, 76, 102; in Maryland, ix, xv, 13–74, 98, 131; in Massachusetts, xxxiv, 3–4, 21, 76–80, 86–87, 102; mother of, 13–14, 87, 126–27; *Narrative* and, xvi–xvii, xxviii–xxix, xxxvii, xl–xli, 6–7, 97, 100, 101, 110, 123–25, 128–29, 131–37; in New Bedford, 3–4, 76–80, 87; in New York City, 74–76, 102, 119; political activities of, 89; praise for, xxvi, xxxiv, xxxvii; religious views of, 59–60, 73, 119; renames himself, 77; responds to critics, xxxvii–xxxviii; in Rochester, 102, 104; runs away, 50, 51–52, 61–66, 70–76, 119, 128; in St. Michaels, 41–46, 52, 105, 110; in Scotland, xiv, xxxv, 117, 132; as slave, ix, xv, xxiii, xxx, xxxiii, xl, 6, 13–74, 94; slave songs described by, 20–21; as speaker, xxix–xxx, xxxv, 4, 87, 103, 109, 122, 125, 128, 131–32; Harriet Beecher Stowe and, xxxix–xli; sunday school run by, 59–60; A.C.C. Thompson and, xxxiii, xxxvi, xl, 133–37; Richard Webb and, whippings of, 27, 46–47, 52–54, 134
Douglass, Helen Pitts, 102
Douglass, Lewis, 105
Dublin, Ire.: abolitionists in, 6, 89; Douglass in, 132; *Narrative* published in, 130, 132
Dumas, Alexander, 125
Durgan and Bailey's shipyard, 34, 37, 106–07

Durgan, John, 107
Durham Street (Baltimore), 105

East Baltimore Mental Improvement Society, 102
Eastern Shore (Md.), 92, 105; economy of, 99; government of, 91; Quakerism in, 113; revivals in, 111–12; slavery in, xxxii, xl, 98, 110, 120; War of 1812 and, 111
Easton, Md., 13, 17, 21, 78, 95; as government center, 91; Douglass jailed in, 64–66; slaves in, 114
Eclectic Review (London), xi
Eden Street (Baltimore), 105
Edinburgh, Scot., 122
Egypt, 7, 90
Elementary Spelling Book, The (Webster), 108
Eli (slave), 50
Elizabeth & Ann (ship), 96
Emancipation: compensated, 91; gradual, 15, 91; Great Britain and, 91; immediate, 87–89, 108, 122; religion and, 43–44; in West Indies, 10
Emancipator (New York), xv
Emancipator and Journal of Public Morals (Jonesborough, Tenn.), 119
England, xxxv, 131; fugitive slaves in, xxii; immigrants to U.S. from, 112; Ireland and, 89; *Narrative* published in, xxiv, 118
Equiano, Olaudah, xx–xxi, xxiv
Europe, 94, 120
Exeter Street (Baltimore), 119
Ewery, Rev. *See* Uriey, William

Fairbank or Fairbanks, Wrightson, 44, 59, 113
Falls Street (Baltimore), 108, 116
"Farewell of a Virginia Slave Mother to Her Daughter Sold into Southern Bondage, The" (Whittier), 110
Fauchet, Abbé, xv
Feby, Harriott, 92
Federalist party, 108
Fell, William, 105
Fell Street (Baltimore). *See* Falls Street (Baltimore)
Fells Point (Baltimore): Douglass resides in, 105, 106, 116–18; ship-yards of, 29, 67, 105–08, 118; wharfs of, 108
Fifth Methodist Episcopal Church (Baltimore), 108
First Continental Congress, 88
Fleet Street (Baltimore), 105
Florence, Mass., 119
Foster, John, xi–xii, xiv
Fountain Street (Baltimore), 105
Fox, Charles James, 107
France, 125

Franklin, Benjamin, 91; as autobiographer, xv, xl–xli

Free blacks: as abolitionists, 5, 77, 89, 119, 122; churches of, 120; in Connecticut, 119–20; discrimination against, 11, 79–80, 90, 116, 125; fugitive slaves and, 118–20, 122; in Maryland, 59, 67–68, 92–93, 102, 104, 111, 116–19, 129; in Massachusetts, 5, 11, 14, 78–80, 89, 119, 122; in New Bedford, 78–79, 122; in New Orleans, 125; in New York, 75, 119, 120; as ship-yard workers, 67–68, 116; temperance and, 120

Free Church of Scotland, 130

Freeland, Elizabeth, 64, 114

Freeland, William, I, 114

Freeland, William, II, 114; character of, 58, 60; Douglass resides with, 57–58, 60, 64; slaves of, 59, 66

Friends. *See* Society of Friends

Fugitive Blacksmith, The (Pennington), 121

Fugitive slave narratives: as abolitionist tool, xv, xvi, xl–xli, 10, 123–24; credibility of, xviii–xix, xxii, xxxvi, 128, 133–34; Douglass and, xv–xvi; editors of, xvii–xix, xxi–xxii; as genre, ix-x, xxv, xxxvi; hostile response to, xxxix–xli, 128; *Uncle Tom's Cabin* and, xxxviii. *See also Narrative* (Douglass)

Fugitive slaves, 35, 136; in Boston, 88; in Canada, xvii, 61; in Connecticut, 120; Douglass as, ix, 4–5, 103, 123–24, 131; in Great Britain, xxii, xxxv, 102–03, 120; in New York, 75, 76, 120; in Pennsylvania, xviii, 59, 122; in Philadelphia, xviii, 122; rendition of, 75, 79, 103, 118, 131; in U.S., xvii–xviii, 11; whites assist, 37, 120

Fugitive Slave Law of 1850, 120

Fuller, Margaret, 125–27

Gardner, Anna, 88

Gardner, George, 105

Gardner, William, 67, 69, 105

Gardner's ship-yard, 29, 105; Douglass works at, 67–69

Garrison, William Lloyd: critics of, xxviii; disunionism and, 91; Douglass and, 3; friends of, 87, 89, 119, 121–22; *Liberator* and, xxv, 87, 90, 124; Massachusetts Anti-Slavery Society and, 88; *Narrative* and, xvii, xxiii, xxv, xxviii, 3–9, 90, 122, 124, 126, 129; temperance and, 87, 122

Garrisonians: blacks as, 89; disunionism and, 12, 90–91; Douglass and, xvii, xxxiv, 3; Garrison and, 87; in Ireland, 89; in Massachusetts, 88; political ideology of, 9, 80

"General Directions for Speaking" (Bingham), 107

Genesis, book of, 94

Genius of Freedom (New York), 119

Georgia, 6, 23, 39

Gibson, Fayette, 101

Gibson, Jacob, 24, 101

Gibson, John Bannister, 102

Glasgow, Scot., xxxv, 132

Goethe, Johann Wolfgang von, xiv

Gore, Austin: Thomas Auld defends, 134; murders slave, 25–27, 90, 101, 134; as overseer, 24–26; portrayal in *Narrative,* xxxiii; slaves whipped by, 25–26; A. C. C. Thompson defends, 135

Graham, George, xxxix–xl

Graham, Joseph, 65, 116

Graham, Thomas: arrests Douglass, 64; *Narrative* criticized by, xxxiv, 116, 134–35

Graham, W.H., 127

Graham's Magazine (Philadelphia), xxxix–xl

Grammatical Institute of the English Language, The (Webster), 108

Grayson County, Va., xxxii

Great Britain: Douglass in, xxii, xxiv–xxv, xxix, xxxiii, xxxv, 102–03, 131–33; fugitive slaves in, xxii, xxxv, 102–03, 120; Ireland and, 89, 107; magazines of, xxv, xxvii; *Narrative* published in, xxiv, 118; parliament of, xx; slave trade and, xx, 117

Great House Farm. *See* Wye House

Gronniasaw, James A., xxiv

Groomes, William, 114

Haddaway's Woods, Md., 111

Ham (biblical character), 15, 94

Hambleton, John, 104

Hambleton, Louisa, 113

Hambleton, Samuel, 104, 110

Hambleton, William, 110; Thomas Auld and, 41, 45; slaves of, 45, 62; stops slave escape, 64–66

Hamilton, Thomas, 32–33, 106–07

Hamilton, William. *See* Hambelton, William

Hamlet (Shakespeare), 115

Hammon, Briton, x

Hancock, John, 91

Happy Alley (Baltimore). *See* Durham Street (Baltimore)

Harris, George (*Uncle Tom's Cabin*), xxxviii–xxxix

Harris, Henry, 59, 61–62, 64–66

Harris, John, 59, 61–62, 64–66

Harrison, Edward, 117

Harrison, Samuel: emancipates slaves, 44, 112; slaves of, 48, 114

Harrison, Thomas, 112

Hartford, Conn., 120
Harvard University, 91
Haverhill, Mass., 110
Henrietta (slave), 32–33
Henry, Patrick: biography of, 88; as orator, 4, 62, 115
Henson, Josiah: as autobiographer, xxxvi–xxxvii, xxxix; Harriet Beecher Stowe and, xxxviii
Hibernian Anti-Slavery Society, xxxiv
Hickey, Thomas, 112
Hickey, William, 44, 112
Hicks, Giles, xxxiii, 26–27, 102
Hildreth, Richard, xviii–xix
Hillsborough, Md., 13, 91; Aulds in, 38, 95, 96, 109; poverty of, 78
Holme Hill Farm, 92–93, 108
Hooker, John, 120
Hopkins, James, 19, 24, 98
Hopkins, Rigby, 57–58, 115
Hopper, Isaac T., xvi, xviii, 120
Howitt, Mary, xxvi
Howitt, William, xxviii
Hughes, Thomas (slave), 120
Hughes, William (slave), 50–51, 53
Hull, Eng., 112
Humphries, Joshua, 44, 112
Hutchinson Family, 131–32
Hydropathy, 119

Iliad (Homer), xxxvi
Independents, 132
Indian captivity narratives, x, xx
Indiana, 95
Indians, x, 91
Ireland: abolitionists in, xxix–xxxi, xxxiv, 6, 35, 89, 132; churches of, 89, 107, 132; Douglass in, xxiv–xv, xxix, 132; England and, 89, 107; political movements in, 6, 89
Irish-Americans, 36–37, 90
Irish Parliament, 107
Isaac (slave), 17, 97

Jake (slave), 17, 97, 129
Jenkins, Sandy, 59, 114; aids Douglass, 52–53; escape plot and, 62–64
Jepson, Jacob. *See* Gibson, Jacob
Jeremiah, book of, 122
Job (biblical reference), 22, 100
John W. Richmond (ship), 76
Johnson, Frederick. *See* Douglass, Frederick
Johnson, Mary Page, 77, 79, 122
Johnson, Nathan, 80, 122; shelters Douglass, 77–79
Judkins, Charles H. E., 132

Keithley, Hester, 106
Keithley, Richard, 106
Keithley, Sophia. *See* Auld, Sophia Keithley
Kemp, Elizabeth Doyle, 52, 114
Kemp, John, 114
Kemp, Joseph, 96
Kemp, Thomas, I, 114
Kemp, Thomas, II, 114
Kent County, Md., 100
Kentucky, 103
Key to Uncle Tom's Cabin, The (Stowe), xxxviii–xxxix
Kinment, the Scotchman, 126

Labor movements, 91
Lady of the Lake, The (Scott), 77, 122
Lake Erie, Battle of, 110
Lambden, Robert. *See* Lambdin, Robert
Lambdin, Robert, 119
Lambdin, Thomas H.W.: murders slaves, 26, 101–2; portrayal in *Narrative,* xxxiii
Lamdin, Thomas. *See* Lambdin, Thomas H. W.
Lane, Lumsford, xvi
Lanman, Thomas. *See* Lambdin, Thomas H. W.
Lattimer, George, 88
Lawrence County, Miss., 103
Lee, Levi, 93–94
Lee, Richard, 95
Leeds, Eng., 118
Lee's Mill, Md., 14
Legion of Honor (France), 125
Lespanard Street (New York City), 76, 121
Lexington Street (Baltimore), 100
Liberator (Boston) xix; Garrison and, 87, 91; influence on Douglass, xv, 80; *Narrative* and, xxv, xxvi, xxxi, 90, 129–30, 133–37; universal reform and, 122
Liberia, 127
Liberty Bell (Boston), xv
"Lion and the Statue" (Aesop), 91
Liverpool, Eng., 132
Lloyd, Anthony, 93
Lloyd, Daniel, 17, 22, 99–100
Lloyd, Edward, I, 96
Lloyd, Edward IV: Aaron Anthony and, 92, 96; plantations of, 96, 99; slaves of, 97
Lloyd, Edward V: Aaron Anthony and, 17, 92; carriages of, 21–22; family of xxxii, 17, 22, 94–97, 99–100; overseers of, 24, 26, 95, 97–98, 101, 134; plantations of, 17, 19–21, 28, 30, 38, 42, 93–94, 96–99, 101–02; portrayal in *Narrative,* xxxiii, 129; slaves of, 16–17, 19–27, 29, 94–100, 129, 134; wealth of, 22, 24
Lloyd, Edward, VI, 97–100
Lloyd, Elizabeth Tayloe, 100

Lloyd, Henry, 100

Lloyd, James Murray, 22, 99

Lloyd Plantation, 21, 27–28

Lloyd, Rebecca, 100

Lloyd, Sally Scott. *See* Lowndes, Sally Scott Lloyd

Lloyd, Sally Scott Murray, 97, 99

Lloyds Cove, 96

Lloyd's Ned. *See* Roberts, Ned

London, Eng.: Douglass speaks in, xxxv

London *Atlas,* xxviii

London *League,* xxviii, xxxi

London *People's Journal,* xxvi

London *Spectator,* xxvii, xxx

Long Island, N.Y., 120

Loudon Slater's Hill (Baltimore), 29,

Louisiana, 6, 99, 125

Louisville, Ky., 103

Lowe, Thomas, 48

Lowndes, Charles, 22, 97, 100

Lowndes, Lloyd, 97

Lowndes, Sally Scott Lloyd, 97, 100; ship named for, 17, 96

Loyal National Repeal Association, 6, 89

Luke, gospel of, 113

Lynch law, 68, 117

Lynn Ladies' Anti-Slavery Society, 102

Lynn, Mass., 123; abolitionists in, 102; Douglass family in, xxxiv, 86, 102

Lynn (Mass.) *Pioneer,* xxx–xxxi, 123–24

Magazines: abolitionist, xv; book reviews in, xxv; British, xxv, xxvii; Indian captivity narratives in, x; in the South, xxxix. *See also* individual magazines

"The Man and the Lion," (Aesop), 10

Marengo Plantation, 101

Maria (slave), 104

Marine Bank (New Bedford, Mass.), 121

Market Street (Baltimore), 109

Marrant, Joseph, x

Martin County, Ind., 95

Martingham, Md., 110

Mary (slave), 32–33

Maryland, 95; compared to North, 77–78; Douglass in, ix, xv, xxiii, 13–74, 131; agricultural products of, 17, 94, 99; free blacks of, 59, 67–68, 92–93, 102, 104, 111, 116–19, 129; government of, 91, 97, 99, 100–101, 116, 118; Mason and Dixon's line and, 88; *Narrative* circulated in, xxxii; Quakers in, 113; slavery in, ix, xv, xxiii, xxxii, xl, 6–8, 10, 13–15, 18, 26, 41, 44, 62–79, 90, 93–94, 98–102, 112–16, 118, 120, 127, 131, 133–37; U.S. Revolution

in, 102; War of 1812 in, 111, 117. *See also* Baltimore; Eastern Shore (Md.); St. Michaels, Md.; Talbot County (Md.)

Maryland Agricultural Society, 94

Maryland General Assembly, 97, 118

Maryland Historical Society, 102

Mason and Dixon Line, 4, 11, 88

Mason, Charles, 88

Massachusetts: abolitionists in xix–xx, 3–13, 87–88, 90–91, 102, 110, 121–22, 124, 131; Douglass family in, xlii, 3–4, 76, 77–80, 86, 87, 102; free blacks in, 5, 11, 14, 78–80, 89, 122; fugitive slaves in, 88, 131; nicknames for, 4, 88; state government of, 121

Massachusetts Anti-Slavery Society, xix–xx; Douglass hired by, 5, 89; Garrison leads, 88; meetings of, 3, 80, 87

Massachusetts Bay Colony, 88

Matthew, gospel of, 122

Matthews, John, 8–9, 90

Matthews, William B., 8–9, 90

McBlair, Alicia, 99

M'Durmond, Mr. *See* McDermott, William

McDermott, William, 21, 99

"Memento," xix, xx

Memoirs of Archy Moore (Hildreth, ed.), xviii

Methodist Episcopal Church: abolitionists in, 83–85, 106; in Maryland, 43–45, 101, 106, 111–13, 115; Methodist Protestant Church and, 115; slaveholders in, xlii, 43–45, 101

Methodist Protestant Church, 115

Methodists' Philadelphia Conference, 112

Mexico, 67

Mexican War, 117

Michaels, D., 76, 121

Michaels, Joseph, 121

Middlebury College, 88

Middletown, Md., 90

Miles River, 17, 29, 96–97, 105

Mirror of Liberty (New York), 119

Mississippi, 99, 103, 110

Mississippi River, 10, 97

"Mr. Sheridan's Speech Against Mr. Taylor" (Sheridan), 107

Mitchell, Peter, 104

Monterey, Battle of, 117

Moore, Archy, xviii

Moral suasion, 89

Mulattoes, 14–15, 125

Murray, Anna. *See* Douglass, Anna Murray

Murray, Bambarra, 102

Murray, Mary, 102

Murray, Sally Scott, 94–95

Mysteries of Paris (Sue), 124

Nantucket, Mass., 3, 80, 87–88, 122
Napoleon I, 43
"Narratives of Fugitive Slaves" (Peabody), xxxvi
Narrative of James Williams (Williams), xix
Narrative of the Adventures and Escape of Moses Roper, from American Slavery (Roper), xxi
Narrative of the Lord's Wonderful Dealings with John Marrant, a Black, Taken Down from His Own Relation (Marrant), x
Narrative of the Life of Frederick Douglass, 8, 30, 96; abolitionists and, xxv–xxvi, xxviii–xxix, xl–xlii, 10, 125; as antislavery tool, xvi–xvii, 10, 123–24; Hugh Auld attacks, 103; authenticity suspected, xxviii, xxix, xl–xxxvi, xl, 133–37; Boston edition of, xxiv, 87, 123; critical reception of, xxv, xxvi–xxxvii, 123–37; Garrison and, xvii, xxiii, xxv, xxviii, 3–9, 90, 122, 124, 126, 129; illustrations in, xxii; Irish editions of, xxviii, xxxiii, xlii, 130, 132; literary reputation of, ix, xi–xii, 124; southern reaction to, xxv, xxxii–xxxvi, 103; Wendell Phillips and, xvii, xxiii, xxviii, 10–12, 126, 131; sales of, 124, 129, 132
Narrative of Uncommon Sufferings and Surprising Deliverance of Briton Hammon, a Negro Man, A (Hammon), x
National Anti-Slavery Standard (New York), xvi, xviii; Douglass reads, xv; *Narrative* and, xxv, xxvi–xxvii, 127–29, 131–33
National Era (Washington, D.C.), 110
National Negro Convention (1832), 122
Neall, James, 95
Nelson, Isaac, xxix, xxxi
New Bedford, Mass., 4; compared to Baltimore, 78; economy of, 78, 87, 121; Douglass resides in, 3, 76, 80, 87; free blacks in, 78–80, 122; racial discrimination in, 79–80
New Bedford Commercial Bank, 121
New Bedford Fire Society, 121
New Bedford Gas-Light Company, 121
New Bedford Institution for Savings, 121
New Bedford Lyceum and Antheneum, 121
New Bedford Monthly Meeting, 121
New Design Farm, 17, 97
New England; abolitionists in, xxv–xxvi, 88, 89, 121; compared to Maryland, 29; fugitive slaves in, 120; secession of advocated, 12. *See also* individual states
New England Anti-Slavery Society, 89, 121; meetings of, xxv–xxvi, 88
New England Magazine, The (Boston), xiv
New Haven, Conn., 120
New Jersey, 112
New Orleans, La., 98, 125

New Orleans, Battle of, 98
New York City, 121, 125; Douglass in, 74–77, 102, 119; free blacks in, 75, 119, 120; fugitive slaves in, 75, 76, 120
New York State, 102, 104, 121; abolitionists in, 88, 120, 125; Douglass in, 74–77, 119; fugitive slaves in, 61, 75, 76, 119
New York Review, xiii, xiv
New York *Tribune,* xxxi; *Narrative* reviewed by, xxviii–xxix, xxx, 125–27
New York Vigilance Committee, 119
Newburyport (Mass.) *Free Press,* 110
Newcastle (Eng.) *Guardian,* xxvii, xxx
Newspapers: abolitionist, xv; book reviews in, xxv; British, xxv; Indian captivity narratives in, x; in the South, xxxix, 8. *See also* individual newspapers
Newport Anti-Slavery Society, 121
Newport, R.I., 76, 121
Newtown, N.Y., 120
Nicholson, Anne G. *See* Storks, Anne G. Nicholson
Nicholson, Joseph, 22, 100
Nicholson, Joseph Hopper, 100
Noah (biblical figure), 94
North: antislavery sentiment in, 128; compared to South, 78; clergy of, xxxvii–xxxviii; economic conditions in, 77–78; free blacks of, 78–79, 118; fugitive slaves in, 11, 88; proslavery sentiment in, xxxvii–xxxviii, 120, 127; racial discrimination in, 11, 79–80, 122. *See also* individual states
North American Review (Boston), xiii, xv
North Carolina, xxi, 12
North Point, Md., 41, 50, 111
North Star (Rochester, N.Y.), xxxv, xxxvii
Northampton Association of Education and Industry, 119
Norwich, Conn., 119
Nova Scotia, 87
Novels, x, xiii

Oberlin *Evangelist,* xxvi
O'Connell, Daniel, 6, 89
O'Connor, Arthur, 107–08
Odyssey (Homer), xxxvi
Oliver Twist (Dickens), xxxi, 124
"On a Man's Writing Memoirs of Himself " (Foster), xi
Overseers, 8–9, 15, 94; Aaron Anthony as, 17; Austin Gore as, 24–26, 90, 101; James Hopkins as, 19, 98; Edward Lloyd V and, 24, 98, 101; James or Philemon Plummer as, 15, 94; William Sevier as, 18–19, 98; slaves whipped

Overseers (*continued*)
by, 24–26; George Townsend as, 98; Noah Willis as, 17, 97–98
Owen, Robert, 88
Oysters, 27, 113

Pacifism, 122
Panorama and Other Poems, The (Whittier), 110
Park Street (Baltimore), 100
"Part of Mr. O'Connor's Speech in the Irish House of Commons, in Favor of the Bill for Emancipating the Roman Catholics, 1795" (O'Connor), 107
Patapsco River (Md.), 111
Paul (Saul), 123
Peabody, Ephraim, xxxvi–xxxviii, xl
Peck's Pamphlets, 129
Pembroke, Jim. *See* Pennington, James William Charles
Penal reform, 91
Pennington, James William Charles, 76, 120
Pennsylvania, 102, 109, 112, 120; abolitionists in, 89, 103; fugitive slaves in, xviii, 50, 122; Mason and Dixon's line and, 88
Pennsylvania Freeman (Philadelphia), 103
Peter (slave), 17, 97
Pettit, Sarah. *See* Bailey, Sarah
People's Journal (London), xxvi
Pharisees, 82–83, 122
Philadelphia, Pa., 41, 102, 109; abolitionists in, 89; churches of, 112; First Continental Congress at, 88; free blacks in, 122; fugitive slaves in, xviii
Philadelphia *Elevator*, xxxii
Phillips, Wendell: biography of, 91; as abolitionist, xxv, 131; *Narrative* and, xvii, xxiii, xxviii, 10–12, 126, 131; temperance and, 91
Philpot Street (Baltimore), 32, 34, 106–08, 116
Pilgrims, 4, 12
Pitt, William, 107
Pitts, Helen. *See* Douglass, Helen Pitts
Plummer, James or Philemon, 15–16, 94
Political abolitionism, 89
Polk, James, 123
Pollok, Robert, quoted, 81, 122
Potomac River, 90
Pratt Street (Baltimore), 98, 105
Presbyterians, 132
President (ship), 112
Presqu'ile (Talbot County, Md.), 99
Price, Thomas, xxi–xxii
Price, Walter, 69, 117
Proslaveryism, 7, 15, 94; Bible used for, 123; in North, 120, 127; slaveholders and, 10
Psalms, book of, 122

Ptolemy I, 90
Puritan conversion narratives, xl–xli

Quakers. *See* Society of Friends

Racism: in North, 11, 79–80, 122; Douglass encounters, 79–80; free blacks against, 11, 79–80, 90, 116, 125
Reconstruction, 96
Reformed Methodist Church, 57, 115
Religion: Douglass and, 59–60, 73, 80–86, 111, 119, 123, 126, 128, 130; Garrison and, 89; revivals and, 81, 111–12; slaveholders and, 80–86, 130
Religious Spectator (Albany, N.Y.), xxviii, xxix, 128–29
Remond, Charles Lenox, 5, 89
Republican party (Jeffersonian), 94
Review of the West India Emancipation (anon.), 129
Rhode Island, 121
Rice, 11
Rich (slave), 17, 29, 97
Rich Neck Manor (Md.), 114
Richardson, Anna, 103
Richardson, Ellen, 103
Ricketson, Joseph, 77, 121
Roberts, Charles, 62, 65–66
Roberts, Ned, 16, 95
Rochester, N.Y., 102, 104
Roman Catholic Church, 89, 107
Roman Empire, 90
Roper, Moses, xxi–xxii, xxiv
Rowe, Joseph H., 38, 109
Ruggles, David: as abolitionist, 119; assists Douglass, 75–76; Darg case and, 120

St. Michaels, Md., 48, 51, 57, 114; Douglass resides in, 41–46, 52, 105, 110; Douglass tried in, 65; free blacks in, 111; government of, 116; Methodists in, 112–13, 115; poverty of, 78; residents of, 26, 41, 59, 62, 96, 101, 105, 119, 134–35; ship-yards of, 96, 101; slaves in, 44, 113, 116
St. Michaels Methodist Episcopal Church, 112–13
St. Michaels River. *See* Miles River
Salem, Mass., 89
Sally Lloyd (ship): Aaron Anthony and, 92, 96; slave crew of, 17, 97
Salvational autobiographies, xl–xli
Sampson, Barnett (slave), 22, 99
Sardis Chapel (St. Michaels, Md.), 115
Saturday Visitor (Baltimore), 130
Scotland, 122; Douglass in xxiv, xxxv, 117, 132

Scott, Walter, 77, 122
Sears, Amanda Auld, 39, 109
Sears, John L., 109
Severe, William. *See* Sevier, William
Sevier, William, 18–19, 98
Shakespeare, William, quoted, 3, 62, 87, 115
Shaw, George C., 76, 121
Shearman, Hannah. *See* Taber, Hannah Shearman
Sheridan, Richard, 35, 107
"Shooting a Slave" (Baltimore *American*), 8
Shurtz & Wilde's Periodical Book Store (Albany, N.Y.), 129
Skaneateles, N.Y., 88
Skinner, Ann Catherine. *See* Anthony, Ann Catherine Skinner
Skinner plantation (Talbot County, Md.), 93
Slatter, Hope H., 130
Slave narratives. *See* fugitive slave narratives
Slave Coast (Africa), 117
Slave Code, 9
Slave driver, 7, 8
Slave patrols, 8, 61
Slave rendition, 75, 79, 103, 118, 131
Slave trade, 81; abolition of, xx, 94; merchants in, 14–15, 18, 23, 39, 65, 98, 110, 117–18; in New Orleans, 98; opposition to, 108
Slaveholders, 98; abolitionists attacks on, xix, 80; character of, xxxvii–xxxviii, 7, 32–33, 42–43, 56, 78–79, 81, 99, 129–30; defend slavery, 10; Douglass criticizes, xxxviii, 14–15, 81; in Maryland, 79, 92, 94, 96, 99–101, 103, 110, 113–15; murder slaves, 36, 90; religion and, 7, 9, 48, 57, 59–60, 80–86, 126, 128, 130, 136; sexual transgressions of, 14; slave escapes and, 70–71; wealth of, 78, 97; whip their slaves, 15, 22, 81; women as, 31
Slavery: in Alabama, xix, 6, 66; in Arkansas, 99, 120; criticism of, xxi, 15; defenders of, xl, 7, 10, 15, 94; in Georgia, 6, 23, 39; in Louisiana, 6, 99; in Maryland, xxiii, xxxii, xl, 6–8, 10, 13–15, 26, 41, 44, 62, 90, 93–94, 98–102, 110, 112–16, 118, 120, 127, 129–30, 133–37; in Mississippi, 99, 103, 110; in North Carolina, xxi; religion and, 7, 9, 15, 44, 48, 57, 59–60, 80–86, 124, 126, 128, 130; severity of, xxiii, xxiv, xxxiii, 6–10; in South Carolina, 12; in Texas, 104; in West Indies, 91
Slavery in Maryland (Carey), 129
Slaves: abolitionists contact, 12; aged, 39–41, 116, 127; breeding of, 48–49; character of, 23, 42, 55–56, 60, 129; children as, xxxiii, 13, 18, 21, 27, 38, 40–41, 127; denied access to the Bible, 131; discontent of, 24–36, 41–42, 60–61, 70–71, 127; education of, xxvi, 36; as fugitives, xv, xvii, xviii; hiring out of, 68–72, 118, 129; holidays of, 55–56; malnourishment of, 10, 18, 23, 27–28, 32–33, 42, 45, 137; manumission of, 44, 112–13; marriages of, 8, 13; murder of, 8–9, 25–27, 36, 90, 101, 134; rebellions of, xvi, xxxiii, 55; religion and, 44, 57, 59–60, 124, 131; as sailors, 17, 29, 96–97, 119; sale of, 14–15, 23, 39, 48, 81–82, 98–99, 103, 110; sexual exploitation of, 81; skills of, 19; songs of, 20–21; as spies, 23; superstition of, 53; treatment of, xxvi, xxxi–xxxii, xxxvii, 6–11, 14, 18, 23–24, 28, 32–33, 39–41, 43, 49, 57, 81, 98–99, 133–37; urban, 28–42, 45, 62, 63, 65–74, 77, 104–06, 109–10, 116–18, 134; whippings of, 11, 14–16, 18–19, 21–22, 24–25, 27, 33, 39, 44–47, 50–54, 57–58, 60, 78, 81, 101, 134, 137. *See also* fugitive slaves
Sloss, Mary, 100
Smith, Bill (slave), 50–51, 54, 114
Smith's Wharf (Baltimore), 29, 105
Society of Friends: as abolitionists, xviii, 87, 89, 113, 120, 121; fugitive slaves and, 120; in Maryland, 113; in Massachusetts, 121
Soulié, Frédéric, 125
South: abolitionists suppressed in, 69; antislavery sentiment in, 15; newspapers in, xxxix, 8. *See also* individual states
South Carolina, 12
Southern Quarterly Review (New Orleans), xxxix, xl
Sparks, Jared, 91
Steuart, R.S., 116–17
Steward, Perry Ward, 13, 92–93
Stewart, General, 130
Stewart, Dr., 129–30
Stewart, Mr., 14
Storks, Anne G. Nicholson, 111
Storks, Levi, 44, 111
Stowe, Harriet Beecher, xxxviii–xxxix
Sue, Eugene, 124
Suffrage, 94
Sugar, 10

Taber, Hannah Shearman, 121
Taber, William C., 77, 121
Talbot County, Md., 97, 105, 116; free blacks in, 93, 104; government of, 91, 101; Methodists in, 43–44, 57–58, 111–12, 115; residents of, 17, 62, 95, 106, 111, 119, 133–37; shipbuilding in, 96, 101, 112; slaveholders of, 79, 92, 94, 96, 99–101, 103, 110, 113–15; slaves of, 13, 26, 93–94, 98–101, 113–15
Talbot Circuit, 111–12
"Tales of Oppression" (Hopper), xvi, xviii
Temperance: free blacks and, 120; Garrison and, 87, 122; Wendell Phillips and, 91

Texas, 104

Text Book of the Origins and History, &c. Of the Colored People, The (Pennington), 120

Thames Street (Baltimore), 116–17

Thompson, A. C. C.: Thomas Auld and, xxxiv–xxxv; as *Narrative* critic, xxxiii–xxxvi, xl, 133–37

Tilghman, Frisbie, 120

Tilghman Peninsula, Md., 111

Time Piece, The (Cowper), quoted, 98–99

Tobacco, 17, 91, 99

Townsend, George, 17, 98

Tribune Buildings (New York City), 127

Truth, Sojourner, 119

Tuckahoe, Md., 13

Tuckahoe Creek (Md.), 91–93

Tuckahoe Farms (Md.), 94

Tuckahoe Neck (Md.), 92

Tweed (ship), 106

Uncle Tom's Cabin (Stowe), xxxviii–xl

Underground Railroad: Douglass describes, 71; free blacks and, 118–20; in New York, 120; Quakers and, 120

United States, xvii, xxv, 92, 103,

U.S. Congress: antislavery petitions to, 108; chaplain of, 112; members of, 19, 94

U.S. Constitution: fugitive slave clause of, 11; Garrisonian criticism of, 11, 91, 123

U.S. Navy, 97, 100

U.S. Revolution: Benjamin Franklin and, 91; in Maryland, 102; in Virginia, 88

Uriey, William, 44, 112

Varian, Ralph, xx

Virginia: Mason and Dixon's line and, 88; U.S. Revolution in, 88, 115

Voices of Freedom (Whittier), 110

Wades Point Farm, 114

War of 1812, 106, 110; in Maryland, 111, 117

Washington, D.C., 8; churches of, 112; Douglass family in, 102; emancipation in, 36; slavery in, 108

Washington, George, 107

Waters, George P., 36, 108

Watson, Henry, xxxvi

Watson, William H., 69, 117

Wayland and Fuller's Letters. See Domestic Slavery Considered as a Scriptural Institution (Wayland and Fuller)

Webb and Chapman, 130

Webb, Richard D. 130, 132

Webster, Noah, 108

Webster's Spelling Book. See American Spelling Book, The (Webster)

Weeden, Daniel, 57, 58, 115

Weld, Theodore Dwight, xvi–xvii, xx, 90, 137

Wesleyan Methodists, 132

West, Garretson, 44, 59, 113, 115

West Indies, 10, 91

Wheat, 17, 50, 94, 97, 99

Whittier, John Greenleaf: poems by, 40, 82, 110, 122; James Williams and, xix

Wild Cat (ship), 38, 109

Wilke Street (Baltimore), 37, 108

Wilkes, William (slave), 22, 100

Wilks Street (Baltimore). *See* Wilke Street (Baltimore)

Wilks, William, 100

Williams, James, xviii–xx

Willis, Noah, 17, 97

Wilmington, Del., 133

Wilson, Nathan, 44, 113

Winder, Charles Sidney, 100

Winder, Edward Stoughton, 22, 100

Winder, Elizabeth Tayloe Lloyd, 100

Winder, Levin, 100

Wingate, Ann, 95

Women's rights: abolitionists and, 91; Garrison and, 87, 89, 122

Woolfolk, Austin, 18, 98

World's Anti-Slavery Convention, 120

Wye Heights, 99–100

Wye House: Douglass at, 29, 96–98; Lloyd family at, 22, 94, 96, 99; overseers of, 24, 98, 101; slaves at, 19–20

Wye Island, 102

Wye River, 96–97

Wye Town, 17, 97